Trauma
Research
Methodology

International Standard Book Number: 0-9629164-8-X
Library of Congress Catalog Card Number: 95-26829
Printed in the United States of America

Library of Congress Cataloging-in-Publication Data

Trauma research methodology / edited by Eve B. Carlson.
        p.   cm.
  includes bibliographical references.
  ISBN 0-9629164-8-X (alk. paper)
  1. Traumatology—Research—Methodology.   I. Carlson, Eve B.
RD93.T6962   1996
617.1'0072—dc20   95-26829
                                                          CIP

Trauma Research Methodology

EDITED BY

Eve B. Carlson,

PH.D.

Sidran

2328 W. Joppa Road, Ste. 15
Lutherville, Maryland 21093
(410) 825-8888

Contents

Preface: Trauma Research Methodology

Eve B. Carlson

Novice trauma researchers face a wide range of new tasks and challenges, but often have no source of practical guidance. A few are lucky enough to have mentors in the field of trauma research, but mentors who are researchers are often extremely busy and may have little time for teaching all of the nitty-gritty details of research. Sometimes, a student's mentor specializes in one type of trauma or population, while the student is interested in another type or population, and methods used to study one are not transferable to the other. Often, the mentor is primarily a clinician and has little knowledge about the specifics of research methodology. Since there are relatively few trauma researchers working in university settings, many students are supervised by researchers or clinicians whose expertise lies outside the field altogether. All of these students could benefit from some advice from experienced trauma researchers.

This book contains just such advice. Readers will find that the chapters span the entire research process, offering practical suggestions on methods for different types of research on different types of subjects. We begin with computerized literature searching, which is the modern version of the age-old foundation of good research: finding out what's already known. After a general chapter on study design and methodological controls, there are two chapters relating to choosing measures. Three chapters focus on specific types of research: epidemiological research, field research, and research on children. A chapter on the emotional and ethical aspects of trauma research explores some of the personally disturbing effects on the researcher of working in this field. The final chapters address the challenging tasks that are goals of most researchers: presenting and publishing their research and obtaining funding for their *next* study.

Though the book was primarily conceived as an aid to graduate students just starting their research careers, more experienced researchers may also find much of it useful. Some methods such as computerized database searching are new to us all. Other topics, such as choosing measures, are familiar issues, but constantly evolving with the field. All of the chapters offer recommendations about how to do and disseminate really good research.

Researchers typically only display the product of their work: the polished conference presentation, journal article, or book chapter. There's no likely outlet and little time for documenting the painstaking methods that distinguish studies that advance the field. But as every researcher knows, the quality of research is wholly dependent on the rigor of the methods. As "first generation" trauma researchers who want to see the field continue to thrive and grow, we hope the second generation will build on, and improve upon, the methods presented here and will return the favor some day by documenting *their* innovations in methodology for the third generation.

1

Searching the Traumatic Stress Literature

Fred Lerner

The literature of post-traumatic stress disorder and other mental-health sequelae of traumatic events is diverse. It is international in origin, interdisciplinary in approach, and eclectic in methodology. In order to facilitate the use of this literature in the study and treatment of PTSD and related mental disorders, the National Center for Post-Traumatic Stress Disorder has undertaken the production of an electronic index. This chapter will describe the PILOTS (Published International Literature On Traumatic Stress) database and suggest effective ways to use it to advance research and clinical work.

Given the excellent indexing of the medical literature provided by the National Library of Medicine's MEDLINE, and the broad coverage of psychology in the American Psychological Association's PsycINFO, some people have questioned the need for a specialized database to cover the traumatic stress literature. It is precisely the breadth of coverage of MEDLINE, PsycINFO, and other large databases that makes a specialized index desirable. The PILOTS database uses an indexing vocabulary designed specifically for the traumatic stress field, one that takes into account the often-divergent terminologies used in the several mental health disciplines. This vocabulary (which is set forth in the PILOTS Thesaurus), especially when used in combination with natural-language terminology and Boolean logic, allows a flexibility and precision not easily attained in more general databases except by expert information specialists. In addition, the PILOTS database is more complete in its coverage of the traumatic stress literature than other databases. MEDLINE provides complete coverage of over 8,000 periodical titles, but until 1994 did not index the *Journal of Traumatic Stress*, the only scientific journal in the world that is entirely devoted to PTSD; nor does it index material published in book form. While PsycINFO includes book material, it also restricts its journal indexing to a predetermined list of titles. In contrast, the scope of the PILOTS database extends to material from any source, in any format—so long as its subject matter is traumatic stress.

In addition to a description of the PILOTS database and a discussion of those features which distinguish it from other indexes relevant to traumatic stress studies, this presentation will discuss methods for effective searching of PILOTS and other bibliographic databases. These will include database selection, search strategy design, and iterative searching techniques.

The Historical Context

Ever since the Royal Society of London began publishing its *Philosophical Transactions* in 1665, scientists have reported their discoveries in the professional journals. It did not take long for the number of scientific journals to exceed the ability of readers to keep up with them. To alleviate this problem, journals began to include brief summaries of papers published in other countries; before long publishers began producing serials consisting entirely of abstracts. During the nineteenth century librarians and learned societies began to prepare indexes to the periodical literature, so that someone walking into a library might be able to extract a particular paper from the thousands of bound volumes weighing down the shelves.

The Royal Society's *Catalogue of Scientific Papers*, which began publishing in 1867, indexed over 1,500 periodicals by author. A few years later, the U.S. Army began producing the *Index-Catalogue of the Library of the Surgeon-General's Office* and *Index Medicus*, two bibliographies that offered a subject approach to the medical literature. The expansion of subject indexing to other disciplines had to wait for the development of classification schemes and lists of subject terms—

no trivial matter, especially when an index is intended to serve a world-wide audience.

The production of an abstract journal or a periodical index naturally lends itself to computerization. Not only is the computer used to simplify the reformatting of weekly or monthly issues into semiannual or annual cumulations, it allows users to mechanize the process of searching for a particular entry, or of locating those entries that satisfy desired criteria. Techniques for this were developed by contractors working for the National Aeronautics and Space Administration, the National Library of Medicine, and the Department of Defense—organizations that shared three characteristics: an immense body of literature, a clientele with a strong incentive to use this literature, and an ample supply of the taxpayers' money with which to facilitate this use.

Over the past three decades, this technology has trickled down from the mainframe to the desktop. For $2,000, a person or organization can purchase everything needed to produce a computer-searchable bibliographic database—and that includes the computer with which to search it. A cottage industry of bibliographers has emerged, in which both professionals and amateurs apply the lessons learned by the database pioneers to make accessible such specialized materials as the contents of science fiction magazines, research studies on sea turtles, and papers on the mental health consequences of experiencing traumatic stress.

An Embarrassment of Riches

The traumatic stress literature is rich and extensive; this poses some special challenges for those who use it. Finding the relevant literature on a trauma-related topic is especially difficult because the field is both diverse and evolving rapidly.

The literature on traumatic stress is interdisciplinary in nature. Valuable papers are published, not only in the psychiatry and psychology journals, but also in those dealing with social work, sociology, criminology, law, and general medicine. Publications devoted to specialized forms of treatment, such as acupuncture or art therapy, or to medical specialties, such as hand surgery or pediatric gynecology, will contain the occasional article or chapter on traumatic stress. While some of these are superficial introductions intended to acquaint practitioners with the concept of Post-Traumatic Stress Disorder, others offer unique information on particular presentations or treatments of PTSD.

Typically, the literature for these different disciplines tends to be indexed in separate databases. The physician or psychologist whose concerns lie within the mainstream of his or her profession has little difficulty in searching the literature. The National Library of Medicine's MEDLINE database sets the standards of design, scope, and accuracy against which other bibliographical projects are measured. It is readily accessible in a variety of formats, is one of the least expensive databases to search, and has an elaborate vocabulary of indexing terms which is updated annually. The American Psychological Association's PsycINFO database is a searchable version of *Psychological Abstracts* with additional entries for book chapters, conference reports, doctoral dissertations, and technical reports. (The CD-ROM version, PsycLIT, omits the dissertations and reports.) PsycINFO is highly regarded by librarians and psychologists for the extent of its indexing vocabulary and the accuracy of its staff-written abstracts.

There are also many specialized databases covering the social science literature as it relates to mental health. *Mental Health Abstracts,* produced by the IFI/Plenum Data Company, emphasizes psychopharmacology, paramedical sciences, and forensic literature in its indexing. *Social Work Abstracts* is produced by the National Association of Social Workers, and indexes not only the core domestic social work journals but also many foreign papers. The *Sociological Abstracts* database includes not only citations and abstracts from the printed version of *Sociological Abstracts,* but also doctoral dissertations, conference papers, book reviews, and material from *Social Planning, Policy & Development Abstracts.* Although there may be considerable overlap between the publications they cover and those indexed in a more general database such as PsycINFO, a database that is prepared from the perspective of a particular discipline may well be more useful to its practitioners.

Similarly, there are well-regarded bibliographical databases covering other fields related to traumatic stress studies. The literature of law is covered by the H. W. Wilson Company's *Index to Legal Periodicals* and by the *Legal Resource Index,* which is produced by the Information Access Company under the sponsorship and editorial guidance of the American Association of Law Libraries. The literature of criminology is covered by the *Criminal Justice Periodical Index,* which is produced by University Microfilms International, and by the *National Criminal Justice Reference Service* (NCJRS), sponsored by the National Institute of Justice. Public policy issues are indexed in the *PAIS International* database, produced by the Public Affairs Information Service. And there are many more such databases.

In addition to the challenge presented by a highly decentralized literature, a trauma researcher must cope with terminology that is constantly changing to reflect the rapid progress of the field. Each of these databases has its own list of subject terms, which highly-trained indexers use to characterize the content of each paper. These terms, along with author names, journal titles, and words occurring in the title or abstract of a paper, can be used to isolate references to publications likely to be relevant to a particular inquiry.

Because the terminology employed by indexers always lags behind the words that active scientists use in describing their research, it is useful to be able to search for all recent papers that cited some particular previous paper. Searching for cited references offers a way of locating articles in a field too new or too specialized to be covered adequately by existing indexing vocabularies. This approach to indexing the literature is provided by the Institute for Scientific Information, whose *SciSearch* and *Social SciSearch* databases are citation indexes. Citation indexing originated in the legal literature, where it is frequently necessary to determine if a judicial decision was amplified or overturned by a later case. Its use in scientific bibliography is based on the assumption that the citation of one publication by a subsequent one implies an intellectual relationship between the content of the two papers. Many studies by information scientists have shown that this assumption is true. Because these databases also allow "key word" searching—that is, searching for articles containing particular words in their titles or abstracts, or additional words or phrases supplied by the author or indexer—it is not necessary to have a specific article in mind before beginning a cited-reference search. Once a pertinent paper is identified using a key word search, any publication in which that paper is cited can then be found. This process can be repeated, allowing the searcher to locate several generations of papers emerging from an evolving area of research activity. Cited-reference searching is a complicated procedure, and the ISI databases are expensive; but in knowledgeable hands they are powerful bibliographic tools.

Choosing a Database

Given this bibliographical abundance, how does one decide where to begin a search of the literature?

The process of literature searching consists of matching concepts that describe the searcher's information needs with concepts that describe the content of existing publications. Computerized database searching, whether done online or on CD-ROM, makes this process much faster and far more efficient than manual searching. But, whether done manually or by computer, a literature search must take into account the features and limitations of the source being used.

The most important of these is the coverage offered by the bibliographical service. This may be defined in terms of language, nationality, time period, subject matter, or source of original publication; there are many other possibilities as well. A database that covers only material published after 1969 will be of limited use to someone interested in a historical approach to a field. One that is limited to English-language materials may serve the needs of a monolingual practitioner, but will not provide the scholar or researcher with access to all the work of European, Asian, and Latin American writers.

Many databases systematically exclude certain formats of publications from their indexing. It is unusual to find references to newspaper articles except in databases devoted specifically to newspaper indexing or in a few business-oriented databases. Technical reports, doctoral dissertations, and other forms of "gray literature" are often excluded from databases, and many do not include books or book chapters. MEDLINE's coverage, like that of many databases, is limited to articles appearing in journals, and only certain journals at that.

Most bibliographical databases index only the journals included on a predetermined list. This list is chosen by the database producers— often with input from an advisory board representing users—to ensure balanced coverage of the field and inclusion of its most important journals. There is an element of positive feedback to this process. The more prestigious journals are indexed in many databases, including the most important ones. This contributes to the greater impact of the papers they publish, which in turn makes writers more eager to submit their work to those journals. Those databases with a reputation for index-ing the highest quality journals tend to be conservative about adding titles to their coverage. It often takes several years for a new journal to be selected: the *Journal of Traumatic Stress*, which published its first issue in January 1988, was not added to the list of serials indexed in MEDLINE until February 1994—and MEDLINE's coverage will not include pre-1994 issues.

The major health-related databases go back only 20 to 30 years in their coverage. (MEDLINE's begins with 1966, PsycINFO's with 1967.) Most database users can accept the chronological limitations of the bibliographical resources that they are using, and are seldom af-fected by the fact that only papers published within the last few decades are indexed. (Unlike work in the humanities, social science and medical publications tend to have a short shelf life.) The most impor-tant restriction on database coverage is the subject matter, which in many databases is defined by the list of sources from which documents are taken to be indexed. So in deciding upon a database to search, the first question to ask is, "Does this database index the publications in which the information I am seeking is likely to be found?"

To determine this, be sure to consult the documentation for the database you are using. The *PsycINFO User Manual* contains a list of the journals indexed in that database, as well as an explicit statement of the dates covered by the database. The National Library of Medi-cine publishes an annual *List of Serials Indexed for Online Users* that includes all titles covered by MEDLINE and other NLM databases. Al-most every database that confines its coverage to a predetermined list of publications issues a list of the titles it covers. In addition, many journals list in each issue the indexes and databases that cover their contents. *Ulrich's International Periodicals Directory*, which can be found in most libraries, lists the abstracting and indexing services that cover each journal.

Not all databases restrict their coverage to a predetermined source list. PsycINFO, for example, indexes not only journals but books and dissertations as well. While a list of the journals is available, the only way to determine whether a particular book or dissertation is likely to be indexed is to have a good idea of the selection criteria employed by PsycINFO's compilers. If a printed bibliography or a database describes itself as containing relevant material from any available source, the obvious question the searcher must ask is "relevant to what?" Knowing how the producers of a bibliography define their subject coverage and determine which publications meet their criteria is an essential part of the decision whether to use it.

Any bibliographical resource worth using will provide potential users with the information they need to make this decision. In a printed bibliography, careful attention should be paid to any definitions of scope or approach contained or implied in the title or subtitle, and to any prefatory or introductory material. With a computerized database, whether searched online, via CD-ROM, or as a file on the user's own hard disk, it is essential to read both on-screen and printed documentation. In many cases, several levels of documentation are offered, ranging from a one- or two-page list of basic search commands to a multivolume series of search manuals, vocabulary lists, and sample searches. Using a bibliography without consulting its documentation is like using a cookbook without reading the recipes—in either case the results are likely to be unpalatable.

Those who plan to search a database frequently should study its documentation before first using it, and have a copy to hand whenever preparing or performing a search. In many cases this material will be available for consultation at the reference desk of the library at which you do your searching. Even if you prefer to perform your own database searches at home or in your office, it is worth visiting the library to use these aids to plan an effective search.

This brings up the issue of mediated versus end-user database searching. When online searching first became a reality, database vendors charged users by the minute. This placed a premium on efficient searching, in which as much preparation as possible was done before logging on to the system. Most searches were performed by experts—highly trained librarians or subject specialists. In the past few years, the tendency has been to price online searching to reflect the value produced by the search rather than the time consumed by it. Under this regimen, the number of items retrieved by the search determines its final price, while the cost of typing search commands and evaluating the preliminary results they produce is negligible. More recently, the availability of databases on CD-ROM or through tape license agreements has allowed many institutions to offer their clientele unlimited searching at a fixed annual price. These developments remove one reason for discouraging information seekers ("end users" in library jargon) from doing their own searching.

But that does not mean that end users *should* do their own searches. Database searching is a complex process, and the continual emergence of new information products, searching features, and communications systems means that keeping one's searching skills up-to-date is a full-time job. If a quick-and-dirty search yielding a few relevant papers is all that's needed, there's no reason why someone comfortable with database searching shouldn't perform his or her own search. But if an exhaustive or authoritative search of the literature is needed—if one is planning a course of treatment for a patient or writing a doctoral dissertation—it is always best, no matter what the subject-matter under investigation or which database has been selected, to work with a reference librarian or other expert searcher to plan and execute a thorough search of the literature.

The PILOTS Database: What It Covers and What It Does Not

As we have seen, until the development of PILOTS, no existing database covered the traumatic stress literature in its entirety. Furthermore, the best available coverage of this literature was provided by immense compendia of bibliographical information, whose very broad scope did not always allow for the precision of searching and ease of use that could be offered by a smaller, more specialized database. And the difficulty of searching a multitude of databases, each reflecting a particular discipline's approach to classification and terminology, each with its own searching vocabulary and record structure, impeded the identification and use of literature from outside the searcher's home discipline.

The PILOTS database was established to make the world's literature on post-traumatic stress disorder and other forms of traumatic stress available to researchers, clinicians, policy makers, students, and others concerned with the mental-health sequelae of traumatic events. The goal of the PILOTS database is to index the traumatic stress literature in its entirety, citing every appropriate publication regardless of its disciplinary, linguistic, or geographical origin.

This is easy to proclaim and hard to implement. For one thing, how does one define "the traumatic stress literature in its entirety"? The compilers of MEDLINE face a relatively easy task in determining whether they have completed their work. A given paper either is published in a journal named in the *List of Serials Indexed for Online Users*, or it is not, but there is no ambiguity. In a database whose contents are chosen on the basis of subject matter rather than provenance, every paper examined requires the exercise of judgment. Inevitably there will be disagreement among those staff members who might be making the selections. ("Inter-indexer consistency" is a popular subject for investigation by information science researchers.) Even a single individual is likely to apply a set of criteria inconsistently, especially when dealing with a rapidly-growing, rapidly-changing field. It is hardly surprising that database users, especially those with strong ties to a particular ideology or discipline, will often regard such a database's selection criteria as ill-conceived or poorly applied—just as anyone who fails to find a favorite writer's latest novel in the catalog of the local public library may have questions about the librarian's book selection policy.

To alleviate this, we use several overlapping methods of searching the literature for papers appropriate for inclusion in the PILOTS database. We scan three weekly editions of *Current Contents on Diskette* (the Clinical Medicine, Life Sciences, and Social and Behavioral Sciences editions) page by page, looking for papers whose titles suggest that their subject matter falls within our purview. When we request reprints from their authors, we enclose a cover letter describing the PI-LOTS database and asking for additional relevant publications. We also search MEDLINE, PsycINFO, and many other databases on a regular basis, using not only "post-traumatic stress disorder" and its synonyms as search terms, but also such phrases as "rape trauma" and "psychatric sequelae." These databases include not only the various medical and mental-health indexes, but also seemingly unrelated databases such as *America: History and Life, Insurance Periodicals Index,* and *Religion Index.*

Many of the resulting citations are to papers already in PILOTS. The others we obtain from their authors or publishers, or from local libraries, interlibrary loan, or document delivery services. In every case, we examine the paper ourselves, determine the correct author and publication information, and assign our own descriptors and other indexing terms. We do not copy any proprietary material from other databases except in a few cases where we have secured licenses or permissions to use it. We are beginning to explore relationships with other organizations interested in the literature of traumatic stress, with a view to agreeing upon bibliographic standards that would allow indexing work done by information centers worldwide to be searched in a single database.

As researchers and clinicians active in traumatic stress work learn of the PILOTS database, many are eager to ensure that their publications are indexed. We often receive unsolicited books, reprints, and photocopies. We are always happy to get them, especially when they originate in countries poorly covered by Western bibliographical services.

Every publication that we receive is examined by an indexer who decides if it should be cited in the database. In doubtful cases, a second opinion is sought. All rejected papers are placed in a file for later evaluation by an invited reviewer. Any paper labeled by MEDLINE, PsycINFO, or certain other authoritative databases as dealing with PTSD is automatically included in PILOTS, even if it was originally rejected by our staff. These acquisition and evaluation procedures are meant to prevent the omission from PILOTS of any papers that properly fall within its scope.

We defined the content of the PILOTS database as "the world's literature on post-traumatic stress disorder and other forms of traumatic stress." By this we mean any published material dealing with:

- post-traumatic stress disorder, as defined in the American Psychiatric Association's *Diagnostic and Statistical Manual of Mental Disorders,*
- any other mental disorders (as defined in DSM-IV and its predecessors) caused by or associated with direct or indirect exposure to an event perceived as traumatic, and
- any mental-health-related consequences of such exposure.

This casts a wide net. It includes not only those papers that explicitly discuss PTSD, but also most of the literature on multiple personality disorder (which DSM-IV has relabeled "dissociative identity disorder") and much of that on borderline personality disorder, both of which are often associated etiologically with childhood trauma. It also includes literature on anxiety disorders, eating disorders, mood disorders, sleep disorders, somatization disorders—all of which may occur as a result of, or in association with, exposure to a traumatic experience.

There are obvious gray areas here. Does an article on depressive symptoms among people recently widowed belong in the PILOTS database? What about a study of somatic symptoms among former prisoners of war? A report on the prevalence of psychiatric disorders among rape survivors seems an obvious choice for inclusion; but what about one that concentrates on the prevalence of rape itself? The first of these papers would not be chosen for PILOTS, though we would occasionally bend the rules and include a comprehensive literature review that could provide PILOTS users with an overview of its topic (and a list of further readings). The second and third would be included in the database. The fourth would be evaluated for its potential usefulness to PILOTS users, and would be included if it were epidemiological rather than journalistic in its approach.

Researchers studying PTSD cannot expect to find that every paper that would be useful to their work will be included in the PILOTS database. There are too many fruitful approaches to investigating traumatic stress, and too many potentially valuable insights to be found throughout the mental health literature, to make that feasible. Insight into the predisposition of some individuals to display the symptoms of PTSD may be gained from studying the etiology of panic disorder; the neuropharmacology of traumatic stress may be elucidated by comparison with schizophrenia. Traumatic stress research will often require the use of other bibliographical databases. But it is our intention to include any published literature directly relevant to traumatic stress that might be found in any other database, thus making PILOTS the database of choice in which to begin a search of this literature.

Users of the PILOTS database should be aware of some types of material that have been deliberately excluded from coverage. Newspaper articles, whether in the general press or in specialist publications, are not included, with the exception of substantial articles appearing in separately-named magazine sections (such as *The New York Times Magazine*). Unpublished conference presentations, manuscripts submitted for publication but not yet in print, and technical reports whose circulation is restricted are also excluded.

There are several classes of material that will be added to the database in the future but which are at present not indexed. These include audiovisual materials, doctoral dissertations, most government documents and general-circulation technical reports, and most material in languages other than English. The traumatic stress literature is abundant, and the PILOTS database staff is small; priorities have to be established and choices have to be made. No doubt there are many valuable films and videotapes about traumatic stress. But how can one index a 90-minute film without spending 90 minutes watching it? In that same time we can index six or eight journal articles. As time and resources permit, as we are able to recruit linguistic expertise (to date we have collected literature in over 20 languages), as inter-institutional cooperation in indexing the traumatic stress literature becomes a reality, these too will be included in PILOTS.

Developing Your Search Strategy

A database search is really a three-step process. First, you put together a search strategy. Then you execute the search. And then you examine the results and modify your search accordingly.

Think of a database search as an exercise in pattern matching. You tell the computer what pattern of letters, words, or phrases you are looking for, and it attempts to match that pattern with those it finds in the database. You can tell the computer where in the database to look for a pattern and you can tell it to search for a combination of patterns. The success of your search depends on the clarity with which you form the pattern you try to match, the accuracy with which you type it into the computer, and the skill and completeness of the database producer. Two out of the three are up to you.

The PILOTS database may be searched in many different ways. Among the possibilities, you can search for

- the writings of a particular author,
- publications from a designated journal,
- papers in which a specific assessment instrument is used,
- material in a particular language,
- studies published in a designated year or period of time, and
- articles and chapters on a particular subject.

There are two basic approaches to searching the PILOTS database: controlled vocabulary and natural language. In *controlled vocabulary* searching, you are instructing the computer to match terms from a prescribed list against those occurring within the records contained in the database. In *natural language* searching, you are telling the computer to match words or phrases that you think might occur in the bibliographical records, regardless of whether they appear on a prescribed list of terms. Using either method, the occurrence of a match should indicate that the paper in which it is found discusses the subject indicated by the word, phrase, or term entered. Each method offers advantages and disadvantages. Many users will find that a combination of both types of searching will produce the best results.

Controlled vocabulary searching takes advantage of the work done by the database producer to standardize the terminology used by the thousands of authors and editors who produce the traumatic stress literature. This standardization is especially important in an interdisciplinary field, as there is no assurance that the terms used by psychiatrists will necessarily match those used by criminologists, or art therapists, or social workers. Even within a discipline, changes in terminology occur over time, or across geographic or ideological boundaries.

We use two vehicles for standardizing terminology in the PILOTS database.

- *Authority* lists ensure consistency in the way that names (of authors, journals, incidents, etc.) are entered in PILOTS. These are continually-updated, alphabetical lists that we maintain at the National Center. When adding new records to the database, we check all names against the appropriate authority lists.

- The PILOTS Thesaurus is a listing of descriptors used to describe the subject content of a document in the PILOTS database. It consists of two parts. One is a hierarchically-arranged table of descriptors that specifies the relationship between broader and narrower terms. For example, you would find "Neuroendocrine Testing" as the narrowest descriptor term in one hierarchy, with the term "Biologic Markers" listed as a broader term, and "Assessment" as the broadest term in that hierarchy. The second part of the Thesaurus is an alphabetical index of descriptors and "entry terms." Descriptors are listed in the alphabetical index along with corresponding broader, narrower, related terms, and unapproved terms for which the descriptor is used. "Entry terms" are non-descriptor terms that a database user might have in mind. If you look up an entry term, you are referred to the appropriate descriptor term. For example, you might look up "Transgenerational Effects" and find that the appropriate descriptor is "Intergenerational Effects."

Natural language searching (sometimes called "free text" searching) allows you to use the terms that you are most comfortable with; it does not require you to use the PILOTS Thesaurus. And it provides a way to locate material on subjects that are too new to be included in the Thesaurus, or that the Thesaurus does not cover well enough for your particular need. However, it is neither as precise nor as complete a way of searching as using a controlled vocabulary. Natural language searching offers too many opportunities to retrieve irrelevant material. For example, searching for the word "shifts" to discover papers on the effects of work schedules in exacerbating PTSD uncovered nothing on that subject—but did turn up several articles discussing paradigm shifts in the sciences underlying traumatic stress studies. That same search would not find an article whose author disdained the word "shifts" in favor of "irregular work hours."

If you simply want to find a few publications relevant to your area of interest, natural language searching is an easy way to go about it. But if you need to make a thorough study of the literature, and you wish to be sure that you do not miss important papers, you should not rely upon natural language searching alone.

Modifying Your Search Strategy

It often happens that a search of PILOTS (or any other database) does not produce the results that you expect. Database searching works best as an iterative process. Don't expect to get definitive results with your first try; plan on doing an exploratory search, and then modify your search strategy according to the results you get. Here are some suggestions:

If your search produces an impossibly large number of citations, examine at least a few of them to see whether you defined your topic too broadly, or used too broad a search strategy.

- If almost all of them are indeed relevant, ask yourself how you can redefine your *objective*. Perhaps you should choose a narrower topic: for example, natural disasters rather than disasters in general.
- If many of the citations your search has retrieved are irrelevant,

you need to refine your *search strategy*. Look at some of the irrelevant citations, and see what they have in common. Does the
same descriptor appear in all of them? If you repeated your
search without using that descriptor would you be eliminating
valuable citations as well as irrelevant ones? If not, you've found
one way of bringing your search results down to a more man-
ageable size. Other methods to refine a search might include re-
stricting your search by language, or by date, or by format.

What if your search has retrieved fewer citations than you think it
should have?

- Perhaps there really *are* very few papers in your area. (Or at least
  very few that have found their way into PILOTS.)
- Or perhaps your search strategy was too narrow. Again, look at
  your results. Find a citation that is directly relevant, and see what
  descriptors were applied to it. Perhaps you might want to add
  one or more of them to your search strategy.
- And don't forget to double check to be sure that you weren't
  done in by a simple typing error. The computer has no way of
  knowing that you meant "alcohol" when you typed "alvohol"!

And what if you could find no relevant citations? Is there a paper
that you know to be relevant? Then search for that paper by author
and title, retrieve the citation, and see how it was indexed in PILOTS.
That might suggest one or more descriptors to use in searching.

Don't be discouraged if your first search strategy doesn't work
perfectly. Experts at database searching often have to modify their
search techniques, especially when working with a database that is new
to them. And don't be surprised if you come across a citation whose
indexing seems strange to you. This is a complex literature, and the indexer is, after all, perforce a generalist. You may well know more
about the topic than the indexer does. And if you find a paper that you
believe has been incorrectly indexed, please let us know. We don't mind
correcting our mistakes.

How to Obtain Copies of Materials Found in PILOTS

Many large database producers offer a document delivery service that for a fee provides users with photocopies of publications discovered by their searches. Smaller organizations are seldom able to provide this service, as they have neither the resources to provide it with existing staff nor the demand to justify adding people dedicated to the task. The National Center for Post-Traumatic Stress Disorder maintains a PTSD Resource Center, which contains every publication indexed in the PILOTS database. However, it has not so far been possible to provide copies of these to PILOTS users. In order to keep the PILOTS database up to date, the Resource Center staff must devote its time to identifying, acquiring, and indexing publications on traumatic stress, as well as preparing the database for searching, writing instructional materials, and providing technical assistance to PILOTS users. It has neither the staff nor the facilities to receive requests, retrieve the documents, make photocopies, and prepare them for mailing, nor is it in a position to make the legal and financial arrangements and keep the detailed records necessary to comply with copyright laws and guidelines.

It may be possible to circumvent these difficulties by contracting with an outside organization to provide a document delivery service to PILOTS users. This contractor would receive orders, handle all the details of fulfillment, and be responsible for all matters of copyright compliance and royalty payments. The National Center is currently exploring this possibility. Meanwhile, these suggestions will help PILOTS users and other traumatic stress workers obtain the journal articles, book chapters, and other materials that they need.

The first place to begin is your local library. If you have access to a medical library, ask the librarian to get copies from the regional medical library system. (All VA medical libraries are part of this system.) Many public and academic libraries belong to networks that make the resources of large libraries available to the clients of smaller ones. In some cases materials can be provided free of charge; otherwise, you may have to pay a small fee for each article you request. (If your request does not come under the "fair use" provision of the copyright laws, there may also be a royalty fee payable to the publisher that your library will have to collect.) Your local librarian will know the fastest and cheapest ways to get what you need.

There are several organizations and companies that specialize in providing rapid copies of publications.

Information brokers offer a complete range of services, from searching databases to providing copies. Document delivery services offer copies of materials from their own resources and often from other library collections. If your needs require it, and you are willing to pay the extra costs involved, you can receive copies by courier or fax. Information brokers can be found in the Yellow Pages, and in the "Brokers Mart" listing published in *Database* magazine. Their trade association is:

- Association of Independent Information Professionals
  203 Pinehurst Road
  Canyon, California 94516
  (510) 530-3635

Document delivery services are operated by private companies, nonprofit organizations, and libraries. They usually offer a wide range of ordering and payment arangements, accomodating users whose needs range from the single article to thousands of papers each year. Many are able to accept orders by electronic mail. In addition to many services that specialize in material on a particular subject or from a particular region, there are several whose resources allow them to offer a comprehensive service. Among these are:

- CARL Systems, Inc. ("Uncover")
  3801 East Florida Avenue
  Building D, Suite 300
  Denver, Colorado 80222
  (303) 758-3030
- University Microfilms, Inc. ("Article Clearinghouse")
  300 North Zeeb Road
  Ann Arbor, Michigan 48106
  (800) 521-0600

- Institute for Scientific Information ("The Genuine Article")
  3501 Market Street
  Philadelphia, Pennsylvania 19104
  (215) 386-0100
- British Library Document Supply Centre
  1 Appleton Street
  Boston, Massachusetts 02116
  (800) 932-3575

These are their American addresses. Your local library can help you locate their offices or agencies serving other countries, and can help you locate other document delivery services.

Conclusion

Any interdisciplinary literature, especially one in which exciting discoveries are continually being reported and controversial opinions frequently expressed, presents both a challenge and an opportunity to those working in the fields it covers. The challenge lies in the fact that the already difficult task of keeping up with the field one was trained in must be repeated in several other, less familiar areas. The opportunity lies in the ability to apply the work of colleagues with an entirely different outlook to problems that often resist the solutions suggested by one's own background.

The ability to identify, evaluate, and benefit from the publications of those working in disciplines cognate to one's own is one of the most powerful tools with which a researcher or clinician can equip him- or herself. A basic understanding of the bibliographic infrastructure of medicine and the social sciences, and a knowledge of the many ways in which bibliographical databases can be searched, are necessary to use the literature effectively. The PILOTS database offers an approach to the traumatic stress literature that has been designed especially to meet the needs of those working in this fast-growing interdisciplinary field.

Access to the PILOTS Database

The PILOTS database is available to users worldwide as a file on the Dartmouth College Library Online System. No account or password is necessary and there is no charge for using the database. Internet users can telnet to lib.dartmouth.edu and at the prompt enter SELECT FILE PILOTS. A PILOTS Database User's Guide may be purchased from the Superintendent of Documents, U.S. Government Printing Office, Washington DC 20402 or downloaded free of charge from ftp. dartmouth.edu (directory /pub/ptsd). Gopher users may connect to gopher.dartmouth.edu and look under Research Resources / Biological Sciences. World Wide Web users can connect to the PILOTS database at http://www.dartmouth.edu/dms/ptsd/. For further information, contact:

Fred Lerner, D.L.S., Information Scientist
National Center for Post-Traumatic Stress Disorder
VA Medical Center (116D)
White River Junction, Vermont 05009
(802) 296-5132 Fax (802) 296-5135
fred.lerner@dartmouth.edu

2

Designing Trauma Studies: Basic Principles

Fran H. Norris

Research design is both a simple and a complex concept. On one level, it simply refers to the plan for conducting the study. Can the question be examined experimentally or are more naturalistic but less rigorous methods required? How many levels of the independent variable will there be and how will subjects be assigned to groups? At the more complex level, research design is the researcher's plan for controlling the sources of variance in the dependent variable. Broadly speaking, the purpose of research design is to maximize experimental variance while minimizing confound, extraneous, and error variance.

Efforts to control sources of variance all contribute to the internal validity of a study. Internal validity can be defined as the degree to which the results of a study really were the effect of the experimental manipulation. Another important aspect of research is external validity, which is the degree to which the results of a study can be generalized or are valid outside the study itself. While methods to increase external validity will not be addressed in this chapter, they are also essential to good research and are covered extensively in Chapter 5 (Fairbank, Jordan, & Schlenger, 1996).

At the outset, I want to make two basic points. The first is that there is nothing unique about trauma studies from the perspective of research design. Depending upon the specific research question, any type of design—experimental, quasi-experimental, or nonexperimental—might be appropriate. Because we cannot manipulate traumatic experiences, research on the *effects* of traumatic experiences is necessarily nonexperimental. However, because we can manipulate exposure to interventions, research on the *treatment* of trauma can be experimental or quasi-experimental. Various components of traumatic experiences, such as fear, can also be studied experimentally, as can aspects of posttraumatic stress, such as the response to reminders of trauma. The second point is that although most textbooks concerning design in psychology assume that one is conducting true experimental research, the same logic, by and large, applies to quasi-experimental and nonexperimental research. Often, it is easier to illustrate design features and strategies using experimental examples, but I will periodically attempt to show that the same basic principles apply to all three types of research designs.

We undertake research because we are interested in knowing whether some predictor or *independent variable* (x) is related to some outcome or *dependent variable* (y). The question, "Does x affect y?" is deceptively simple; the answer is anything but. It means, first of all, that x and y must covary. That is, can the researcher show that when x varies (increases or decreases), y varies (increases or decreases)? Traditionally, research psychologists perform some type of statistical test to provide evidence that an observed relation is reliable. Although they take different forms, practically all statistical tests are some sort of effect/variability ratio. So, to understand research design, we should start by reviewing what this ratio means conceptually.

Controlling Variance

Variables and Variance
As an example, let's consider the relation between fear (x) and need for affiliation with other people (y). We have chosen an experimental test of the hypothesis. We will create a situation wherein some subjects are exposed to a frightening stimulus and some are not, and then see if the first group exhibits a greater need to affiliate with other people than does the second group. Following tradition, we'll refer to the subjects who were exposed to the stimulus as *experimental subjects* and those who were not exposed as *control subjects*.

Four Hypothetical Frequency Distributions

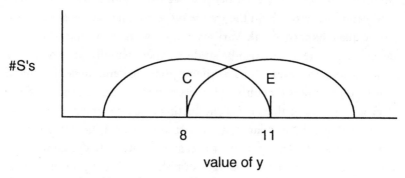

Figure 1.   The effect of x is small relative to the variability in y.

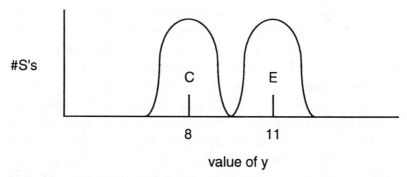

Figure 2.   The effect of x is the same as in Figure 1, but the variability in y is smaller.

In this example, need for affiliation is the dependent variable. It is easy to overlook what that means, but understanding variability may be the key to grasping how the research process works. What is a variable? Somewhat redundantly, a variable is something that varies or changes. It is an entity that takes on different values. Intelligence is a variable; scores on an intelligence test are values. Sex is a variable, male is one value, female another. A dependent variable is an entity that we have measured, maybe using a psychological scale of some type, because we believe it will be affected by the independent variable. The traditional labels of "independent" and "dependent" seem less arbi-

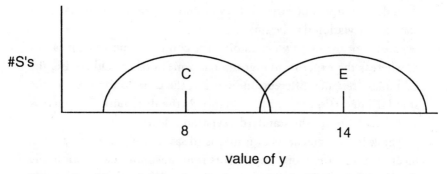

Figure 3. The variability in y is the same as in Figure 1, but the effect of x is greater.

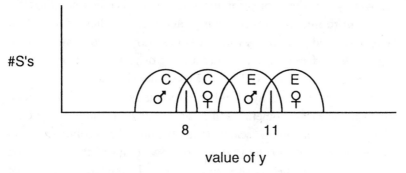

Figure 4. The variability in y has been blocked by sex.

trary when one remembers that the value of the dependent variable *depends upon* the value of the independent variable.

To view how much dispersion there is in the sample as a whole, it is useful to examine the frequency distribution of y. Three hypothetical distributions are shown in Figures 1-3. How do we summarize all the data represented by a frequency distribution? Traditionally, we reduce the data by calculating measures of central tendency, such as the mean, and measures of variability, such as the standard deviation. The standard deviation is useful because it is readily interpreted as the average distance from the mean of all of the scores. If the individuals we are studying are heterogeneous (or diverse) on need for affiliation, the standard deviation will be large. If they are homogenous (or similar), the standard deviation will be small.

In each of the first two examples, the control group has a mean of 8, whereas the experimental group has a mean of 11. Otherwise, the examples are quite different. In Figure 1, the distribution is wide (the standard deviation is high). In Figure 2, the distribution is narrow within each group (the standard deviation is low).

Think for a moment what it means to say a group or sample has a mean of a specific value (e.g., 8). Is it an absolute, unquestionable Truth? No, it is simply an approximation of reality—our best guess of some underlying, unknowable population value. There is a high probability that the population mean is really 7 or 9. There is a smaller probability that the population mean is 6 or 10. I sometimes illustrate this point to my class by collecting each student's height in inches. Here, a defined *population* (the class) has a known population mean (e.g., 67"). Different *samples*, drawn using dice, do not always have a mean height of 67 inches, though it is usually close to this value. But sometimes, by chance, my sample has too many short students, yielding a smaller mean; sometimes, it has too many tall students, yielding a larger mean. In real life, scientists rarely know the absolute truth, so they have established rules that govern how confident they should be in the accuracy of their observations. Generally, the larger the sample and the narrower the distribution, the more confident we are that our obtained mean is close to the actual mean. Then we say that the mean has a small *confidence interval*. Conversely, the smaller the sample and the wider the distribution, the larger the confidence interval.

In assessing the effects of x, we have to think about the mean as this interval rather than as a point. For this reason, we cannot judge whether two groups representing two levels or values of x are really from two different populations simply by knowing that one group has a mean of 8 and the other has a mean of 11. This effect can be evaluated only by considering its size relative to the total variability of y. In the first example, the confidence intervals are large—let's say 6-10 in the control group and 9-13 in the experimental group. Since these intervals overlap, it is difficult to conclude that the two sample means are reliably different. The true population means could arguably be 10 in both groups. In the second example, however, the confidence intervals around the means are small—let's say they are 7–9 in the control group and 10–12 in the experimental group. Even if the true population means are at the edges of the intervals, 9 and 10, we can be confident the groups are in fact different on the dependent measure. In summary, an effect of a given size is meaningful if the total variability in y is low but not if the total variability in y is high.

Now look at Figure 3. The control group looks just like it did in Figure 1. In this case, however, the effect of fear was strong enough to shift the experimental group further up the scale. Even though the subjects within each group vary considerably, it would be fairly safe to conclude the effect of the fear-arousing stimulus was meaningful.

The point of all this is that if we want to show that x is related to y, or in this case, that the exposed group has higher need for affiliation than the unexposed group, then we can improve our chances of verifying this effect statistically by either (a) decreasing the overall variability within the distributions, such as in Figure 2; or (b) increasing the distance between the two distributions, such as in Figure 3.

Thus, to repeat, researchers have to be concerned with the variability in their data. Research design provides a way to control the sources of variance in a study. "Sources of variance" is simply the delineation of why y—in this case, need for affiliation—varies. Why do some people exhibit relatively little need to affiliate with others, whereas some people need other people very much? Why does even the same person sometimes show one level of need and sometimes show another? What are the sources of this variance?

Sources of Variance

There are different ways of categorizing the sources of variance, but I have found the following scheme, drawn from Kerlinger's (1986) text, most useful.

First, there is *experimental* or *treatment* variance. This is the portion actually due to the independent variable. It is that part of the variance in which the researcher is substantively interested. In my example, it is the part that can be attributed to the fact that some subjects were exposed to a fear-arousing stimulus and some were not. In an epidemiological study of trauma, it might be the percentage of the variance in psychopathology accounted for, or predicted, by the number of traumatic events experienced.

Second, there is *confound* variance. This is the portion due to variables other than the independent variable whose effects are entangled with it. When two variables are confounded, we are measuring the effects of both, when we intend to measure only the effect of one. For example, it was once thought that coffee drinking was a contributory cause of heart disease, but smoking was confounded with coffee drinking in those studies. (Smokers drink more coffee.) Likewise exposure to traumatic events may be confounded with exposure to an impoverished environment or poor family functioning. Confounds are possible in experimental as well as nonexperimental studies. In my fear-affiliation study, if I ran all of my control subjects in the morning and all of my experimental subjects in the evening, then time of day would be a confound. Perhaps people are naturally more sociable in the evening than in the morning. If so, it would be impossible for me to isolate the effects of the experimental stimulus from time of day.

Third, there is *extraneous* variance. These are the true difference across participants in a study. Subjects bring with them differences in individual ability and personality and demographic characteristics that will affect their scores on the dependent variable in ways that have nothing to do with the experimental manipulation. It would be naive to think that fear is the only cause of an individual's need to affiliate. People naturally vary on this trait. Similarly, an individual's depression score at any given point in time will be a function of innumerable causes, no matter how powerful the influence of traumatic events.

Finally, there is *error* variance. This is the fluctuation or variation in scores due to chance or transient factors. Errors in measurement, which are difficult to avoid in psychological research, add further variability to the data.

All sources of variance can be understood as variability in the data that occurs either between or within groups. Because both experimental and confound variance differ systematically between groups, it is customary to consider them together as *between-groups* variance. In

Figure 3, the two groups could be different because of the experimental treatment; if my study was not well designed, they could also be different because of some confound. Likewise, it is customary to group extraneous and error variance together under the broader label of *within-group* variance. A simple way to think of the within-group variance is as the collection of factors that explain why subjects who are treated identically in a study do not perform identically.

Now, let's return to the observation that most statistical tests represent some effect/variability ratio, i.e., they are a ratio of the between-groups variance and the within groups variance: V_b/V_w. Logically, if the independent variable had an effect, the between-groups variance should be greater than the within-groups variance. So, it is to our advantage to do whatever we can to increase the numerator, decrease the denominator, or both. However, we should not seek to increase the numerator at the cost of being wrong.

Research design is our primary strategy for doing just this. The goals of research design are to a) maximize experimental variance, b) minimize confound variance, c) minimize extraneous variance, and d) minimize error variance. When we have done these things we have both an *internally valid* and *efficient* research design. I will discuss these first three goals in some detail. The last, minimizing error variance, is largely an instrumentation issue and will be discussed only briefly in this chapter. However, because in many ways it is the most basic issue, I will discuss it first.

Minimizing Error Variance
Error variance is the variance in the dependent measure that is due to chance or transient factors. To the extent that errors of measurement are present in a measuring instrument (whether a questionnaire, observer, or piece of equipment), that instrument is unreliable. Reliability can be defined as the relative absence of errors of measurement; in other words, it is the precision or consistency of an instrument. Reliability is not the same attribute as validity. Reliability means that you will get the same value, more or less, upon repeated measurements of the same individual. A scale can be perfectly reliable and still not be

valid if it does not measure what you intend to measure. Error variance is not the result of systematic biases but of random influences that even out over time.

In classic measurement theory, an *obtained score* can be broken down into two components, a *true* component and an *error* component. It is symbolized: $X = T + e$. T is what we would get with a perfect, error-free instrument. The greater proportion of the score considered true, the more reliable the measure. In terms of this chapter's outline, experimental and extraneous variance would both be part of the true score variance since they both reflect true differences among individuals in the dependent variable. When there is only a single observation, it is impossible to distinguish an observed score from a true score. Therefore, estimates of an instrument's reliability (Vtrue/Vtotal) are made using multiple observations, for example, by assessing the same individuals at two points in time, by using two observers of the same phenomenon, or by analyzing the internal consistency of multiple items that should, more or less, be measuring the same thing.

Some reasons for error reside in the subjects themselves, such as their guessing, momentary inattention, lapses in memory, fatigue and consequent mistakes, and transient emotional states. Other reasons reside in the procedures, such as poorly trained or tired observers and unclear instructions.

The goal of minimizing error variance in research design thus directs us to be systematic and consistent in our procedures, precise in our definitions, clear in our questions and directions, thorough in our training, and critical when selecting psychological measures. If reliability cannot be established from previous literature, pilot work is essential. Neither clever designs nor sophisticated statistics can compensate for poor measures or procedures.

Maximizing Experimental Variance

There are three strategies to consider here. First, the researcher must consider what constitutes an adequate manipulation and/or measurement of the independent variable. The levels of the independent variable should be as different as possible. If I am using a true experiment to study fear and affiliation, was the experimental stimulus actually capable of arousing fear in the experimental group? Was I likewise careful *not* to arouse fear in the control group in some unanticipated way? Or, let's say I intend to study the effects of domestic violence by comparing a group of women who have requested services *because* of abuse to a group of women who have requested services for reasons *other than* abuse. Seasoned researchers in this area would immediately know that they cannot assume the comparison group does not include some women who have been abused. It would be important to measure the extent of exposure among all study participants and then either to eliminate abused women from the comparison group or to control for their abuse experiences in some other way.

The second strategy is to make sure that the dependent measures are sensitive. Will they tap the effects you want them to tap? Ceiling and floor effects (where criteria are set too low or too high) are good examples of situations where the measures are not sufficiently sensitive to experimental variance. For example, if the measure of affiliation used did not have a wide enough range to measure an extremely high need for affiliation in the fear-exposed group, then a ceiling effect would occur, making it less likely that the true difference between the experimental and the control group would be detected. Good measures of dependent variables allow for a range of measurement that is sufficiently wide: very few subjects in either the experimental or the control group should earn scores at the extreme ends of the range.

Valid measures are another component of sensitivity. Relations are theorized between *constructs*, i.e., hypothetical entities such as fear and need that cannot be directly observed. Relations are tested between operational manifestations of those constructs. *Construct validity* has many facets but, in its essence, it means that you are measuring what you intend to measure. The true influence of fear on affiliation could be strong, but my test of this relation quite weak, if my dependent measure has poor construct validity.

The third strategy is to make sure that you have adequate statistical *power*. If you plan to use statistical tests, do you have enough subjects to show an effect even if one is present? This relates to the issue of statistical decision making. Most researchers are trained carefully to avoid the problem of "Type I error." This type of error happens when the researcher concludes that an effect is present when one is not (that is, an effect of that size could have occurred by chance). Power, or rather lack thereof, is related to the problem of "Type II error." In this case, the error is in concluding that an effect is not present when one, in fact, exists. It's the situation that exists when your groups "look" different but your statistical tests tell you they're not different enough. This is often an issue for trauma studies that require specialized research participants, for example, rape victims or refugees or people meeting criteria for current PTSD. Although trauma is all too common from a population perspective, researchers still find it quite challenging to recruit sufficient numbers of individuals who have experienced the event of interest within a specified time interval and geographic area. Therefore many trauma studies have fewer participants and less power than would be ideal.

Power, then, refers to the probability that experimental variance will be detected. It does not increase experimental variance but the same ratio of Vb/Vw is interpreted differently as the sample size increases. When *n* is small, the ratio must be fairly large before you can trust it. When *n* is large, a smaller ratio can be considered as evidence of a reliable effect. A "reliable" effect is not the same as a large effect or a clinically meaningful effect; it just means you would expect to find the effect again if you were to conduct the study again. The most useful resource I have found for choosing sample size is Cohen's (1992) power primer for psychologists. (I keep a photocopy of this article on my desk.)

Minimizing Confound Variance

To be able to claim that the independent variable caused a change in the dependent variable, the researcher must show that the independent variable and only the independent variable produced the change. Often, a confound results in a spurious relation, i.e., it appears that the first variable, x, causes the second variable, y, but in reality both x and y are both caused by a *third variable, z*.

When a study is free of confound variance, we say it is *internally valid*. Because procedures to minimize confound variance compose such an integral aspect of research design, I will elaborate on the concept of confounding variables and provide a few basic definitions. Campbell and Stanley (1963) identified a number of threats to internal validity. Receiving considerable acceptance by the scientific community, their monograph provides researchers with a useful checklist for considering whether or not common confounds or threats have been ruled out.

A *selection* confound refers to differences between groups that arise due to biases in the assignment of subjects to conditions. That is, subjects in one group differ from subjects in another in ways other than level of the independent variable. My favorite example is taken from Durso and Mellgren's (1989) undergraduate research text: A scientist is interested in testing the effects of drugs on spatial ability in rats. He goes to the dump and catches 10 rats, gives them Drug A, and tests how long it takes them to learn a maze. He then goes back to the dump, catches 10 more rats, gives them Drug B, and then tests them. These rats learn to run the maze more quickly, so the scientist concludes that Drug B is better. The rival hypothesis? The second group of rats have superior speed and intelligence, which is why he didn't catch them the first time he went to the dump. Drug type was confounded with natural superiority in his research.

In trauma research, selection confounds are seldom as obvious. The threat is ubiquitous in studies of the effects of trauma because we can never establish unequivocally that exposure to trauma is the *only* difference between individuals who have experienced a given event and individuals who have not. The threat would be equally severe in studies of the treatment of trauma, if we were limited to naturalistic research methods. It is not reasonable to assume, for example, that people who self-select one type of treatment (e.g., behavior therapy) are equivalent to people who select another type of treatment (e.g., psychopharmacology), let alone to people who choose no treatment at all.

The issue of equivalent groups is even more complicated when a study involves more than one session. Even if groups are initially comparable, there is no assurance that they will remain so if some subjects drop out. Differential attrition or *mortality* can be very problematic in treatment studies. For example, individuals who drop out of stressful treatments involving exposure to traumatic memories may differ in important ways from individuals who drop out of more benign treatments, such as support groups. If individuals who are not likely to be cured are scared away by the first session, and thus do not complete the study, the success rate among those who complete all sessions is higher than the success rate legitimately should be. This internal validity issue should be distinguished from the external validity issue that occurs when many subjects drop out of both conditions. Generalizability can be threatened even if the loss is not differential across groups.

Another potential threat is *maturation*. This confound refers to changes in the dependent variable that occur due to the passage of time — growing older, tired, or becoming well. A researcher conducting a "pre-experimental" study contrasting pre- and post- treatment scores of rape victims receiving crisis intervention services might mistakenly conclude that observed improvement was an effect of treatment, when it was actually only a natural tendency to improve over time.

History refers to events that take place at the same time as the treatment that are not related to it but nonetheless influence the dependent variable. Whereas maturation refers to changes that are *internal* to the subject, history refers to changes that are *external* to the subject. Such confounds range from subtle (time of day, weather) to severe (major political events). In intervention research, it is imperative to show that it was the intervention itself and not some other co-occurring event that caused observed changes in the dependent measure. My own personal experience with a history confound occurred when my colleague, Krys Kaniasty, and I were preparing for our longitudinal study of Hurricane Hugo. As a frame for selecting individual participants in the research, we selected four cities that differed in the nature of their experience with the hurricane: Charleston, SC had been both threatened (forewarned) and struck by the hurricane; Charlotte, NC was struck without forewarning; Savannah, GA had been threatened but not struck; and Greenville, SC had been neither threatened nor struck. In August 1990, we were revisiting stricken neighborhoods and searching for comparison sites to add to our survey. The final stop of our journey was Savannah where we celebrated the completion of this phase of our work on a patio overlooking the Savannah River. While chatting about our study, we saw a huge navy vessel leaving the Savannah harbor. Along the river banks people with flags and flowers were bidding farewell to one of the first military installments sent to the Persian Gulf. Yet it was not until January 1991 that we fully realized that this threat to world peace was somewhat ironically a methodological threat to our by-then in-progress study. The U.S. entry into the war started a little more than a month before the second wave of data collection began in Charleston and Savannah, cities with major military bases. It was quite possible that the nature and extent of exposure to this additional stressor would vary in complex and confusing ways across other factors of interest to us, such as the nature of experience with the hurricane (defined here by the city of residence).

As a trauma researcher, I like this example for a number of reasons. First of all, there was no way we could have known when planning a follow-up study of Hurricane Hugo that an event of this proportion would happen. We could not control history! However, we could measure it, and that, in fact, is what we did. We added a sizable battery of questions pertaining to the Persian Gulf War to our interview schedule and analyzed that data thoroughly before attempting to evaluate the effects of Hurricane Hugo. In this way, if necessary, the effects of the war could have been controlled statistically when assessing the effects of the hurricane. The lesson here is to be sensitive to threats, to prevent those threats that can be prevented, and to measure the rest. That is the best we can do in studies of this type.

Some threats to validity arise because measurement error can rarely be totally eliminated in research. These threats, however, are reasonably well controlled when a control group has been included in the design. A *testing* threat arises when taking a test influences subsequent experience with a test. Many students, for example, score more highly on the SAT or GRE the second time they take it, even though their true level of scholastic aptitude has not changed. This issue is not as serious as many others in trauma research, where dependent variables are usually concerned with emotional states rather than accuracy of performance on measures with right and wrong answers. An *instrumentation* threat arises when the instrument (rather than the subject) changes. This threat is easiest to see in the context of observational research; observers may change their standards or become more or less vigilant over the course of a study. An example here might be a school-based intervention following some collective trauma (shooting incident, natural disaster) where the dependent variables include measures of classroom behavior (e.g., disruptiveness). Instrumentation would have occurred if observers changed their standards for disruptiveness as the study progressed. Instrumentation confounds are preventable with clear operational definitions, careful observer training, and ongoing monitoring (perhaps through videotape). A threat that occurs less frequently but can be quite serious is *statistical regression*. High scores will tend to get lower and low scores will tend to get higher upon retesting. Keeping in mind that measurement errors tend to be random, an observed score that is very high is likely to be higher than the underlying true score and so is more likely to decrease than increase on a subsequent testing. Thus whenever groups are formed on the basis of extreme scores, the researcher can count on the groups' scores regressing toward the mean whether any intervention occurs or not. For example, if research subjects are classified as high and low PTSD on the basis of a measure of PTSD, the first group predictably will improve more than the second when they are subsequently re-assessed. No psychological theory would be needed to explain this observation.

The strategy used to minimize confound variance is the key distinction between the three most basic categories of research designs: true experimental designs, quasi-experimental designs, and nonexperimental (correlational) designs. Let's consider the true experiment first. In a traditional laboratory experiment, confound variance is minimized through *randomization* and *tight experimental control*. Both methods assume there is a control group, that is, some group that is equivalent to the experimental group in all ways other than exposure to the independent variable. Random assignment means that each subject has an equal and independent probability of being assigned to each group. Therefore, a person with a given attribute should have an equal chance of being assigned to any condition. This is the single best way to insure that the groups *start out the same*. They are probabilistically equivalent.

Tight control means the groups are *treated the same* in all ways other than exposure to the independent variable. It is achieved through careful attention to procedures and details. It means everyone gets identical instructions and attention. A classic example is the use of a placebo in drug treatment research. A placebo is a medically inert substance that is provided to control subjects so that they receive the same level of attention and possess the same expectation of recovery as the treatment group. In this way, *subject reactivity* (or bias) is controlled. Careful procedures are also needed to control *experimenter reactivity* (or bias). Continuing with the drug treatment example, the evaluator should not know which subjects are receiving the placebo and which are receiving the active drug.

Because no method compares with randomization and tight control in terms of eliminating confound variance, true experiments should be used whenever possible. Even the simplest possible design—two groups of randomly assigned subjects who are assessed after exposure to the independent variable—is strong in terms of eliminating confound variance. Within the trauma field, treatment studies are now usually held to this standard. A number of different techniques make randomization feasible even in real world settings where ethics prohibit denial of treatment. One technique is the *wait-list control group*, wherein participants are randomly assigned to immediate treatment or to a waiting list for subsequent treatment. Both groups are measured when the first group enters and completes the intervention. A second technique is to assign participants randomly to the treatment of interest or to a *nonspecific therapy control group*, for example, treatment specifically geared to PTSD versus social skills training for kids. A third technique is to assign participants randomly to a new treatment, perhaps an experimental drug, versus a *treatment-as-usual control group*, who receive the drug commonly used to treat that disorder.

Of course, many investigators are interested in phenomena that cannot be studied in true experiments. Researchers do not assign children randomly to classrooms and they certainly do not assign people randomly to traumatic events. When an investigator finds that random assignment is absolutely out of the question, he or she should consider using a quasi-experimental design. Quasi-experimental designs look much like true experimental designs. A treatment is implemented by the investigator after groups are formed. The key difference between a true experiment and a quasi-experiment is that, in a quasi-experiment, assignment to groups is not determined randomly. The most common strategy is to identify a *nonequivalent control group*, i.e., a group of subjects who appear to be roughly comparable to the experimental group except on the variable of substantive interest. The effects of a violence prevention effort might be tested by comparing a classroom of children who received the intervention with a classroom (another *intact group*) composed of children who are roughly comparable except that they did not receive the intervention. Sometimes, a comparison group must be formed via purposive sampling, a method which is similar but not identical to matching, which will be discussed in a separate section further on in this chapter. In this case, the investigator handpicks the elements of the comparison group so that key attributes (e.g., age, sex) are distributed in desired ways.

In nonexperimental research, the researcher exerts even less control over the assignment or selection of subjects. Nonexperimental research involves measuring phenomena as they occur naturally and then seeing if x and y correlate. Most correlational studies have a *cross-sectional design*, which means that x and y have been measured at the same point in time. Often, in studies of this type, information on traumatic events is collected *retrospectively*, meaning the subject looks back and reports on the past. In correlational research, the primary strategy for minimizing confound variance is to use *statistical controls*. For example, if testing the relation between criminal victimization (x) and anxiety (y), the researcher typically would control for the effects of background characteristics, such as socioeconomic status (z), before testing the effects of crime. This process is illustrated in Figure 5. The shaded area represents the *total correlation* between x and y, and the darkly shaded area represents the *partial correlation* with the confound (z) controlled. This represents an improvement over drawing conclusions based only upon the bivariate correlation between crime exposure and anxiety which may be confounded with background characteristics. That is, persons of lower SES may experience more crime (the correlation between x and z) and be more anxious for many reasons other than their exposure to crime (the correlation between y and z).

Sometimes, the method of statistical control is supplemented by the

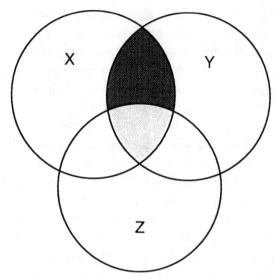

Figure 5. Total correlation (shaded area) and partial correlation (darkly shaded area) between x and y, as influenced by a confound, z.

method of purposive sampling. For example, a sample of children who have experienced residential fires might be compared to a group of children who are selected because they come from similar households in the same neighborhoods. Or, each child in an abused sample might be asked to identify a friend who is very much like him or her. The friends collectively serve as controls. These designs may appear similar to quasi-experiments but, unless there are pre-event measures available, they do not achieve quasi-experimental status.

Minimizing Extraneous Variance
As stated earlier, we generally know at the outset of a study that many variables other than the independent variable affect the dependent variable. It is almost overwhelming to consider, for example, how many causes there might be of a given individual's depression score at a given point in time. Childhood history, recent events, biological conditions, simply whether he or she has been having a good or bad day can all be

expected to exert some influence. Need for affiliation likewise stems from a multitude of stable and transient factors. Randomization or some other confound-minimizing strategy may prevent these factors from being confounded with the independent variable, but to the extent that extraneous factors increase the variability of scores within groups, they still make it difficult to detect effects.

Controlling for extraneous variance is difficult to do well in correlational research having a cross-sectional design. We generally must rely upon statistical controls to control for extraneous variance as well as to control for confound variance. For this reason, the covariates included in a regression equation (a technique that tests the relation between a set of predictor variables and the dependent variable) are not always necessarily confounds. For example, sex (a common covariate) does not have to be confounded (correlated) with crime exposure (the independent variable) for it to have methodological value in an equation predicting depression (the dependent variable), assuming sex is correlated with depression in the population under study.

Historically, homogeneous sampling was the leading technique for controlling extraneous variance in experimental research. In a homogeneous sample, subjects vary little on factors other than those of substantive interest to the research. In the past, researchers often limited their studies to college students or to white men of a given age cohort (say 30 to 50). This technique was effective, but the efficiency came at a very high cost to the generalizability of the research. In current health research, homogeneous sampling is no longer considered acceptable.

Design Features for Controlling Variance

Fortunately, there are lots of other ways to reduce extraneous variance in experiments and quasi-experiments. A skilled researcher can select and combine various features so as to create the most efficient research design possible for a given question. I will now describe the most generally applicable features used in research design. Many of these features also help the researcher to identify, if not necessarily eliminate, potential confounds in the research. I'll discuss how the various features accomplish this as well.

Blocking

Blocking is a very useful and widely applicable design strategy. It involves building the attribute variable (the source of the extraneous variance) into the design as a second independent variable or factor. For example, a researcher might know that men and women differ considerably on the dependent variable, making sex a source of extraneous variance that could cloud observed effects. A simple way to control this variance is to make sex a second independent variable in the design. The term, *factorial design*, refers to any between-groups design that has two or more factors. When one of the factors is an attribute variable, such as sex, rather than an experimental variable, we sometimes say that subjects have been blocked on sex, and refer to the attribute variable as a *blocking variable*.

Factorial designs have many advantages over one-way designs. One advantage is greater efficiency. Returning to the ratio, Vb/Vw, for reference, it is almost like we can take some of the variance out of the denominator and move it to the numerator. In the fear-affiliation example, blocking on sex could be very useful. In Figure 1, sex could easily contribute to the wide variability within each group. By blocking, the data can be examined apart from the extraneous influence of sex, as shown in Figure 4. The within-group variability is much smaller when groups are defined using both the experimental and blocking variables (Figure 4) than when they are defined using the experimental variable only (Figure 1). In a sense, blocking offers the advantages of homogeneous sampling without its disadvantages.

In addition, factorial designs allow the investigator to examine how the experimental and attribute variables combine to influence the dependent variable. A detailed discussion of the interpretation of main effects and interactions can be found in almost any statistics or research design text. The presentation here will be quite brief. A *main effect* is the effect of one independent variable on the dependent variable without regard to the other independent variables in the design. In my example, I might have a main effect of fear (exposed > unexposed), a main effect of sex (women > men), or both.

An *interaction* means that the effect of one independent variable (e.g., fear) depends upon the level of the other (e.g., sex). The best way

Figure 6a.

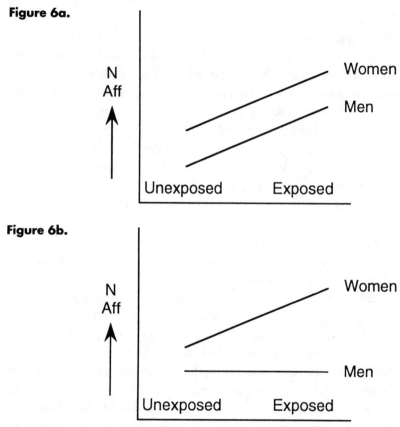

Figure 6b.

Figure 6.   Hypothetical Data. A Gender X Fear interaction is present
in Figure 6b, but not in Figure 6a.

to see whether an interaction is present or not is to plot the data as in
Figure 6. When the lines are parallel, as in 6a, there is no interaction.
The effect of fear in this example is the same among women and men
even though women are overall more affiliative. When the lines are not
parallel, such as in 6b, there is an interaction. Here, fear increased the
need to affiliate among women but not among men. Not only did this
design feature of blocking allow us to reduce extraneous variance, it
allowed us to describe the phenomenon all the better.

Blocking is useful regardless of whether one is using an experimental or quasi-experimental design. An analogous procedure can also be used in nonexperimental (correlational) designs. For example, correlations, or full regression models, can be tested within subgroups of a sample and compared across them. An investigator who is concerned that SES might be a source of confound or extraneous variance when examining a given relation might simply control for SES before assessing the effects of trauma, as illustrated in Figure 5. However, a different and more informative approach would be to test the relation within subsamples defined by SES.

Pretesting

Another common and very useful design feature is pretesting. A pretest is a measure of the dependent variable that is taken before a study begins. Traditionally (Campbell & Stanley, 1963), a *randomized pretest-posttest design* is symbolized as follows:

$$
\begin{array}{ccc}
O & X & O \\
O & & O
\end{array}
$$

The Os stand for observations and the X for experimental treatment. A *nonequivalent control group design* also relies on a pretest for its control over confound and extraneous variance. This quasi-experimental design looks just like the pretest-posttest design, except that a dotted line is used to symbolize the lack of random assignment to groups, as shown below.

$$
\begin{array}{ccc}
O & X & O \\
\cdots\cdots\cdots\cdots\cdots\cdots\cdots\cdots\cdots\cdots \\
O & & O
\end{array}
$$

It is easiest to show the advantages of pretesting by contrasting the pretest-posttest design to the *posttest only design*. In its simplest form, a true experiment requires only a single assessment, taken after the treatment occurs. The design is internally valid. Selection is ruled out because of randomization. History is ruled out because the effects of a co-occurring event, if any, should be reflected in the control group's scores as well as in the experimental group's scores; thus the difference between the two groups is still due only to the independent variable. Likewise, if subjects were naturally improving or worsening around the time of assessment, that maturation effect should occur among both experimental and control subjects. Once again the difference between the groups is due only to the independent variable. But even though it has controlled for confound variance, this basic posttest only design has done nothing to control for extraneous variance.

Consider an intervention study that aims to enhance the coping strategies available to gay adolescents as they confront harassment or even abuse in school. The dependent variable is positive coping, i.e., the number of instances of healthy coping (as opposed to unhealthy instances such as self-medication or social withdrawal) on some inventory of coping behaviors. You believe you can apply advances in cognitive therapy toward improving the efficacy of these adolescents' coping attempts. You randomly assign subjects to two groups: one group (E) receives the cognitive intervention; the other (C) participates in a discussion group. Both groups attend the first group session, report a week later for the second session, and at that time complete the coping inventory as it relates to the past week. Your hypothesis is supported if the experimental group has a statistically higher scale score average than the control group. Let's say you used a posttest only, so had available only the posttest data in Table 1 below. There is a difference between groups averaging 20 units, but there's also lots of within-group variability.

Now say you had included a pretest by administering the coping inventory at the beginning of the first session. You obtained the data shown below. Under most circumstances (Kenny, 1975), the appropriate dependent variable is a *difference score* rather than the posttest score. Can you see how this is much more efficient? The procedure dramatically reduced the range of individual differences. The pretest removed the influence of absolute healthiness of coping, which varied considerably, so that you could look at *change* in coping, which varied less.

Pretests have other advantages as well. Most importantly, they provide a check on the researcher's assumptions that subjects have been

Table 1. Hypothetical Data

Experimental Group			Control Group		
Pretest	Posttest	Difference	Pretest	Posttest	Difference
70	100	30	80	80	0
60	80	20	70	60	−10
110	120	10	90	100	10
180	200	20	190	180	−10
30	50	20	20	30	10
Mean	110	20		90	0
Range	150	20		150	20

assigned in such a way that experimental groups are equivalent. In a true experiment, a pretest is not essential but it nonetheless provides a check on random assignment. Although the laws of probability mean that randomized groups should be equivalent, occasionally, by chance, the groups may not be the same. A pretest provides a way of knowing if you were among the unlucky experimenters for whom random assignment has failed.

Another major advantage of using a pretest arises in studies that involve more than one experimental session or assessment point. As noted earlier, subject mortality or attrition poses a threat even in true experiments. Pretests do not eliminate subject attrition, but they help the researcher to assess the extent to which attrition was differential across groups. Generally, we are comfortable assuming that the study has remained internally valid if the subjects who dropped out of one group are comparable to the subjects who dropped out of the other.

In a quasi-experiment, a pretest is essential because one cannot count on randomization to produce equivalent groups. Kenny (1975) presents a useful and more advanced discussion of how to analyze pretest-posttest data depending upon an underlying model of selection into treatment groups. In cases where intact groups are examined, change score analysis is the appropriate method, but in cases where assignment to treatment is determined (a) by the participant's pretest or (b) by self-selection, other methods are required, such as analysis of covariance (ANCOVA, case a) or ANCOVA with reliability correction (case b).

Pretests (pre-event measures) are equally valuable in nonexperimental designs. When available, premeasures not only make the research more sensitive to the true effects of the predictor or independent variables (e.g., traumatic events) but reduce the confounding issues inherent in correlational data. Some correlational studies use a *longitudinal design*, meaning that the study involves two or more assessment points. Even better, some of these studies use a *prospective design*, meaning there is a measure of the dependent measure (y) taken before the measure of the event (x) and the outcome (y). If the effects of pre-event symptoms on postevent symptoms are controlled statistically, a stronger argument can be made that the relation between the traumatic event and subsequent pathology is not due to some unidentified confound. Pre-event measures are rare in trauma research, but they are not impossible to obtain if you are alert to opportunities as they arise.

Sometimes the opportunity arises to supplement a retrospective design with a prospective design. For example, my colleagues and I conducted a study of criminal victimization in which we screened a large random sample of households in Kentucky (N = 12,226) and selected samples of 171 recent violent crime victims, 338 recent property crime victims, and 298 nonvictims for more in-depth interviews. We attempted to assess the psychological symptoms (among other variables) of each person three times at six-month intervals and concluded the study with *n*s of 105, 227 and 190 for the three groups, respectively. For the most part, we studied the experiences of these 105 and 227 victims for whom we did not have precrime measures. As you might expect, there were statistically strong differences between these groups in the severity of symptoms: crime victims were more symptomatic than nonvictims, and violent crime victims were more symptomatic than property crime victims. These findings held when various background characteristics (potential confounds) were controlled, but we still could not establish unequivocally that crime exposure was not confounded with precrime psychological state. Nonetheless, because a substantial number of "nonvictims" experienced crimes over the course of the longitudinal study, we were able to supplement these retrospective analyses with prospective analyses that included precrime measures. For example, the effects of violent crimes occurring during the study on later depression held even when precrime depression was controlled. These analyses thus strengthened support for our conclusions that it was the crime itself and not some other confound that caused the observed elevations in psychological distress.

I can provide an even more opportunistic example from my research on natural disasters; in fact, it was this research opportunity that led me into the field of trauma research in the first place. As a student, I worked with Stan Murrell on a panel study of older adults' mental health. A *panel study* is a longitudinal study in which the same individuals are assessed repeatedly, such as in the crime study described above. This panel of older adults was interviewed about their recent stressful life events, resources, and mental health five times at six-month intervals. During the course of that study, a major flood occurred in eastern Kentucky, an area where a number of our respondents lived. I later received funding from NIMH to conduct additional interviews with respondents in the stricken area and adjacent counties about the extent of their exposure to the floods. These data were merged with the previously collected data, resulting in a tremendously rich set of data that included predisaster as well as postdisaster measures of psychological symptoms, physical health, and social support. The particular disaster we studied was not as catastrophic as are many, the number of primary victims was relatively small, and the sample varied widely in their scores on the dependent variables. I suspect that if we only had postflood data, the effects of the flood would have been very difficult to see. However, the ability to include predisaster measures made the design very sensitive to *changes* in symptoms and support co-occurring with the floods. Thus the design was simultaneously both more conservative (eliminating the threat that disaster reports were confounded with psychological states) and more sensitive (eliminating the extraneous variability in psychological states.)

Pretests also have a disadvantage in some types of intervention research. When using a pretest, the researcher must consider whether the pretest itself contributed to the observed outcome. A pretest might have motivated subjects to work harder or provided them with important information. Would the treatment have been as effective without the pretest to set the stage? This effect is generally considered an external validity issue rather than an interval validity issue. Solomon's Four Groups Design can be used if the researcher is seriously concerned about interactions between the pretest and treatment. This design essentially combines a posttest-only design with a pretest-posttest design, as illustrated below:

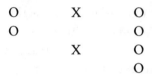

This design allows the researcher to make a number of interesting comparisons. Random assignment is assumed. The difference between the first and second group shows the effect of X in the presence of a pretest; the difference between the third and fourth group shows the effect of X in the absence of a pretest. The difference between the first and third group shows the effects of the pretest in the presence of treatment, whereas the difference between the second and fourth group shows the effects of the pretest in the absence of treatment. As you might imagine, this design is labor and subject intensive. Whether or not it is worth all the trouble depends upon the question under study. The design is probably quite useful if you want to export the treatment (X) to a real world setting where pretests would be unlikely to occur. It is less useful if pretests are likely to be a part of the intervention anyway (e.g., psychotherapy, educational initiatives).

Matching

Another feature, matching, is sometimes useful, generally when the sample is not large enough for blocking to be feasible. Matching means that subjects are paired in terms of a pre-existing characteristic. The pairing is useful only when the *matching variable* is correlated highly with the dependent variable. One member of each pair is assigned randomly to the experimental group, the other member to the control group. The dependent variable is then the difference in performance between members of the pair. On the average, if the experimental variable is unrelated to the outcome variable, the difference should be zero. The data look much like pretest-posttest data within a single group.

In the context of a true experiment, matching reduces confound variance that may arise when the sample size is so small that the laws of probability cannot assure equivalent groups. It reduces extraneous variance because difference rather than absolute scores are analyzed.

Matching is one of the most misused terms in research design. It means that cases are paired and that differences between members of pairs constitute the dependent variable. Often what the researcher really intends is to create a comparison group that is similar to some natural group (e.g., rape victims, fire survivors) in terms of its sex, race, age, or SES composition. In this case, the data are not paired for analysis. This procedure is better described as purposive sampling than matching.

Using Same Subjects

Another way to reduce extraneous and confound variance is to use the same subjects in all conditions. Instead of randomly assigning Ss to different levels of the independent variable, the investigator exposes each subject to all levels in some predetermined sequence. Subjects must be randomly assigned to sequence, however. *Within-subject designs* are the ultimate in control over selection bias because subjects in all groups are identical rather than merely probabilistically equivalent. Each subject is his own control. Moreover, because each subject is assessed more than once, variance due to individual differences across subjects can actually be isolated and removed, thereby yielding a highly sensitive design.

An example here could be basic research on the nature of posttraumatic stress. Perhaps we are interested in demonstrating physiological reactivity to traumatic stimuli among trauma victims. We could study this phenomenon using a between-groups design by randomly assigning subjects to three independent groups: the first group would be exposed to neutral stimuli, the second would be exposed to traumatic stimuli, and the third would be exposed to otherwise noxious or unpleasant stimuli. This design is sound; the physiological arousal of the three groups could be simply measured and compared. However, because trauma victims are difficult to obtain for research purposes, the *n* is likely to be small. Thus, to support the research hypothesis, between-group differences (those attributable to stimuli) will have to be substantially greater than within-group differences (individual differences in physiological states).

This dilemma is immediately resolved if we use a within-subjects design, in which each subject is exposed to all three stimuli (as illustrated by the data in Table 2). Not only do you get more data per subject (10 people provide as much information as 30 in the between-groups design), it becomes possible to isolate variations in performance across stimuli (intra-individual) from absolute differences in performance (inter-individual). Person A may always have higher scores than Person B, but each person may receive his own highest score when exposed to the traumatic stimuli. When the data are described in this way, you can begin to see how any given score (the score of one subject in one condition) can be predicted if you know which subject was performing (the Subject factor) and which condition she was performing under (the Stimuli factor). Study the data below and you will see how these patterns emerge. The main point here is to see how the influence of individual differences in physiological reactivity can be completely eliminated by using a within-subjects design.

The potential threat in within-subjects designs consists of various types of order and carry-over effects across conditions. This threat is easily preventable by *counterbalancing* so that some subjects are first assigned to Condition A, then to Condition B, whereas other subjects are first assigned to Condition B, then A. As with any between-subjects manipulation, assignment to order should be random.

Within-subjects designs have so many advantages over between-groups designs that it is unfortunate that they are limited to situations where exposure to one level of the independent variable does not meaningfully interfere with the effects of exposure to another level. If the investigator was testing the difference between two psychotherapeutic interventions, it would be impossible to undo the effects of one therapy while exposing the subject to the second. However, the method

Table 2.   More Hypothetical Data

	Raw scores				Deviation scores		
	Neutral Stimuli	Noxious Stimuli	Traumatic Stimuli	Mean	Neutral Stimuli	Noxious Stimuli	Traumatic Stimuli
S1	2	2	5	3	–1	–1	2
S2	4	4	7	5	–1	–1	2
S3	5	4	9	6	–1	–2	3
S4	9	8	10	9	0	–1	1
S5	10	12	14	12	–2	0	2
Mean	6	6	9	7	–1	–1	2

is useful for laboratory studies that yield insights into the cognitive, perceptual, or psychophysiological processes underlying PTSD.

Mixing Features to Create Research Designs

In general, these features are not mutually exclusive and can be combined with one another. Blocking and pretesting can be combined easily and effectively. Did older children (grades 4-6) show greater attitudinal change in response to a school-based anti-violence intervention than did younger children (grades 1-3)? Similarly, the strategies of blocking and using the same subjects can be combined quite well. The same subjects can be used at each level of the independent variable (e.g., type of stimulus) and blocked according to a pre-existing attribute variable (e.g., sex or type of trauma). As in all factorial designs, the investigator could then examine whether the independent and attribute variables interact (e.g., men show greater physiological reactivity than women; combat victims show greater physiological reactivity than rape victims.) Blocking is not likely to be combined with matching because the latter is generally used when the former is not feasible. However, pretesting and matching can be used together; in fact, a pretest sometimes constitutes an excellent matching variable. Pretesting and matching do not add anything to within-subjects designs because each subject already serves as his own control.

Summary: The Process of Designing a Study

Research design is first and foremost a logical process. The research question, phrased in the manner of a hypothesized cause and effect relation between two or more variables, comes first. We should create designs that answer our questions rather than ask questions that fit familiar designs. If you, the reader, are in the process of planning or conducting a study, ask yourself the questions outlined below. If you can answer them positively, you probably have a sound experiment or study in the works.

How am I minimizing error variance? Have I made sure that study procedures will be carried out systematically and consistently? Are my questions and directions to subjects worded clearly and unambiguously? If observers, confederates, or interviewers are involved in the research, have they been thoroughly trained? Have they been given adequate time to practice? Are my chosen measures reliable according to previous literature or my own pilot work?

How am I maximizing experimental variance? Is there an adequate implementation of treatment? Are the levels of the independent variable different enough to elicit different thoughts, feelings, or behaviors? Are operational definitions sufficiently sharp to create mutually exclusive categories? Do I have valid and sensitive dependent measures? Will they reflect differences in thoughts, feelings, or behaviors? Have I been careful to avoid ceiling or floor effects? Do I have adequate power, i.e., is my *n* adequate to detect an effect of a size reasonable to expect for the relation under study?

How am I minimizing confound variance? Is the independent variable something than can be studied with a true experiment, wherein I, the investigator, have complete control over who is exposed and who is not to different levels of the treatment? If yes, is the nature of the variable such that using the same subjects in all conditions is feasible? If I cannot use a within-subjects design, and I am therefore going to use a between-groups design, is my sample size adequate to depend upon random assignment to eliminate confounds, or should I use matching before randomly assigning each member of the pair to Condition A or B? Does a thoughtful consideration of the ethical issues point toward using an untreated, wait-list, non-specific treatment, or treatment-as-usual control group? Regardless of which I choose, have I developed my procedures sufficiently to insure that all groups are treated the same (attention, time, instructions, etc.) in all ways other than exposure to the independent variable? Have I done anything to cue subjects that I want them to behave in certain ways?

If I do not have complete control over assignment to levels of the independent variable, do I at least have some control? If I cannot control who gets the treatment, can I at least influence when they get it, so that pretesting can be used? Can I find an intact group, or create a group through purposive sampling, that is sufficiently comparable to serve as a non-equivalent control group, that I can simultaneously pretest, thereby creating a quasi-experimental design? How will I insure that my treatment and nonequivalent control groups are treated the same (attention, time, instructions, etc.) in all ways other than exposure to the independent variable?

If I have no experimental control, have I carefully researched, identified, and measured all variables deemed to be meaningful sources of confound and extraneous variance so that I can use statistical controls as part of my nonexperimental or correlational study? Have I been too quick to conclude that only a cross-sectional and retrospective design is feasible or necessary, given the phenomenon to be studied? Pretending for the exercise that resources are no concern, what would it take to study the phenomenon using a longitudinal and prospective design?

Regardless of whether my basic approach is to be an experimental, quasi-experimental, or nonexperimental study, have I carefully reviewed (perhaps using a checklist of some kind) how my specific design for my specific question in my specific setting controls for the various threats to internal validity, such as selection, maturation, history, mortality, statistical regression, instrumentation, and reactivity? Can some of these threats be ruled out on logical grounds if the design does not eliminate the threat?

How am I minimizing extraneous variance? The plan for controlling extraneous variance may overlap with the plan for controlling confound variance because many design features help to minimize both. According to my answers above, will I be using a pretest or some other form of repeated measurement? If yes, am I confident that this procedure will adequately control for the study's extraneous variance as well? If no, can I add a pretest to the design simply for this reason without otherwise jeopardizing the study's validity? Have I considered and identified one or more subject attributes that would be useful to treat as blocking or matching variables?

Closing Words. Design is so complex that it often takes several exposures to these concepts before one begins to feel competent in designing studies. If you could not answer all of the questions above, keep working! Consult other reference materials on designing trauma studies, such as the chapters by Baum et al. (1993) and Kulka and Schlenger (1993). Scour the literature for studies that have dealt with the specific issues that are puzzling you. Find a consultant or collaborator or mentor. Experienced researchers can often detect design problems that may not be apparent to novice researchers. Do pilot work. When you both know the answers and understand the questions, you probably have a good to excellent understanding of research design.

References

Baum, A., Solomon, S., Ursano, R., Bickman, L., Blanchard, E., Green, B., Keane, T., Laufer, R., Norris, F., Reid, J., Smith, E., & Steinglass, P. (1993). Emergency/disaster studies: Practical, conceptual, and methodological issues. (pp. 125–133). In J. Wilson & B. Raphael (Eds.) *International handbook of traumatic stress syndromes.* New York: Plenum Press.

Campbell, D. & Stanley, J. (1963). *Experimental and quasi-experimental designs for research.* Chicago: Rand-McNally.

Cohen, J. (1992). A power primer. *Psychological Bulletin, 112,* 155–159.

Durso, F. & Mellgren, R. (1989). *Thinking about research: Methods and tactics of the behavioral scientist.* New York: West.

Fairbank, J., Jordan, B. K., & Schlenger, W. E. (1995). Designing and implementing epidemiologic studies. In E. B. Carlson (Ed.), *Trauma research methodology.* Lutherville, MD: Sidran Press.

Kenny, D. (1975). A quasi-experimental approach to assessing treatment effects in the Nonequivalent Control Group Design. *Psychological Bulletin, 82,* 346–360.

Kerlinger, F. (1986). *Foundations of behavioral research*. New York: CBS College Publishing.

Kulka, R. & Schlenger, W. (1993). Survey research and field designs for the study of posttraumatic stress disorder. (pp. 145–155). In J. Wilson & B. Raphael (Eds.) *International handbook of traumatic stress syndromes*. New York: Plenum Press.

3

Choosing Self-Report Measures and Structured Interviews

Susan D. Solomon, Terence M. Keane, Elana Newman, Danny G. Kaloupek

When designing a study, one of the first tasks you will face is to choose what measures to use. Almost every trauma-related study should include some measure of posttraumatic stress disorder (PTSD) symptoms and some measure of exposure to traumatic events. This chapter discusses the strengths and weaknesses of various instruments available for measuring posttraumatic stress disorder (PTSD). Which of these is the best will depend on the purpose for which it is being used. We will also briefly discuss some measures of exposure to traumatic events.

The kind of research question you are asking may dictate the need to use a certain kind of instrument. One important consideration is whether PTSD is the central focus of a study or whether it is peripheral to the study's purpose. For example, if a research question requires a case-control design study that compares people who are exposed to an event and develop PTSD to people who are exposed to that same event but do not develop PTSD, you want to be sure that the people designated as PTSD are truly cases. In that particular kind of study, where there is a strong need for accuracy in determining caseness, you

The opinions or assertions contained herein are the private ones of the authors and are not to be considered as official or to reflect the views of the National Institutes of Health or the Department of Veterans Affairs. The authors would like to thank Ellen Gerrity and Gladys Hammond for providing background information for this chapter.

might want to rely on multiple measures for assessing PTSD. In contrast, if the study is intended to determine the long-range outcome of exposure to a particular violent experience, you may want to assess not only PTSD but also many other outcomes as well (e.g., substance abuse, depression, marital and occupational functioning). In that case you may want to chose a single brief measure of PTSD, to allow sufficient time to assess these other domains.

Many self-report measures and structured interviews have been developed to assess the symptoms of PTSD in adults. This wide array of instruments poses a challenge to you when you are trying to select the most appropriate measure for your research study. Since the assessment of PTSD is tied to the diagnosis itself, this chapter begins with a discussion of some problems with the definition of PTSD as they affect assessment. The chapter then reviews the more commonly used instruments for assessing PTSD in adults, in terms of their advantages and disadvantages for particular uses.

Research Constraints Imposed by the Diagnosis

To meet criteria for the diagnosis as it was defined in DSM-III-R (American Psychiatric Association, 1987) an individual must have "experienced an event that is outside the range of usual human experience" (Criterion A). Symptoms that are predicted to result from this exposure cluster into three distinct groups: 1) four symptoms relating to reexperiencing the trauma (Criterion B), such as intrusive distressing recollections or recurrent dreams; 2) seven symptoms relating to avoidance of stimuli associated with the trauma or numbing of general responsiveness (Criterion C), such as avoidance of trauma-related thoughts or diminished interest in people or activities; and, 3) six symptoms of persistent increased arousal (Criterion D), such as difficulty in sleeping or concentrating. To qualify for the diagnosis of PTSD, an individual must present at least one reexperiencing, at least three avoidance, and at least two arousal symptoms. While these criteria were recently revised for DSM-IV (American Psychiatric Association, 1994) (e.g., the stressor has been redefined to include both objective and subjective elements; physiological reactivity has been moved to the reexperiencing cluster; duration requirements are changed), the basic symptoms and the way they are clustered have remained fundamentally the same. For present purposes these changes in the DSM are quite minor; as a result the instruments reviewed in this chapter, although developed and tested prior to the DSM-IV revision of the criteria, remain current and timely. However, both past and present formulations of this diagnosis create difficulties for the assessment of PTSD.

One problem with the diagnosis is that the stressor (the "cause") is built into the PTSD criteria. This makes it difficult to assess PTSD as a response (the "effect"). For example, many individuals who have all of the Criteria B, C, and D symptoms will not be counted as having PTSD if their stressor (e.g., job loss) does not fit Criterion A (see Scott and Stradling, 1994 for case examples). Other individuals who have, at some point in their lives, been through a traumatic event (e.g., combat veterans) may be counted as PTSD cases even if the event they report that they are currently reexperiencing is a confrontation with their supervisor (i.e., not physically threatening as is required by the stressor criterion). In order to really learn about cause and effect it is necessary to use a measurement strategy that optimally separates the two: i.e., one that assesses PTSD symptoms independently of stressors.

That being said, however, we recognize that the nature of the relation between the traumatic event and the PTSD symptoms requires some means of being able to link these two factors. In terms of measurement, the issue is a question of who should be required to make this link. The respondent may see no connection between his or her Criterion C and D symptoms and the traumatic event he or she has experienced. Yet on some scales the questions are worded so that the symptom will not be counted unless the respondent says it resulted from the traumatic exposure. In these cases, some instruments are requiring knowledge not available to the respondent and will therefore fail to identify C and D symptoms. For this reason scales that separate the traumatic event from the C and D symptoms are rated more highly in this review than those that do not.

A related problem is that DSM diagnostic criteria and most self-report measures and structured interviews assume that the subject has experienced a single trauma. Since symptoms are linked to a single traumatic event, these measures and interviews constrain subjects who have experienced multiple traumas to report only symptoms related to one event. Clearly, for many subjects, this will result in underreporting of symptoms or a false negative diagnosis.

Another problematic aspect of the DSM system for assessing PTSD is the division of the diagnosis into three distinct categories of symptoms (Criteria B, C, and D), with arbitrary requirements for a specific number of symptoms in each category. It is not at all apparent that this particular grouping of symptoms and the specific cutoff criteria for each symptom group add anything meaningful to our understanding of the diagnosis. A major disadvantage of this categorization strategy, however, is very clear: it substantially reduces the probability of detecting a statistically significant difference between respondent groups because non-parametric tests (used for analyzing categorical data) are always less powerful than parametric tests (used for analyzing continuous data). Furthermore, PTSD is most appropriately conceptualized as a dimensional construct, and like all other mental health disorders, is best represented as a continuum; that is, rather than being clearly present or absent, PTSD is actually a matter of degree. Where one draws the line on a dimensional PTSD measure above which someone is to be called a case is subject to some debate. Yet the DSM calls for artificially considering PTSD as a dichotomy. We view such clear-cut distinctions about the disorder and among symptom criteria as premature given the available technology, and have rated more highly those instruments that allow PTSD to be measured on a dimensional scale rather than just on a categorical one.

Most instruments described in the following sections have attempted to address one or more of these diagnostic limitations, with varying degrees of success. The importance of these limitations, and the usefulness of any particular instrument, will depend on the purpose of the research. This chapter describes the characteristics of the major instruments in use today for measuring PTSD in adults, with the objective of helping researchers determine which of these instruments is most suitable for their own study purposes.

Self-Report Instruments

Self-report measures are popular for many reasons. As Spiro, Shalev, Solomon, and Kotler (1989) note, self-report measures are more easily standardized than clinicians' assessments and less intrusive than physiological measures. Since these measures provide information about how respondents view their symptoms in a context that is not influenced by direct interaction with an interviewer, they may increase the response accuracy for individuals who would be reluctant to reveal their experiences to another person directly. Self-report measures are relatively inexpensive to use, since they take less time to administer than structured clinical interviews and can be administered by trained paraprofessionals. As a result, self-report measures are often included in studies using structured interviews, in order to provide multiple measures of PTSD (Keane, Wolfe, & Taylor, 1987). Some of these tools are used primarily as screening instruments, since only those scoring high are subjected to more time-consuming and costly interviews. Accordingly, their use can realize a substantial savings in research costs.

To date, a variety of PTSD self-report measures have been developed. Tables 1, 2, and 3 present characteristics of the most frequently used and/or psychometrically advanced self-report measures to assess PTSD and its associated symptoms in traumatized populations. As Table 1 indicates, none of the self-report scales provide information about the recency, onset, and/or duration of PTSD symptoms.

Table 1 examines the following properties of the items in each self-report instrument: a) the number of items; b) whether or not the instrument assesses symptom frequency, severity, recency, onset, and/or duration; c) whether the measure is designed to produce a categorical or dimensional outcome for each symptom; and d) the time period for which the symptoms are measured. (Table 4 offers the same information for the structured clinical interviews.)

Table 2 shows how each self-report scale as a whole assesses properties of the PTSD diagnosis: a) whether the scale yields a DSM PTSD diagnosis; if so, b) whether the diagnosis is a categorical or dimensional one; c) if the measure assesses other psychiatric diagnoses or symptom clusters; d) whether the scale has been tested on the general population

Table 1.   Item Properties of Self-report Scales

Scale	# Items	Frequency	Intensity	Recency/ Onset/ Duration	Time Period	C/D
				Items Assess		
Miss	34 (combat) 39 (civilian)	Y[a]	Y[a]	N	NS	D
MMPI-PK	49	N	N	N	NS	C
Penn	26	Y[a]	Y[a]	N	past W	D
PSS-S	17	Y	Y	N	past 2W	D
SIP	47	N	Y	N	past 4W	D
PCL	17	N	Y	N	past M	D
CR-PTSD	28	Y[a]	Y[a]	N	past 2W	D
IES	15	Y	N	N	past W	D

Y=Yes; N=No; C=Categorical; D=Dimensional; NS=Not Specified; W= Week; M= Month; [a] = some items measure frequency and some items measure intensity; Miss= Mississippi Scale; MMPI-PK=Keane PTSD Scale; Penn=Penn Inventory for PTS; PSS-S=PTSD Symptom Scale Self-report; SIP= Self-rating Inventory for PTSD; PCL= PTSD Checklist; CR-PTSD=Crime-Related PTSD Scale; IES=Impact of Event Scale

or on special sub-populations; and e) whether the measure includes the assessment of symptoms associated with multiple traumas. (See Table 5 for similar information about the structured clinical interviews.)

Table 3 highlights available information about each self-report instrument's strengths: a) whether it can be administered by trained paraprofessionals; b) whether assessment of Criterion C and D symptoms of PTSD are linked to a particular traumatic event and require the respondent to make this link; c) and whether self-report measures have demonstrated a high degree of test-retest reliability (the extent to which test scores are consistent over time); d) convergent validity (the degree to which test scores correlate with scores on another measure of PTSD; e) sensitivity (the probability that those *with* the diagnosis will be correctly identified by the test score); and f) specificity (the probability that

Table 2. Instrument Properties of Self-report Scales

Scale	DSM-III-R PTSD Diagnosis	C/D	Assesses Comorbidity	Population Tested On	Multiple Traumas
Miss	Slight Deviations	D	N	Veterans Clinical	N
MMPI-PK	Large Deviations	No DX	N	Veterans Clinical	TNA
Penn	Slight Deviations	C & D	N	Veterans Disaster	TNA
PSS-S	Exact	C & D	N	Veterans Rape	N
SIP	Exact	C & D	DESNOS	Military Clinical	TNA
PCL	Exact	C & D	N	Military General	N
CR-PTSD	Large Deviations	No DX	Y (SX)	Crime	TNA
IES	Large Deviations	No DX	N	General	N

Y=Yes; N=No; C=Categorical; D=Dimensional; DX=Diagnosis; SX=Symptoms; TNA=Trauma not assessed; Miss= Mississippi Scale; MMPI-PK=Keane PTSD Scale; Penn=Penn Inventory for PTS; PSS-S=PTSD Symptom Scale Self-report; SIP= Self-rating Inventory for PTSD; PCL= PTSD Checklist; CR-PTSD=Crime-Related PTSD Scale; IES=Impact of Event Scale

those *without* the diagnosis will be correctly identified). (See Table 6 for the strengths and psychometric properties of the structured clinical interviews for PTSD). In Table 6, reliability results may refer to test-retest reliability or to interrater reliability (the extent to which test results are the same when administered or scored by different interviewers).

The standards shown in Table 3 for convergent validity and specificity may not apply to measures that assess multiple traumas, do not require Criterion A for the diagnosis, and/or do not link Criterion C and D symptoms to a particular event. If the validity of such a measure was studied using a diagnostic interview which was more narrow in its assessment (assessing for only a single trauma, requiring Criterion A,

Table 3.   Special Strengths and Psychometric Properties of
Self-report Scales

Scale	Parapro. Admin.	C & D Symptoms Linked to Trauma	Reliability >.75	Converg. Validity >.75 (Scale)	Sensitivity >.80	Specificity >.80
Miss	Y	Y	Y	N	Y	Y
MMPI-PK	Y	Y	Y	Y (CAPS)	Y	Y
Penn	Y	Y	Y	Y (Miss.)	Y	Y
PSS-S	Y	Y	N	Y (SCID)	N	Y
SIP	Y	N	Y	Y (CAPS, Miss)	Y	N
PCL	Y	Y	Y	Y (Miss, IES)	Y	Y
CR-PTSD	Y	Y	ND	ND	N	Y
IES	Y	N	ND	Y (PCL)	Y	N

Y=Yes; N=No; C=Categorical; D=Dimensional; ND=No Data; Miss=Mississippi Scale;
MMPI-PK=Keane PTSD Scale; PENN=Penn Inventory for PTS; PSS-S=PTSD Symptom
Scale Self-report; SIP= Self-rating Inventory for PTSD; PCL=PTSD Checklist; CR-
PTSD=Crime-Related PTSD Scale; IES=Impact of Event Scale

and linking symptoms to trauma), then one would expect the new measure to appear to have lower convergent validity and lower specificity.
For example, subjects with multiple traumas would be likely to report
more symptoms on the new measure than on the diagnostic interview
(resulting in lower convergent validity for the new measure). Furthermore, the standard diagnostic interview would be likely to identify
some subjects as PTSD-negative who actually were PTSD-positive (if
all of their symptoms were considered). These differences in diagnosis
between the self-report measure and the diagnostic interview would result in an erroneously low specificity levels for the new measure.

Mississippi Scale for Combat-related PTSD (Keane, Caddell, & Taylor, 1988)

Available in both combat and civilian versions, the 35- and 39-item scales have performed effectively in both clinical (Keane, Wolfe & Taylor, 1987; McFall, Smith, Rozell, Tarver, & Malas, 1990) and community (Kulka et al., 1991) settings. The Mississippi Scale was originally developed to assess the severity of DSM-III PTSD symptoms, and also assesses a number of features associated with PTSD. Ratings are made on a 5-point Likert scale measuring PTSD symptom severity. Requiring 15 minutes to administer, the Mississippi scale has been demonstrated to have excellent psychometric properties. Several versions of the Mississippi Scale have been developed to make it applicable to other populations. The Mississippi Scale seems to function as a very good indicator of PTSD, although not every symptom of the disorder is directly assessed.

PK subscale of the MMPI (Keane, Malloy, & Fairbank, 1984)

This scale consists of 49 items that were initially successful in differentiating PTSD from non-PTSD patients. However, subsequent studies have found a significantly lower rate of correct classification (Watson, 1990). The PK subscale seems to work as well when it is applied as a separate measure as it does when imbedded in the MMPI (Herman, Weathers, Litz, Keane, & Joaquim, 1993). As a separate measure it takes approximately 15 minutes to administer. The scale was revised slightly for MMPI-2 by deleting three item repetitions (Lyons & Keane, 1992). The scale does not comprehensively reflect DSM PTSD symptoms and may be most useful for analyses of the many archived datasets which include the MMPI, but no measure of PTSD.

Penn Inventory for Posttraumatic Stress (Hammerberg, 1992)

This 26-item scale is unique in that it is the only PTSD scale to have been developed and validated on different trauma populations (accident survivors, combat veterans, and veteran psychiatric patients in different cultures), although to date it has not been validated with women. Requiring only 15 minutes to complete, the scale yields dimensional ratings of all DSM-III-R symptoms of PTSD as well as related symptoms, and its psychometric properties are excellent. Its items are designed to apply to all types of traumatic events.

PTSD Symptom Scale Self-Report (PSS-S) (Foa, Riggs, Dancu, & Rothbaum, 1993)

The PSS-S consists of 17 items rated on a 4-point scale from "not at all" to "very much," permitting the scale to be used as either a categorical or dimensional measure. The scale is brief, taking only 5 to 10 minutes to complete. However, since it has been used only on rape victims, there is no psychometric data for other traumatized samples. Another disadvantage of this scale is that respondents are required to link their C and D Criterion symptoms of PTSD to a particular traumatic event; as discussed earlier, this may lead to under-reporting of these symptoms. In addition, its 2-week symptom window makes it more useful as a measure of change over time than as a measure of DSM-III-R PTSD, since the diagnosis is tied to a different time frame. A modified version of this scale includes both frequency and intensity ratings (Falsetti, Resnick, Resick, & Kilpatrick, 1993). Unlike the PSS-S, this modified version allows assessment of symptoms related to multiple traumatic events. The Falsetti et al. (1993) measure has been tested on treatment-seeking and community samples with good psychometric results.

Self-rating Inventory for PTSD (SIP) (Hovens, 1994)

The SIP consists of 47 items, 22 of which are the core symptoms of DSM-III-R criteria for PTSD. The remaining items assess associated features of PTSD, especially the "Disorders of Extreme Stress Not Otherwise Specified" (DESNOS) category of symptoms believed to be found in chronically traumatized populations (proposed for, but ultimately not included in, DSM-IV). The items are rated independently of the traumatic stressor, and are assessed on a 4-point Likert scale, allowing for a dimensional measure of PTSD. Tested on war traumatized and psychiatric patients in the Netherlands, the scale has been found to have good psychometric properties, and appears to discriminate not only between PTSD and non-PTSD cases, but also between non-PTSD cases who have been through a traumatic event and those have not.

PTSD Checklist (PCL) (Weathers, Litz, Herman, Huska, & Keane, 1993)

Requiring only 5 to 10 minutes to complete, the PCL is a 17-item measure that provides a dimensional measure of PTSD, with each of its items measured on a 5-point scale. The scale offers the advantages of being brief and of possessing excellent psychometric properties. It is available in three versions: one with reexperiencing items written generically to apply to military experiences, one written generically to apply to any traumatic event, and one written to apply to a specified event.

Symptom Checklist 90-R Scales (SCL-90-R) (Derogatis, 1977)

The SCL-90-R is a commonly used 90-item inventory designed to reflect psychological symptom patterns. A subset of items comprise the Global Severity Index, the scale's best single indicator of the severity and range of subjective distress. A number of attempts have been made to derive a PTSD scale from items on the SCL-90-R, since such a scale can be incorporated into a research protocol without requiring an additional PTSD measure. Because the SCL-90-R has been so widely used, a PTSD scale derived from it also permits analysis of existing data sets not originally designed to examine PTSD. Perhaps the best known of these SCL-derived scales is the Crime-Related PTSD Scale (CR-PTSD) (Saunders, Arata, & Kilpatrick, 1990). This 28-item measure was successful in discriminating women with crime-related PTSD from noncases in a community population. Green (1991) developed a 12-item SCL-90-R PTSD subscale for disaster survivors that discriminated cases from non-cases as well as the CR-PTSD in a non-clinical population. However, Green notes that there is no evidence that either scale has greater predictive validity for PTSD than the Global Severity Index of the SCL-90-R.

Impact of Event Scale (IES) (Horowitz, Wilner, & Alvarez, 1979; Zilberg, Weiss, & Horowitz, 1982)

This scale is the oldest and most widely used self-report instrument for assessing the psychological consequences of exposure to traumatic events and has been administered to several different kinds of traumatized and bereaved populations. Due to its widespread use this measure is often included within a battery of PTSD measures, to allow for cross-study comparisons of results. A 15-item measure, the IES takes approximately 10 minutes to complete. While easy to administer, the usefulness of this measure is limited by its exclusive emphasis on the intrusive and avoidant symptoms, rather than the full range of PTSD symptoms. Further, respondents must be able to link their symptoms to a single traumatic event, potentially leading to an underestimate of these symptoms.

Structured Clinical Interviews

When the central purpose of the study requires obtaining an accurate diagnosis of PTSD, use of a structured clinical interview is recommended (Green, 1990; Resnick, Kilpatrick, & Lipovsky, 1991; Wolfe & Keane, 1993). Structured clinical interviews allow for a detailed exploration of PTSD symptomatology. The interview method provides organization and consistency, while permitting respondents to discuss their experiences in their own words. The interview format also provides the flexibility needed to gather qualitative information and can potentially increase comprehension, since interviewers can rephrase questions to insure that a respondent understands them. Some of the interviews described below are measures solely of PTSD. Others imbed the PTSD assessment in an extensive interview which includes the assessment of other mental disorders. Tables 4, 5, and 6 describe the specific properties of each of these interviews. All of these interviews offer the advantage of yielding an exact DSM diagnosis of PTSD.

PTSD Symptom Scale Interview (PSS-I) (Foa, Riggs, Dancu, & Rothbaum, 1993)

The PSS-I is a 17-item semi-structured interview that assesses the severity of PTSD as a continuous measure. Requiring only about 10 minutes to complete, the PSS-I has been designed for use by paraprofessional interviewers, making its administration relatively inexpensive. Its psychometric properties are promising, although thus far it has been

Table 4. Item Properties of Structured Interviews

Scale	# Items	Items Assessed					Time Period	C/D
		Frequency	Intensity	Recency	Onset	Duration		
PSS-I	17	Y[a]	Y[a]	N	N	N	past 2W	C&D
SI-PTSD	28+	Y[a]	Y[a]	N	N	Y	worst ever recent past	C&D
PTSD-I	21	Y[a]	Y[a]	N	Y	N	worst M past M	C&D
CAPS	30+	Y	Y	N	N	N	worst M past M	C&D
SCID	19	N	N	Y	Y	Y	worst ever past 5Yr	C&D
DIS	13+	Y	Y	Y	Y	Y	<2W, 4W 6M, 1Yr, >1Yr	C
ADIS-R	17	Y_a	Y_a	Y_b	Y_b	Y_b	1W, 1M	D

Y=Yes; N=No; C=Categorical; D=Dimensional; Yr=Year; [a] = some items measure frequency and some items measure intensity; [b] = property is assessed for the entire scale; PSS-I=PTSD Symptom Scale Interview; SI-PTSD=Structured Interview for PTSD; PTSD-I=PTSD Interview; CAPS=Clinician Administered PTSD Scale; SCID=Structured Clinical Interview; DIS=Diagnostic Interview Schedule; ADIS-R=The Anxiety Disorders Interview-Revised

validated only with female victims of sexual and criminal assault, and its sensitivity and specificity are unknown. A disadvantage of this scale is that respondents are required to link their C and D Criterion symptoms of PTSD to a particular traumatic event, which may lead to under-reporting of these symptoms. Further, its two-week window departs from that of the DSM.

Structured Interview for PTSD (SI-PTSD) (Davidson, Smith & Kudler, 1989)
The 28-item SI-PTSD takes approximately 15 to 25 minutes to administer. A positive and unique feature of this interview is that it uses

Table 5. Instrument Properties of Structured Interviews

Scale	DSM-III-R PTSD Diagnosis	C/D	Assesses Comorbidity	Population Tested On	Multiple Traumas
PSS-I	Exact	C & D	N	Assault	N
SI-PTSD	Exact	C & D	N	Veterans	N
PTSD-I	Exact	C & D	N	Veterans	N
CAPS	Exact	C & D	N	Veterans	TNA
SCID	Exact	C	Y	General Clinical	N
DIS	Exact	C	Y	General Clinical	Y
ADIS-R	Exact	C & D	Dep, Anx	Veterans	N

Y=Yes; N=No; C=Categorical; D=Dimensional; Dep=Depression; Anx=Anxiety; TNA= Trauma not assessed; PSS-I=PTSD Symptom Scale Interview; SI-PTSD=Structured Interview for PTSD; PTSD-I=PTSD Interview; CAPS=Clinician Administered PTSD Scale; SCID=Structured Clinical Interview; DIS=Diagnostic Interview Schedule; ADIS-R=The Anxiety Disorders Interview-Revised

Table 6. Special Strengths and Psychometric Properties of Structured Interviews

Scale	Parapro. Admin.	C & D Symptoms Linked to Trauma	Reliability >.75	Converg. Validity >.75 (Scale)	Sensitivity >.80	Specificity >.80
PSS-I	Y	Y	Y	Y (SCID)	ND	ND
SI-PTSD	Y	Y	Y	Y (SCID)	Y	Y
PTSD-I	Y	Y	Y	Y (DIS)	Y	Y
CAPS	N	N	Y	Y (SCID)	Y	Y
DIS	Y	Y	ND	ND	Y	N
SCID	N	Y	Y	N	Y	Y
ADIS-R	Y	Y	ND	Y (Expert)	Y	Y

Y=Yes; N=No; C=Categorical; D=Dimensional; ND=No Data; PSS-I=PTSD Symptom Scale Interview; SI-PTSD=Structured Interview for PTSD; PTSD-I=PTSD Interview; CAPS=Clinician Administered PTSD Scale; SCID=Structured Clinical Interview; DIS=Diagnostic Interview Schedule (general population); ADIS-R=The Anxiety Disorders Interview-Revised observer ratings to measure "constricted affect," in addition to obtaining the more common assessments of feelings of estrangement, detachment, and diminished interest. The interview provides both categorical and dimensional ratings of DSM-III PTSD symptoms. Another strength is that the SI-PTSD's ratings are directly tied to the severity or frequency of particular behaviors for each symptom (e.g., nightmares are rated by frequency and disruption caused, using behavioral anchors such as waking up sweating or shouting). The authors of the SI-PTSD scale report promising psychometric properties, although thus far the SI-PTSD has been validated only with veterans. A disadvantage of the SI-PTSD is its use of the problematic "worst ever" time period to assess lifetime PTSD. This may result in an overestimate of lifetime PTSD, in that all reported symptoms may not have been experienced concurrently. Another disadvantage may have the opposite effect: like most structured interviews, the SI-PTSD requires respondents to be able to link their C and D Criterion symptoms of PTSD to a particular traumatic event, thereby constraining the reporting of these symptoms.

PTSD Interview (PTSD-I) (Watson, Juba, Manifold, Kucula, & Anderson, 1991)

The 21-item PTSD-I is a 10-minute interview that provides both categorical and dimensional ratings of PTSD symptoms and overall diagnosis. One of the few instruments to assess onset, frequency *and* severity of symptoms, the PTSD-I's other advantages include its excellent psychometric properties, its brevity, and its ability to be administered by a lay interviewer. A disadvantage of the PTSD-I is that it lacks interviewer probes; further, its questionnaire-like format and reliance on the interviewee's responses makes it subject to the limitations of self-report methods. Another disadvantage of the instrument is that it has thus far been tested only on veterans.

Clinician-Administered PTSD Scale (CAPS) (Blake et al., 1990; Blake et al., 1995; Weathers, 1993; Weathers, Blake et al., 1993)

Designed to overcome many of the limitations of other structured PTSD interviews, the CAPS addresses both the 17 primary PTSD symptoms and 13 associated characteristics, including impairment in social and occupational functioning. Its symptoms are behaviorally defined and its one-month time frame for current symptoms is consistent with DSM criteria. A weekly version is also available for detecting change over time (e.g., within the course of treatment). The CAPS generates both categorical and dimensional indices of PTSD. It also assesses specific criteria for both intensity and frequency of symptoms, thereby allowing an individual who has occasional intense symptoms to meet diagnostic criteria as well as a person who has more frequent but less intense symptoms. In addition, the CAPS is the only interview to assess the C and D criterion symptoms without reference to a particular traumatic event; indeed, trauma exposure is not assessed at all in this instrument since it is intended for use in conjunction with a separate trauma exposure measure. This sensitive procedure allows for a more complete and accurate reporting of the C and D symptoms, and thus a greater likelihood of meeting diagnostic criteria than the other interviews, all of which require the respondents themselves to make the link between their symptoms and a particular event. These strengths, coupled with its strong psychometric properties, make the CAPS an excellent choice for use in research. Its major disadvantages include the length of time required for administration (45 to 90 minutes), and the lack of validation to date with non-veterans. And, like most instruments, the CAPS does not assess symptom recency, onset and/or duration, information that may be of importance for some study purposes.

Structured Clinical Interview for DSM-III-R (SCID) (Spitzer, Williams, Gibbon, & First, 1990)

The SCID is designed to provide a comprehensive clinical assessment of DSM Axes I and II, making its use advantageous in studies of PTSD comorbidity. The PTSD module of the SCID offers other advantages as well, not the least of which is its usefulness for cross-study comparisons with other traumatized populations, as it has been used in a broad range of PTSD studies. The SCID-PTSD module typically takes a skilled clinician only 15 to 30 minutes to administer and has been found to have very good psychometric properties. Apart from the DIS (see below), the SCID is the only instrument to include an assessment of the recency, onset, and duration of PTSD symptoms. On the minus side, however, the SCID includes no assessment of the frequency and intensity of these symptoms. Another disadvantage of the SCID is that it provides only categorical assessments of both the symptoms and the diagnosis, and thus is insensitive to changes in symptom patterns over time. In addition, the SCID measures lifetime PTSD symptoms irrespective of when they occurred, based on the respondent's memory of their "worst ever" experience, a procedure which is likely to lead to an overestimate of lifetime PTSD. Finally, the SCID interview must be administered by a trained clinician, a costly requirement for research studies.

Diagnostic Interview Schedule (DIS) (Robins, Helzer, Croughan, Williams, & Spitzer, 1981)

The DIS is a semi-structured interview that a trained technician can administer, making it relatively less costly than the SCID for obtaining diagnostic information. The DIS as a whole is designed to measure most of the major psychiatric diagnoses and is therefore useful in assessing comorbidity with PTSD. The 13-item PTSD section is brief, requiring only about 15 minutes to administer for each traumatic event. Another advantage of the DIS is that it has been used in many community-based studies, thus facilitating cross-study comparisons. In addition, it may be used to assess the effects of multiple traumatic events.

A shortcoming of the DIS is its reliance on categorical ratings, thereby limiting its ability to detect ranges of symptoms and changes over time. Furthermore, like most interviews, the DIS requires the interviewee to directly associate each PTSD symptom with a specific traumatic event, resulting in a potential underestimate of criterion C and D symptoms. The DIS has also been criticized for using only one initial screening question to determine if the PTSD module should be administered (Resnick, Kilpatrick, & Lipovsky, 1991). However, this shortcoming can be overcome by using better concurrent measures of trauma exposure. Probably the most serious criticism of the DIS has revolved around its psychometric properties. The few studies assessing the DSM-III version of the DIS were discouraging. While some evidence supported its usefulness in clinical settings (see Watson, 1990), the DSM-III version of the DIS was found to greatly underestimate the number of PTSD cases in the National Vietnam Veterans Readjustment Study (NVVRS; Kulka et al., 1991). However, it should be noted that the DIS was considerably modified for DSM-III-R, and a study using this revised version in an HMO population showed improved sensitivity (Breslau, Davis, Andreski, & Petersen, 1991). The instrument was recently revised again for DSM-IV, and now provides a very comprehensive picture of PTSD core symptoms (Robins, personal communication, August 1994). Nevertheless, there is a need for psychometric evaluation of the newer version in field studies before its utility can be determined.

The Anxiety Disorders Interview-Revised (ADIS-R; DiNardo & Barlow, 1988; DiNardo, Moras, Barlow, Rapee, & Brown, 1993)

The ADIS-R is designed to provide a comprehensive assessment of anxiety and mood disorders, so it is particularly useful for studies of PTSD comorbidity with affective or other anxiety disorders. The ADIS-R PTSD module takes approximately 15–25 minutes for a trained mental health professional to administer. The ADIS-R is the only interview that includes a section about trauma-related panic symptoms, a feature that may be most useful when the relationship between panic disorder and PTSD needs to be explored. Unfortunately, the ADIS does not provide specific prompts or anchors for coding the presence or absence of PTSD symptoms, and thus frequency and intensity cannot be distinguished. In addition, little psychometric data on the performance of the PTSD module of the ADIS-R is available.

Choosing a PTSD Measure

Which measure of PTSD is best will vary according to your study's purpose and your resource constraints. For studies that are broad in scope (e.g., epidemiological studies), you might lean toward using a measure that is brief and can be administered by a paraprofessional. In studies where an accurate determination of PTSD "caseness" is of paramount importance (e.g., treatment effectiveness studies, biological studies), you may wish to include an in-depth structured clinical interview that yields an exact measure of the diagnosis, including its one-month time frame. Regardless of study purpose, use of a measure that yields a dimensional diagnosis, that measures the intensity of the symptoms, that assesses PTSD symptoms separately from exposure, and that has strong psychometric properties for the population of interest is highly recommended. Tables 1 through 6 have been designed to assist in making an instrument selection.

However, no single measure can definitively determine whether or not an individual has PTSD; all measures are imperfect and contain error. If resources permit, we suggest you use multiple measures of PTSD. Multiple measures are recommended for two reasons. First, no existing single PTSD measure can be viewed as conclusive (Keane, Wolfe, & Taylor, 1987; Malloy, Fairbank, & Keane, 1983; Kulka et al., 1988), since a respondent may have difficulty with a particular test format or demonstrate response bias on a particular test. Use of multiple measures minimizes the impact of such extraneous factors. Second, different PTSD instruments have different psychometric strengths, and combining them can maximize the overall efficiency and predictive power of the entire test battery. For example, tests that are high in sensitivity can be used to insure that no PTSD cases will be missed, and then measures strong in specificity can be used to eliminate individuals that are not true cases (Newman, Kalopek, & Keane, in press).

Of course, when multiple measures are used, discrepancies among the PTSD indicators often occur. Therefore some method must be established for reconciling apparent contradictions. Clinical judgment or statistical algorithms may serve this purpose. PTSD caseness can also be substantiated by seeking information from other sources, such as collateral informants or psychophysiological indices (Keane, Wolfe, & Taylor, 1987). Measures of cognitive performance and behavioral functioning can also strengthen confidence in the accuracy of the diagnosis.

Measures of Exposure to Traumatic Events

Regardless of how PTSD is assessed, it is advisable to also include a separate measure of exposure to traumatic events. Any investigation of cause and effect requires use of a measurement strategy that assesses PTSD symptoms independently of types of stressors. While an in-depth review of trauma exposure measures is beyond the scope of this chapter (cf., Newman, Kaloupek, & Keane, 1995), some of the available instruments to assess level and type of exposure to traumatic events are presented in Table 7. This table provides a summary of the psychometric properties, administration time, populations examined empirically, and extant evidence for test-retest reliability of some these measures.

In reviewing Table 7 some caveats are in order; in particular, none of these measures has been assessed for its validity. In general, the development of measures of trauma exposure has lagged behind the development of instruments to measure PTSD, despite the fact that such assessments are critical to our understanding. One reason for this lag may be the difficulties involved in accurately measuring exposure to traumatic events. One epidemiological study of rape found that over

Table 7.   Psychometric Measurement of Trauma Exposure

Scale	Modality	Trauma Type	Admin. Time in Minutes	Gender Used in Validation	Reliability	Internal Consistency (kappa)	DSM-IV Criteria
CES	SR	Combat	5	Men	.97	.85	N
WWTSS	SR	Military	10	Women	.91	.89	N
HTQ	I	Torture	40	Both	.23–.9[a]	ND	Y
TSS	I	Mulitple	10	ND	ND	ND	ND
PSEI	I	Multiple	25–90	Both	ND	ND	Y
ETI	I	Childhood	60	ND	ND	ND	N
ELS	SR, I	Multiple	45–90	Both	ND	ND	Y

Y=Yes; N=No; SR=Self-report; I=Interview; [a] =Higher test-retest reliability was found for personal trauma (e.g., torture) rather than general events (e.g., lack of water); ND=No Data; CES=Combat Exposure Scale (Keane et al., 1984); WWTSS=Women's War-Time Stressor Scale (Wolfe et al., 1993); HTQ=Harvard Trauma Questionnaire (Mollica et al., 1992); TSS=The Traumatic Stress Schedule (Norris, 1990); PSEI=Potential Stressful Events Inventory (Falsetti et al., 1994); ETI=The Early Trauma Inventory (Kriegler et al., 1990); ELS=Evaluation of Lifetime Stressors (Krinsley et al., 1994)

50% of 260 identified rape victims had also been victims of physical and/or sexual assaults that were distinct from the rape incidents (Kilpatrick, 1990). Another study found that 33% of college sophomores were exposed to four or more traumatic events (Vrana & Lautenbach, 1994). These and other findings indicate that trauma histories are often complex, suggesting the need for correspondingly complex strategies for assessing trauma exposure. Yet existing trauma measures generally fail to distinguish discreet, continuous, sequential, and multiple stressors (cf., Sutker, Uddo-Crane, & Allain, 1991).

A second problem with these instruments is that stressors have been variously categorized by event types, victim's subjective appraisal of their experience, and by salient aspects of the exposure (e.g., extent of physical injury and ability to escape; Sutker, Bugg, & Allain, 1991). Except for the Potential Stressful Events Inventory (Falsetti, Resnick, Kilpatrick, & Freedy, 1994; Kilpatrick, Resnick, & Freedy, 1991) and the Evaluation of Lifetime Stressors (Krinsley et al., 1994), these scales do not incorporate both the objective *and* subjective elements of an experience, as required by the new DSM-IV Criterion A definition of a stressor.

Conclusion

This chapter has reviewed some available PTSD instruments in order to help researchers select measures that are best suited to their particular study's goals. It is our hope that the rapid proliferation of PTSD instruments witnessed in recent years is coming to an end and that future research in PTSD assessment will concentrate on refining and validating existing instruments in populations exposed to different types of traumatic events. Through systematic efforts at refinement, our understanding of PTSD will be incrementally enhanced, since the use of standardized measures will allow us to compare the effects of traumatic events across different studies, and to compare the effectiveness of interventions to ameliorate the negative consequences of exposure to these events.

References

American Psychiatric Association. (1987). *Diagnostic and statistical manual of mental disorders* (3rd ed. rev.). Washington, D.C.: American Psychiatric Association.

American Psychiatric Association. (1994). *Diagnostic and statistical manual of mental disorders* (4th ed.). Washington, D.C.: American Psychiatric Association.

Blake, D. D., Weathers, F. W., Nagy, L. N., Kaloupek, D. G., Klauminser, G., Charney, D. S., & Keane, T. M. (1990). A clinician rating scale for assessing current and lifetime PTSD: The CAPS-1, *Behavior Therapist, 18*, 187–188.

Blake, D. D., Weathers, F. W., Nagy, L. N., Kaloupek, D. G., Gusman, F., Charney, D. S., & Keane, T. M. (1995). The development of a clinician-administered PTSD scale. *Journal of Traumatic Stress, 8*, 75–90.

Breslau, N., Davis, G. C., Andreski, P., & Peterson, E. (1991). Traumatic events and posttraumatic stress disorder in an urban population of young adults. *Archives of General Psychiatry, 48*, 216–222.

Briere, J. (in press). *Professional manual for the Trauma Symptom Inventory.* Odessa, Florida: Psychological Assessment Resources.

Briere, J. & Conte, J. (1993). Self-reported amnesia for abuse in adults molested as children. *Journal of Traumatic Stress, 6*, 21–31.

Davidson, J. R. T., Smith, R. D., & Kudler, H. S. (1989). Validity and reliability of the DSM III criteria for posttraumatic stress disorder: Experience with a structured interview. *Journal of nervous and mental disease, 177*, 336–341.

Derogatis, L. R. (1977). *The SCL-90 manual 1. Scoring, administration and procedures for the SCL- 90.* Baltimore: Johns Hopkins University School of Medicine, Clinical Psychometrics Unit.

DiNardo, P. A., & Barlow, D. H. (1988). *Anxiety Disorders Interview Scale - Revised.* Albany, NY: Center for Phobia and Anxiety Disorders.

DiNardo, P. A., Moras, K., Barlow, D. H., Rapee, R. M., & Brown, T. A. (1993). Reliability of DSM-III-R anxiety disorder categories: Using the Anxiety Disorders Interview Schedule - revised (ADIS-R). *Archives of General Psychiatry, 50*, 251–256.

Falsetti, S. A., Resnick, H. S., Resick, P. A., & Kilpatrick, D. G. (1993). The Modified PTSD Symptom Scale: A brief self-report measure of Posttraumatic Stress Disorder. *The Behavior Therapist, 16*, 161–162.

Falsetti, S. A., Resnick, H. S., Kilpatrick, D. G., & Freedy, J. R. (1994). A review of the Potential Stressful Events Interview: A comprehensive assessment instrument of high and low magnitude stressors. *The Behavior Therapist, 17*, 66–67.

Foa, E. B., Riggs, D. S., Dancu, C. V., & Rothbaum, B. O. (1993). Reliability and validity of a brief instrument for assessing post-traumatic stress disorder. *Journal of Traumatic Stress, 6*, 459–474.

Green, B. L. (1990). Defining trauma: Terminology and generic stressor dimensions. Special Issue: Traumatic stress: New perspectives in theory, measurement, and research. *Journal of Applied Social Psychology, 20*, 1632–1642.

Green, B. L. (1991). Evaluating the effects of disasters. *Psychological Assessment, 3*, 538–546.

Hammerberg, M. (1992). Penn Inventory for posttraumatic stress disorders: Psychometric properties. *Psychological Assessment, 4*, 67–76.

Herman, D. S., Weathers, F. W., Litz, B. T., Keane, T. M., & Joaquim, S. G. (1993). Keane PTSD scale of the MMPI-2: Reliability and validity of the embedded and stand-alone versions. Unpublished manuscript.

Horowitz, M. J., Wilner, N. R., & Alvarez, W. (1979). Impact of Event Scale: A measure of subjective distress. *Psychosomatic Medicine, 41*, 208–218.

Hovens, J.E. (1994). *Research into the psychodynamics of posttraumatic stress disorder.* The Netherlands: Eburon Press.

Keane, T. M., Caddell, J. M., & Taylor, K. L. (1988). Mississippi Scale for Combat-Related Posttraumatic Stress Disorder: Three studies in reliability and validity. *Journal of Consulting and Clinical Psychology, 56*, 85–90.

Keane, T. M., Fairbank, J. A., Caddell, J. M., Zimering, R. T., Taylor, K. L., & Mora, C. A. (1989). Clinical evaluation of a measure to assess combat exposure. *Psychological Assessment, 1*, 53–55.

Keane, T. M., Malloy, P. F., & Fairbank, J. A. (1984). Empirical development of an MMPI subscale for the assessment of combat-related posttraumatic stress disorder. *Journal of Consulting and Clinical Psychology, 52*, 888–891.

Keane, T. M., Weathers, F. W., & Kaloupek, D. G. (1992). Psychological assessment of post-traumatic stress disorder. *PTSD Research Quarterly, 3*, 1–8.

Keane, T. M., Wolfe, J., & Taylor, K. L. (1987). Post-traumatic stress disorder: Evidence for diagnostic validity and methods of psychological assessment. *Journal of Clinical Psychology, 43*, 32–43.

Kilpatrick, D. G. (1990). *The epidemiology of potentially stressful events and their traumatic impact: Implications for prevention.* Paper presented at the 6th Annual Meeting of the International Society for Traumatic Stress Studies, New Orleans, LA.

Kilpatrick, D. G., Resnick, H. S., & Freedy, J. R. V. (1991). *Potential Stressful Events Inventory.* Charleston, SC: Crime Victims Treatment and Research Center, Medical University of South Carolina.

Kriegler, J., Blake, D., Schnurr, P., Bremner, D., Zaidi, L. Y., & Krinsley, K. (1990). *Early Trauma Interview.* Unpublished interview.

Krinsley, K., Weathers, F., Vielhauer, M., Newman, E., Walker, E., Young, L., & Kimerling, R. (1994). *Evaluation of Lifetime Stressors Questionnaire and Interview.* Unpublished manuscript.

Kulka, R. A., Schlenger, W. E., Fairbank, J. A., Hough, R. L., Jordan, B. K., Marmar, C. R., & Weiss, D. S. (1988). *National Vietnam veterans readjustment study (NVVRS): Description, current status, and initial PTSD prevalence estimates.* Research Triangle Park, NC: Research Triangle Institute.

Kulka, R. A., Schlenger, W. E., Fairbank, J. A., Jordan, B. K., Hough, R. L., Marmar, C. R., & Weiss, D. S. (1991). Assessment of Posttraumatic Stress Disorder in the community: Prospects and pitfalls from recent studies of Vietnam veterans. *Psychological Assessment, 3,* 547–560.

Lyons, J. A. & Keane, T. M. (1992). Keane PTSD scale: MMPI and MMPI-2 update. *Journal of Traumatic Stress, 5,* 111–117.

Malloy, P. F., Fairbank, J. A., & Keane, T. M. (1983). Validation of a multi-method assessment of posttraumatic stress disorders in Vietnam veterans. *Journal of Consulting and Clinical Psychology, 83,* 488–494.

McFall, M. E., Smith, D. E., Rozell, D. K., Tarver, D. J. and Malas, K. L. (1990). Convergent validity of measures of PTSD in Vietnam combat veterans. *American Journal of Psychiatry, 147,* 645–648.

Mollica, R. F. & Caspi-Yavin, Y. (1991). Measuring torture and torture-related symptoms. *Psychological Assessment, 3,* 581–587.

Mollica, R. F., Caspi-Yavin, Y., Bollini, P., Truong, T., Tor, S., & Lavelle, J. (1992). The Harvard Trauma Questionnaire: Validating a cross-cultural instrument for measuring torture, trauma, and posttraumatic stress disorder in Indochinese refugees. *Journal of Nervous and Mental Disease, 180,* 111–116.

Neal, L. A., Busuttil, W., Rollins, J., Herepath, R., & Turnball, G. (1994). Convergent validity of measures of post-traumatic stress disorder in a mixed military and civilian population. *Journal of Traumatic Stress, 7,* 447–455.

Newman, E., Kaloupek, D., Keane, T. M. (in press). Assessment of PTSD in clinical and research settings. In A. C. McFarlane, B. van der Kolk, & L. Weisaeth (Eds.), *Comprehensive text on post traumatic stress.* Cambridge: Cambridge University Press.

Norris, F. H. (1990). Screening for traumatic stress: A scale for use in the general population. *Journal of Applied Social Psychology, 20,* 1704–1718.

Resnick, H. S., Kilpatrick, D. G., & Lipovsky, J. A. (1991). Assessment of rape-related posttraumatic stress disorder: Stressor and symptom dimensions. *Psychological Assessment, 3,* 561–572.

Robins, L. N., Helzer, J. E., Croughan, J. L., Williams, J. B. W., & Spitzer, R. L. (1981). *NIMH Diagnostic Interview Schedule, Version III.* Rockville, MD: NIMH, Public Health Service (Publication number ADM-T-42-3 {5–81, 8–81}).

Saunders, B. E., Arata, C. M., & Kilpatrick, D. G. (1990). Development of a crime-related post-traumatic stress disorder scale for women within the Symptom Checklist-90-Revised. *Journal of Traumatic Stress, 3,* 439–448.

Schlenger, W. E., Kulka, R. A., Fairbank, J. A., Hough, R. L., Jordan, B. K., Marmar, C. R., & Weiss, D. S. (1992). The prevalence of post-traumatic stress disorder in the Vietnam generation: A multimodal, multisource assessment of psychiatric disorder. *Journal of Traumatic Stress, 5,* 333–363.

Scott, M. J., & Stradling, S. G. (1994). Post-traumatic stress disorder without the trauma. *British Journal of Clinical Psychology, 33,* 71–74.

Spiro, S. E., Shalev, A., Solomon, Z., & Kotler, M. (1989). Self-reported change versus changed self-report: Contradictory findings of an evaluation of a treatment program for war veterans suffering from post traumatic stress disorder. *Evaluation Review, 143,* 533–549.

Spitzer, R. L., Williams, J. B., Gibbon, M., & First, M. B. (1990). *Structured Clinical Interview for DSM-III-R — Patient edition (SCID-P).* New York: Biometrics Research Department, New York State Psychiatric Institute.

Sutker, P. B., Uddo-Crane, M., & Allain, A. N. (1991). Clinical and research assessment of posttraumatic stress disorder: A conceptual overview. *Psychological Assessment, 3,* 520–530.

Sutker, P. B., Bugg, F., & Allain, A. N. (1991). Psychometric prediction of PTSD among POW survivors. *Psychological Assessment, 3,* 105–110.

Vrana, S. & Lauterbach, O. (1994). Prevalence of traumatic events and post-traumatic symptoms in a nonclinical sample of college students. *Journal of Traumatic Stress, 7,* 289–303.

Watson, C. G. (1990). Psychometric posttraumatic stress disorder techniques: A review. *Psychological Assessment, 2,* 460–469.

Watson, C. G., Juba, M. P., Manifold, V., Kucula, T., & Anderson, P. E. D. (1991). The PTSD Interview: Rationale descriptions, reliability, and concurrent validity of a DSM-III based technique. *Journal of Clinical Psychology, 47,* 179–188.

Weathers, F. M. (1993). *Empirically derived scoring rules for the Clinician Administered PTSD Scale.* Unpublished manuscript.

Weathers, F. W., Litz, B. T., Herman, D. S., Huska, J. A., & Keane, T. M. (1993). *The PTSD Checklist: Description, use, and psychometric properties.* Unpublished manuscript.

Weathers, F. W., Blake, D. D., Krinsley, K. E., Haddad, W. H., Huska, J. A., & Keane, T. M. (1993). *Reliability and validity of the Clinician-Administered PTSD Scale.* Unpublished manuscript.

Wolfe, J., Brown, P. J, Furey, J., & Levin, K. B. (1993). Development of a War-Time Stressor Scale for women. *Psychological Assessment, 5,* 330–335.

Zilberg, N. J., Weiss, D. S., & Horowitz, M. J. (1982). Impact of events scale: A cross validation study and some empirical evidence supporting a conceptual model of stress responses syndromes. *Journal of Consulting and Clinical Psychology, 50,* 407–414.

4

Psychophysiological Measures and Methods in Trauma Research

Danny G. Kaloupek, J. Douglas Bremner

As the importance of physiological aspects of posttraumatic stress disorder (PTSD) becomes more evident, many researchers are interested in measuring physiological variables in their PTSD studies. But even for those with the requisite expertise in psychophysiology, the special technical and methodological considerations of this kind of research make it daunting. Fortunately, relatively "low-tech" psychophysiological measures can yield valuable results in the study of PTSD, and the necessary technology is increasingly available to medical and psychological researchers. In this chapter, we will review recent PTSD research on peripheral sympathetic nervous system variables and describe a number of technical and methodological considerations that are relevant to such studies. Finally, we will briefly review research on additional psychophysiological variables and discuss the directions we expect research in this area to be taking in the future.

It has long been recognized that alterations in physiological responsivity are associated with exposure to traumatic stress. Terms such as Soldier's Irritable Heart, which was applied to veterans of the American Civil War, captured the syndrome of increased heart rate and blood pressure responsiveness to reminders of the original trauma. At the time it was thought that the stress of war was associated with an impairment of cardiac function which led to these symptoms, which are now included in the reexperiencing cluster for the DSM-IV diagnosis of posttraumatic stress disorder. Later, Freud thought of combat-related psychopathology as being related to conflicts over whether or not to run from the battlefield. His influence led to a general understanding of physiological reactivity to trauma as an expression of an unresolved conflict. With the First and Second World Wars came a renewed interest in a possible direct physiological basis for the enduring symptoms associated with the psychological trauma of combat. Kardiner (1941) advanced the hypothesis that excessive sympathetic activity was responsible for symptoms such as increased physiological responsiveness to reminders of the original trauma.

Since the time of the Second World War the psychophysiology paradigm has been widely applied in the study of the sympathetic nervous system in patients with PTSD. Kolb (1984) has pointed out that many of the symptoms of PTSD, including sleep disturbance, hypervigilance, physiological arousal, and exaggerated startle response, could possibly be related to alterations of sympathetic systems. He described the phenomenon of increased physiological reactivity to reminders of the original trauma as a "conditioned emotional response." In principle, this response can be studied in controlled conditions in the laboratory using psychophysiological techniques.

The typical psychophysiological challenge paradigm involves the measurement of physiological signals at rest and during exposure to reminders of a previously experienced traumatic event. Bioelectrical signals generated from the body are conducted by surface electrodes and transducers. The signals are then filtered, amplified, and recorded for later interpretation of their biological or psychological significance. Physiological variables most often examined in relation to PTSD include heart rate, systolic and diastolic blood pressure, skin conductance, and electromyographic (EMG) activity of the frontalis, corrugator, zygomaticus or orbicularis oculi muscles. These variables reflect, in part, activity of the peripheral sympathetic nervous system. This system is activated during the stress response, in addition to being linked to central catecholaminergic systems which play an important role in mobilization in response to stress.

The procedure generally begins with a baseline rest period followed by exposure to trauma-related and neutral cues. The format of trauma reminders utilized in the psychophysiology paradigm has included slides (with or without accompanying sounds) that depict the general type of trauma (e.g., combat), and imagery scripts, which are descriptions of the traumatic experiences from the perspective of the affected individual. Comparisons are then made between reactions to trauma-related material and either baseline levels or reactions to neutral material. The use of slides and sound tracks has the advantage of being consistent from one subject to the next, while the script technique has the advantage of being more specific to the individual's traumatic experience. Psychophysiological responses, in general, have the advantage of being direct measures of a construct which is felt to be a central component of PTSD.

Prins, Kaloupek, and Keane (1995) recently reviewed the evidence relating psychophysiological variables to PTSD diagnosis and concluded that there is strong support for the hypothesis that individuals with PTSD show greater autonomic reactions when they are exposed to trauma-related stimuli than do individuals without PTSD. In addition, they noted that there are often differences in baseline levels of autonomic activity between groups differing with respect to PTSD (e.g., Blanchard et al., 1982; Pallmeyer et al.,1986; Pitman et al., 1987; Gerardi et al., 1989). These differences in baseline levels appear to be an example of autonomic elevation due to subjects' anticipation of trauma-related presentations in later portions of the protocol. This is a potentially important distinction because it means that the higher physiological readings (e.g., for heart rate) are not due to a biologically stable elevation in autonomic activation but instead are the result of entering a potentially threatening situation.

Prins et al. (1995) note that the strongest evidence for physiological differentiation of PTSD is found in relation to combat-related trauma, and the most consistent indicator is heart rate. Combat veterans with PTSD show significantly more heart rate reactivity to combat stimuli than various comparison groups (i.e., normal controls, non-veterans with other psychiatric diagnoses, combat veterans with no mental disorder) across protocols that have utilized standardized audio or audio-visual combat stimuli (Blanchard et al., 1982; Pallmeyer et al., 1986; Blanchard et al., 1986; Gerardi et al., 1989; Blanchard et al., 1989; Malloy et al., 1983; Pitman et al., 1987; McFall et al., 1990; Pitman et al., 1990; Orr et al., 1993; Shalev et al., 1993). Significant differences are also evident with respect to skin conductance, and they were most clear when the idiographic imagery procedure was used. Finally in terms of subjective distress, Vietnam veterans with PTSD consistently report more distress to combat material than do Vietnam veterans without PTSD, regardless of the psychophysiological assessment format used.

Despite the frequent replication of differential psychophysiological response by PTSD subjects to trauma cues, including demonstrations with traumatized populations other than combat veterans (e.g., Shalev, Orr, & Pitman, 1993; Blanchard, Hickling, Taylor, Loos, & Gerardi, 1994), as many as 40% of patients with PTSD do not show the expected differential reactivity. In fact, Prins et al. (1995) highlight a general trend across studies that indicates better performance by psychophysiological assessment in identifying individuals who do not qualify for an interview-based PTSD diagnosis than in identifying those who do qualify for the diagnosis. There are several possible reasons for this limited accuracy, some of which are addressed in the following sections concerning misconceptions about psychophysiology, factors that need to be considered when planning for psychophysiological protocols, and factors that reduce assessment accuracy.

Psychophysiological Measures: Common Misconceptions

Psychophysiological measures can provide converging evidence for diagnosis, index hyperarousal and reactivity in a manner that doesn't rely on self-report, and supply quantitative information for evaluating treatment effectiveness. These considerations can provide strong justification for the cost and effort of using physiological measures. On the other hand, psychophysiological assessment sometimes has an exaggerated image as a truly objective means for detecting an individual's psychological state. This and other common misconceptions about psychophysiological methods need to be dispelled as a first step in understanding their value.

Misconception #1. Psychophysiological measures are objective, immune to faking, and capable of providing a direct window on the true psychological state of an individual. While these methods can provide unique information, they are not inherently more valid nor more objective than typical assessment methods involving self-report or interviews. In addition, psychophysiological assessment is subject to ambiguous outcomes just like any other assessment method. In clinical application, findings often aren't fully consistent with a PTSD diagnosis (or absence of such). Insofar as faking is concerned, there is limited evidence on the issue in the context of PTSD. Gerardi, Blanchard, and Kolb (1989) suggest that veterans with PTSD have modest ability to suppress responding, but many of those without PTSD can increase responding purposely. Given this evidence, it is important to realize that all of the current challenge protocols (i.e., involving presentation of trauma-relevant depictions) require some degree of active cooperation by the individual being assessed. The ability to shift attention, imagine other scenes, and generate physical movements that affect physiological reactions are all options which, if exercised selectively, would have the potential to allow dissimulation.

Misconception #2. Psychophysiological measures are relatively interchangeable as indicators of arousal. There is ample evidence that measures are differentially sensitive to emotional and psychological states and behaviors. Fowles (1980) in particular has explored some of the differential value of heart rate and skin conductance as psychophysiological indicators. As a simple example, it appears that heart rate will better index responding associated with active avoidance behavior, while skin conductance will better index active inhibition. Thus, the fact that a measure can be conceptualized as psychophysiological in nature does not guarantee that it will be appropriate for the application in question. Conversely, it should be noted that the concept of arousal is itself problematic because it implies a sort of unidimensional energy underlying all emotion, cognition, and behavior. This overly simplified perspective can lead to inappropriate interpretation and cross-study mixing of evidence. It is important to instead think in terms of the state to be indexed and the underlying autonomic activity that is expected to couple to this state most closely.

Misconception #3. There is a constant reciprocal relationship between sympathetic and parasympathetic activity in the autonomic nervous system. It is commonly taught that the fight or flight (sympathetic) and inhibitory (parasympathetic) branches of the autonomic nervous system have a fixed relationship. When activity is high in one, it is necessarily low in the other. This is quite incorrect. These two subsystems have independent and complimentary effects, as well as their better known reciprocal effects (Berntson, Cacioppo, & Quigley, 1991). This is an important distinction because it affects the selection of measures and the interpretation of findings. For example, it cannot be assumed that an increase in heart rate is uniquely due to increased sympathetic activity. It could be the result of at least three patterns of activation: 1) sympathetic activation, 2) parasympathetic withdrawal, or 3) concurrent activation in both subsystems, which might be dominated by sympathetic effects. Psychophysiological studies of PTSD have not addressed this distinction thus far, but future efforts will perhaps do better in this regard.

Planning for a Trauma-Oriented Psychophysiology Lab

The first step in planning for a new lab or the upgrade of an existing lab is to outline and prioritize the uses it will be expected to serve. Considerations that need to be taken into account include the aims of the recording, the range of measures to be examined, the level of flexibility required in setup, the relative ease of use, capacity for data storage and manipulation, and the environment in which measurements will occur. Some concrete questions in relation to each of these considerations are listed below.

Aims of Recording
Is the recording primarily for clinical or research purposes or both? In some respects this is becoming a false distinction as managed care and other influences increase the need for careful, systematic recording in the clinical setting. Nonetheless, the particulars of the clinical or research application(s) in question will determine what the equipment must be able to do.

Range of Measures

Heart rate and skin conductance are the most typical measures in the literature to this point. Do you require others? Are you willing to use back or chest leads to get a stable heart rate signal, or will other less intrusive attachments (e.g., limb leads or photoreflective finger clip) be preferable despite the problems with signal loss that may occur? How much time are you willing or able to spend with preparation and attachments for each recording session? The time required for setup can range from 1–2 minutes to 10 minutes or more, depending on number and type of measures.

Level of Flexibility

Will the equipment be dedicated to a single protocol or modified for different protocols as they arise over time? The advantages to having a dedicated function for lab equipment extend all the way from the planning stage through implementation and long-term use. For example, it is easier to specify the precise equipment features that the protocol requires, training of technicians can be simplified, and there is less likelihood of inadvertent loss of recordings due to incorrect setup. This latter problem often arises when equipment is used for multiple purposes that require different configurations or settings. Checklists can be used to verify proper setup, but mistakes still occur. On the other hand, it may not be practical or economical to limit use to a single protocol, and the ability to adapt to different applications may be one of the factors that recommend one brand or model of equipment over another. Whatever the situation, it can be anticipated that, in general, more flexible equipment will be more technically complex to use.

Ease of Use

What level of technical support will be available both initially during implementation and later during extended use? It is important that even the simplest recordings are subject to scrutiny by someone with technical familiarity with the equipment and the indices in question. Expert guidance should be sought from the perspectives of safety, as well as reliability, and validity of measurement. Likewise, it can be advantageous to have some staff devoted to the recording process so that training can be detailed and procedures have greater likelihood of being applied systematically. Will non-technical staff (e.g., clinical care providers) be expected to conduct their own recordings? If so, ease of use will be one of the foremost considerations.

Data Storage and Manipulation

What will be done with the recordings? Will they merely be displayed back in real-time for the purposes of biofeedback, or will some retention and processing be in order? While there may be some modest applications for which data retention isn't worthwhile, it is probably a good idea to purchase equipment with some built-in or accessory means of data storage. Certainly any research application will require this capacity. Even in the clinical realm, however, it is increasingly important to have data on hand as documentation of assessment or treatment efforts.

The Recording Environment

Will the recording always be done in one place or will it need to be portable so that it can move from room to room? Will it be desirable, or possible, to conceal the equipment from view? Will recording need to allow for physical movement either in a relatively confined space or in the real-world environment? Reasonably good quality equipment is available for applications that range from ambulatory recording through portable recording that can be moved readily from room to room, to stationary recording restricted to one setting. The advantages of portability should be weighed carefully against the challenges it creates. Ambulatory recording can be highly idiographic and may have very direct relevance to the problems in behavior, emotion, or functioning that a person reports. However, it can be a substantial challenge to summarize the volume of data that often results, and there are a number of uncontrolled influences on physiological systems (e.g., activity or speaking) that complicate the scoring and interpretation of data. Both ambulatory and portable equipment have increased opportunity for damage due to accidents and misuse. Bumps and jars can also cause more subtle problems by affecting calibration settings. Portable equipment also may be used in a variety of physical environments where factors such as temperature, humidity, noise, seating comfort, and visual clutter vary and introduce error into the measurement process. By contrast, despite the loss of flexibility, an identified recording space can be prepared to serve its purpose optimally and to do so systematically for all recording sessions.

The Need for Consultation

The critical second step in planning for psychophysiological measurement is to arrange for expert consultation. It is not the first step only because it is important to think through some of the previously listed considerations before contacting the potential consultant. Even if there are many uncertainties remaining after you proceed as far as you can on your own, you should at least be able to show initiative by taking responsibility for the effort. This approach also makes it much easier to discuss what it is that you need in the way of consultation services. Such preparation will be viewed quite positively by potential consultants who might otherwise be reluctant to become involved with a project where the need for assistance appears too great. Initiative on your part gives a sense of active involvement which is both warranted and wise in your quest for a good consultant.

Sample Psychophysiological Paradigms

The choice of procedures for a psychophysiological protocol depends on the purpose and aim of the study. The most common use thus far has been with traumatized individuals for diagnostic purposes (Keane et al., 1987). An example of one protocol which could be used for a diagnostic screening for combat-related PTSD is as follows:

0–5 min.   Resting baseline followed by Subjective Units of Distress Scale (SUDS) ratings.

5–11 min.   Six one-minute presentations of neutral slides and accompanying music soundtrack, each followed by a SUDS rating.

11–16 min.   Resting baseline followed by SUDS ratings.

16–22 min.   Six one-minute combat slides and accompanying combat
             sounds soundtrack, each followed by a SUDS rating.
22–27 min.   Recovery period followed by a SUDS ratings.

Rule of thumb criteria that might be used as indicators of psychophysiological reactivity: 1) a 5 beats per min. greater heart rate
maximum during the combat slide presentation when compared to the
neutral slide presentation, and; 2) a greater than 50 point difference in
SUDS scores between the highest rating for a combat slide presentation
compared with the highest rating for a neutral slide presentation. Although the example only includes heart rate, in general, use of more
physiological measures that indicate differential reactivity to the
trauma cues increase confidence in the diagnostic interpretation.

The acoustic startle paradigm provides another noninvasive measure of the physiological correlates of PTSD, although the diagnostic
relevance of this index has not been determined. Increased eyeblink
startle magnitude has been found in Vietnam combat veterans with
PTSD in comparison to Vietnam combat veterans without PTSD with
80-100 dB noise bursts (Pallmeyer et al., 1986; Butler et al., 1990). An
increase in heart rate and skin conductance during the startle paradigm
has also been reported in patients with civilian PTSD in comparison to
controls (Shalev et al., 1992). Not all studies have produced positive
findings, however (Paige et al., 1990; Ross et al., 1989). Startle testing
requires the development of a laboratory for the delivery of sound
bursts at specific decibel ranges in a controlled environment, with the
capacity for measurement of the oculomotor reflex. Consultation with
an experienced startle investigator is advisable before attempting studies of this type.

Factors That Can Reduce the Accuracy of Psychophysiological Assessment

Task Compliance

One of the most basic considerations, but one which is too easily overlooked, is the need to maximize compliance with the assessment task.

This means, for example, maximizing compliance with instructions to sit quietly and rest, to view audiovisual presentations, or to make ratings of distress at the appropriate time. More subtle factors come into play as well because of the emotionally-evocative nature of the material being presented. It may be very difficult for those being tested to stay engaged with a task that causes them distress. They may try to limit distress by turning away, distracting themselves, or focusing artificially on some mundane feature of the display. They may also self-regulate physiological responding by using physical maneuvers (e.g., deep breathing) that dampen autonomic response. Conversely, because motor activity can itself elevate physiological activity, fidgeting and other such extraneous movements during the procedure can increase reactivity.

Many of these factors can be mitigated by careful planning of the phrasing and delivery of instructions. However, some of the factors are substantially beyond the ability of the clinical investigator to compel or control. For example, it would be unethical to arrange the presentation of trauma-related material in such a way that the individual could not readily escape or terminate the procedure. The best alternative then becomes a matter of documenting any significant violations of the protocol. Recordings of eye movements and closures, large muscle movements, and respiration are among the types of auxiliary physiological measures that might be used to identify departures from the protocol. This information, in turn, can be used as a basis for eliminating or adjusting intervals during which formal task compliance was in question.

The issue of compliance also can be viewed from a broader perspective that takes into account the clinical value of behavior exhibited during psychophysiological challenge procedures. Many of the compliance failures during psychophysiological testing are meaningful behavioral indicators of distress. The fact that someone is unable to view or attend to the trauma-related material can be as important clinically as the fact that someone else shows a larger heart rate reaction to trauma-related material than to neutral material. In the context of most clinical evaluations, the psychophysiological protocol offers the only opportunity to observe the individual as he or she typically functions in the presence of trauma cues. It is a good idea to capitalize on this opportunity by having some means of unobtrusive observation during the test procedure. It is highly advantageous to follow the testing with a structured debriefing to question the individual in detail about self-protective or self-regulatory behavior used during testing. Not surprisingly, a number of things that are reported during the debriefing are sufficiently subtle or unobservable to escape detection by others. With the debriefing, it is almost always possible to collect clinically useful information of some type. Given that the aim is to collect meaningful physiological and behavioral information, a broad perspective on the procedures makes it likely that at least one or the other will result from testing and contribute to the clinical formulation.

Factors That Affect Physical State

One of the most basic considerations for psychophysiological measurement is physical comfort. Laboratory temperature or humidity should be sufficiently well controlled to not cause discomfort. Seating needs to be comfortable and to remain so for the duration of the testing period. Similarly, headphones or other attachments must be designed and adjusted so as to be well tolerated for the duration of their use. On a more basic level, one of the most disruptive, though readily preventable, discomforts is the full bladder. Routine bladder emptying is highly recommended in advance of any physiological testing.

Medications can also constitute a strong influence on physiological responding, particularly drugs with clear autonomic effects (e.g., beta blockers). In clinical settings, it is often not feasible to conduct psychophysiological testing on medication-free individuals. Unfortunately, the impact of many medications is either unknown or difficult to quantify at the individual level. Thus it is generally not possible to specify a dose-related formula for adjusting the responding of medicated individuals to estimate their unmedicated status. At minimum, however, it is a good idea to at least document the medication status of anyone who is tested so that its impact can be considered in the course of interpreting the physiological findings.

Nicotine and caffeine also can have a pronounced influence on physiological systems that are typically monitored in PTSD assessments. Unfortunately, their effects are not uniform across physiological systems and the impact of withdrawal can be as problematic as that due to consumption (e.g., Hughes, 1993; Lane & Williams, 1985; Lyvers & Miyata, 1993; Perkins, Epstein, Jennings, & Stiller, 1986; Ratliff-Crain, O'Keeffe, & Baum, 1989). The result of these complications is a common practice of requesting that individuals refrain from smoking or drinking caffeine for some period (often 30 minutes or more) prior to the psychophysiological assessment. This seems to be a reasonable step, though it is worth recognizing that some people may find the period of abstinence long enough to cause discomfort. Additionally, it is a good idea to question and document the person's usual daily intake (e.g., cups of caffeinated beverages, number of cigarettes), the amount consumed to that point on that day, and the actual amount of time since last intake. As with medications, there is no available means for translating this information into a formal adjustment, but it can be useful to the process of interpretation of findings.

Limitations of Physiological Measures

As noted earlier, there are no easily obtained, error-free measures of autonomic nervous system activity, let alone measures specific to the condition of PTSD. This consideration is compounded by the limited specificity that measures demonstrate with respect to important behavioral or psychological influences. For example, skin conductance responses are commonly observed when attention is drawn to a new stimulus regardless of content, as well as when a stimulus has threat value and elicits an emotion such as fear. It is therefore necessary to rely on convergence of measures, both physiological and nonphysiological, to develop a picture of the disorder. This sort of construct-oriented approach is further aided by careful planning of tasks and selection of measures. The aim is to reduce the likelihood of multiple influences and alternative explanations for an observed pattern of findings.

In this context, it is highly advisable to include a resting baseline period prior to any significant psychophysiological data collection, and to have a set recovery period after the task is complete. Recommendations about baseline length (e.g., Hastrup, 1986) point to a minimum of 10 to 15 minutes for studies that examine psychophysiology in relation to acute laboratory stressors. Recovery periods of 5 to 10 minutes are probably sufficient. Recordings from these periods can provide critical context for interpretation of data. A concrete (and fairly common) example of their importance is the case where someone shows fairly high physiological activity throughout a diagnostic assessment procedure, including initial baseline, and then shows a substantial decrease in activity during recovery. This pattern suggests that the absence of differential response across sections of the procedure (e.g., neutral vs. trauma-related presentations) is due to a high level of anticipatory responding. Such anticipation can be sufficiently strong to elevate responding during reference periods and to preclude differences between baseline and reference periods. If this hypothesis is supported by other information (e.g., from observation or a debriefing interview), it favors interpretation of the evidence as consistent with PTSD. In contrast, simple comparison between neutral and trauma presentation periods in this example without consideration of the baseline and recovery would lead to a presumably incorrect conclusion that the evidence is inconsistent with a PTSD diagnosis.

Limitations Associated with Using Physiological Measures to Make a Diagnosis

One problem associated with using physiological measures to make a diagnosis that the multiple symptom options available under the diagnosis of PTSD make it possible to obtain a diagnosis of PTSD without the presence of psychophysiological reactivity. The fact that reactivity per se is not required by the diagnostic criteria opens the way for heterogeneity among cases and makes it understandable that there might be a limited association between diagnosis and results of formal psychophysiological measures. Even apart from this source of variation, it is important to recognize that the foundation of the PTSD diagnosis is subjective information that isn't necessarily comparable to information recorded directly from physiological systems. For example, research on autonomic perception and response covariation (e.g., Eifert & Wilson, 1991; Spinhoven, Onstein, Sterk, & Haen-Versteijnen, 1993; Tyrer,

Lee, & Alexander, 1980) makes it clear that self-reports of psycho-physiological reactivity are not interchangeable with observations or recordings of such activity.

From another angle, it is clear that several forms of psychopathology often accompany PTSD, particularly depression, anxiety, and substance abuse (Davidson & Fairbank, 1993; Keane & Wolfe, 1990). Evidence from outside the trauma context suggests that these conditions can have independent impact on psychophysiological responding (e.g., Lahmeyer & Bellur, 1987; Sayette, Smith, Breiner, & Wilson, 1992; Storrie, Doerr, & Johnson, 1981) and thereby complicate the interpretation of physiological evidence. Some effort to quantify comorbid problems in these areas is, therefore, well justified when PTSD is the target of interest.

Individual Biological Influences
Without going into detail, it is clear that individual differences that can influence psychophysiological reactivity arise from subject characteristics such as age, sex, race, menstrual cycle, and physical fitness level. Their relationship to sustained and reactive features of autonomic activity have been established in studies employing psychophysiological methods, and quantification of this information is highly encouraged whenever such methods are applied. There are few examples from the trauma literature that directly demonstrate the impact of these factors; however, one study by Shalev et al. (1993) did find that female subjects with PTSD demonstrated 33% greater physiological responding to their trauma script than male subjects with PTSD. More examples like this can be expected as the literature on the psychophysiology of trauma develops.

Appropriateness of Trauma Cue Presentations
The final influence to be noted as a potential explanation for imperfect association between psychophysiological responding and PTSD diagnosis is cue adequacy. A question that must be asked each time a trauma-related psychophysiological challenge is administered is how well the challenge material matches the individual's traumatic event. In this respect there may be an advantage to idiographic approaches to

trauma cue selection. While standardized presentations benefit from uniformity and their potential for allowing tight experimental control, they suffer the disadvantage of variable degree of correspondence with individual experience. Idiographic presentations may be designed to closely approximate the internal (memory) representations of the traumatic experience and thereby improve the validity of assessment.

As a related point, Anderson and McNeilly (1991) have recently argued for a contextual approach to psychophysiological research. Basically, this involves viewing psychophysiological responding as a function of the ecological niche that the person inhabits at the time of assessment. It is important to consider the testing situation from the first-person perspective, to think about the meaning and potential sources of threat cues for traumatized individuals. This outlook will both help to improve the application of psychophysiological methods and increase the likelihood that the information obtained from all aspects of the procedure is of value to clinical care and scientific advancement.

Measurement of Other Physiological Variables in PTSD

Other methods have been utilized in the assessment of physiological corrrelates in PTSD. We briefly review below research methods which are more complicated to institute than the psychophysiology paradigm. These methods can provide important information about the neurobiology of PTSD.

Studies of neurotransmitter function have provided evidence for alterations in catecholaminergic function in PTSD which are consistent with findings from the psychophysiology literature. Increases in urinary norepinephrine and epinephrine have been found in PTSD patients in comparison to patients with other psychiatric disorders and healthy controls (Kosten et al., 1987; Mason et al., 1988). Other investigators, however, have found no difference in urinary levels of norepinephrine or cortisol in patients with PTSD in comparison to Vietnam veterans without PTSD (Pitman et al., 1990a), or in plasma levels of norepinephrine at baseline in Vietnam veterans with PTSD in comparison to healthy controls (McFall et al., 1992; Blanchard et al., 1991). An increase in plasma epinephrine (McFall et al., 1990) and norepinephrine (Blanchard et al., 1991) has been shown following exposure to traumatic reminders in Vietnam veterans with PTSD in comparison to healthy subjects. A decrease in platelet adrenergic alpha$_2$ receptor number, possibly secondary to high levels of circulating catecholamines, has been observed in PTSD patients in comparison to healthy controls (Perry et al., 1987). Although these studies do not consistently support an increase in basal sympathetic function in PTSD, they do suggest that patients with PTSD may have an increased responsiveness of the sympathoadrenal system.

Pharmacological studies are also consistent with alterations in noradrenergic function in patients with PTSD. The alpha$_2$ antagonist, yohimbine, blocks the noradrenergic presynaptic autoreceptor, resulting in an increase in firing of noradrenergic neurons and an increased release of norepinephrine in the brain. Yohimbine administration results in flashbacks in 40% and panic attacks in 70% of Vietnam veterans with combat-related PTSD, an increase in PTSD-specific symptomatology, increased MHPG, blood pressure, and heart rate response in patients with PTSD in comparison to normal healthy controls (Southwick et al., 1993).

Furthermore, we are currently studying Vietnam combat veterans with PTSD and healthy subjects using positron emission tomography (PET) and [^{18}F]2-fluoro-2-deoxyglucose (FDG) in the measurement of brain metabolism following administration of yohimbine or placebo. Brain metabolism correlates with neuronal activity, therefore PET measurement of metabolism is a good indicator of functional activity of the brain. We know from studies in animals that high levels of norepinephrine release in the brain will have the effect of reducing brain metabolism in the cerebral cortex, whereas lower levels of norepinephrine release in the brain may actually cause an increase in metabolism. We hypothesized that if PTSD is associated with an increase in sensitivity and an increase in norepinephrine release in the brain relative to controls following yohimbine challenge, that there would be a relative decrease in metabolism with yohimbine compared to controls. Consistent with this, we found that yohimbine administration is associated with a relative decrease in metabolism in cerebral cortical areas in PTSD compared to controls, namely in temporal, parietal, prefrontal, and orbitofrontal cortex (Bremner et al., 1995).

Findings from psychophysiological studies are also of potential value for understanding alterations in memory function in patients with PTSD (van der Kolk et al., 1989; Charney et al., 1993; Bremner et al, 1993). Exposure to trauma-related slides and sounds or scripts of the individual's traumatic event often results in the recall of trauma-related memories and associated affect. The psychophysiology challenge paradigm offers a means for studying pathological traumatic recall, which is an important part of the symptomatology of PTSD.

As reviewed in greater detail elsewhere (Bremner et al., in press), pathological traumatic recall involves a variety of brain structures which are involved in memory and which are probably abnormal in patients with PTSD. The amygdala mediates the startle response and conditioned emotional responses to traumatic cues such as loud noises. The hippocampus plays an important role in short-term recall, and also is involved in conditioned responses to complex spatially-related cues. A decrease in volume of the right hippocampus (possibly related to neuronal damage secondary to high levels of glucocorticoids, which are associated with traumatic stress) with deficits in short-term verbal memory has also been associated with PTSD (Bremner et al., 1993b; Bremner et al., in press).

Future Directions for Psychophysiological Research

Psychophysiological research has provided a great deal of useful information for the study of PTSD. Psychophysiology studies have demonstrated a robust and reproducible increase in heart rate, skin conductance, and blood pressure with exposure to traumatic reminders with a variety of methodologies and patient populations. These increases also are seen at baseline, in anticipation of contact with such reminders. Future studies are needed to expand this evidence to topics of clinical relevance such as the relationship between alterations in memory function and psychophysiological responding in patients with PTSD. For example, brain blood flow and metabolic correlates of the increased physiological arousal seen during the paradigm could provide important information about brain correlates of pathological remembering in patients with PTSD. Psychophysiology as a predictor of treatment response, for both psychotherapy and psychopharmacology, should be explored as well (Solomon, Gerrity, & Muff, 1992). Finally, the psychophysiology paradigm could also be used to examine important trauma-related symptom areas such as dissociation. The relative noninvasiveness and increasing ease of use of psychophysiology equipment encourages wider application in these areas in years to come.

References

Anderson, N. B. & McNeilly, M. (1991). Age, gender, and ethnicity as variables in psychophysiological assessment: Sociodemographics in context. *Psychological Assessment, 3*, 376–384.

Berntson, G. G., Cacioppo, J. T., & Quigley, K. S. (1991). Autonomic determinism: The modes of autonomic control, the doctrine of autonomic space, and the laws of autonomic constraint. *Psychological Review, 98*, 459–487.

Blanchard, E. B., Kolb, L. C., Pallmeyer, T. P., & Gerardi, R. J. (1982). A psychophysiological study of posttraumatic stress disorder in Vietnam veterans. *Psychiatric Quarterly, 54*, 220–229.

Blanchard, E. B., Kolb, L. C., Gerardi, R. J., Ryan, P., & Pallmeyer, T. P. (1986). Cardiac response to relevant stimuli as an adjunctive tool for diagnosing post-traumatic stress disorder in Vietnam veterans. *Behavioral Therapist, 17*, 592–606.

Blanchard, E. B., Kolb, L. C., Prins, A., Gates, S., & McCoy, G. C. (1991). Changes in plasma norepinephrine to combat-related stimuli among Vietnam veterans with posttraumatic stress disorder. *Journal of Nervous and Mental Disease, 179*, 371–373.

Blanchard, E. B., Hickling, E. J., Taylor, A. E., Loos, W. R., & Gerardi, R. J. (1994). The psychophysiology of motor vehicle accident related post-traumatic stress disorder. *Behavior Therapy, 25*, 453–467.

Bremner, J. D., Davis, M., Southwick, S. M., Krystal, J. H., & Charney, D. S. (1993a). The neurobiology of posttraumatic stress disorder. In J. M. Oldham, M. B. Riba, & A. Tasman (Eds.), *Review of psychiatry*, Vol. 12 (pp. 141–155). Washington, D.C.: American Psychiatric Press.

Bremner, J. D., Scott, T. M., Delaney, R. C., Southwick, S. M., Mason, J. W.,

Johnson, D. R., Innis, R. B., McCarthy, G., & Charney, D. S. (1993b). Deficits in short-term memory in posttraumatic stress disorder. *American Journal of Psychiatry, 150,* 1015–1019.

Bremner, J. D., Innis, R. B., Ng, C. K., Staib, L., Duncan, J., Bronen, R., Zubal, G., Rich, D., Krystal, J. H., Dey, H., Soufer, R., & Charney, D. S. (1995). PET measurement of central metabolic correlates of yohimbine administration in posttraumatic stress disorder. Unpublished manuscript.

Bremner, J. D., Krystal, J. H., Southwick, S. M., & Charney, D. S. (1995). Functional neuroanatomical correlates of the effects of stress on memory. *Journal of Traumatic Stress,* vol. 8, 527–553.

Bremner, J. D., Randall, P., Scott, T. M., Bronen, R. A., Seibyl, J. P., Southwick, S. M., Delaney, R. C., McCarthy, G., Charney, D. S., Innis, R. B. (in press). MRI-based measurement of hippocampal volume in combat-related posttraumatic stress disorder. *American Journal of Psychiatry.*

Butler, R. W., Bratf, S. L., Rausch, J. L., Jenkins, M. A., Sprock, J., & Geyer, M. A. (1990). Physiological evidence of exaggerated startle response in a subgroup of Vietnam veterans with combat-related PTSD. *American Journal of Psychiatry, 147,* 1308–1312.

Charney, D. S., Deutch, A. Y., Krystal, J. H., Southwick, S. M., & Davis, M. (1993). Psychobiologic mechanisms of posttraumatic stress disorder. *Archives of General Psychiatry, 50,* 294–299.

Davidson, J. R. T. & Fairbank, J. A. (1993). The epidemiology of posttraumatic stress disorder. In J. R. T. Davidson & E. B. Foa (Eds.), *Posttraumatic stress disorder: DSM-IV and beyond* (pp. 147–172). Washington, D.C.: American Psychiatric Press.

Dobbs, D., & Wilson, W. P. (1960). Observations on persistence of war neurosis. *Disorders of the Nervous System, 21,* 606–691.

Eifert, G. H. & Wilson, P. H. (1991). The triple response approach to assessment: A conceptual and methodological reappraisal. *Behavior Research and Therapy, 29,* 283–292.

Gerardi, R. J., Blanchard, E. B., Kolb, L. C. (1994). Ability of Vietnam veterans to dissimulate a psychophysiological assessment for post-traumatic stress disorder. *Behavior Therapist, 20,* 229–243.

Hastrup, J. L. (1986). Duration of initial heart rate assessment in psychophysiology: Current practices and implications. *Psychophysiology, 23,* 15–18.

Hughes, J. R. (1993). Possible effects of smoke-free inpatient units on psychiatric diagnosis and treatment. *Journal of Clinical Psychiatry, 54,* 109–114.

Kardiner, A. (1941). *The traumatic neuroses of war.* New York: Hoeber.

Keane, T. M., Wolfe, J., & Taylor, K. L. (1987). Post-traumatic stress disorder: Evidence for diagnostic validity and method for psychological assessment. *Journal of Clinical Psychology, 43*, 32–43.

Keane, T. M., Fairbank, J. A., Caddell, J. M., & Zimering, R. T. (1989). Implosive (flooding) therapy reduces symptoms of PTSD in Vietnam combat veterans. *Behavioral Therapist, 20*, 245–260.

Keane, T. M. & Wolfe, J. (1990). Comorbidity in post-traumatic stress disorder: An analysis of community and clinical studies. *Journal of Applied Psychology, 20*, 1776–1778.

Kolb, L. C. (1984). The post-traumatic stress disorder of combat: A subgroup with a conditioned emotional response. *Military Medicine, 149*, 237–243.

Kosten, T. R., Mason, J. W., Ostroff, R. B., & Harkness, L. (1987). Sustained urinary norepinephrine and epinephrine elevation in posttraumatic stress disorder. *Psychoneuroendocrinology, 12*, 13–20.

Lahmeyer, H. W. & Bellur, S. N. (1987). Cardiac regulation and depression. *Journal of Psychiatric Research, 21*, 1–6.

Lane, J. D. & Williams, R. B. (1985). Caffeine affects cardiovascular response to stress. *Psychophysiology, 22*, 648–655.

Lyvers, M. & Miyata, Y. (1993). Effects of cigarette smoking on electrodermal orienting reflexes to stimulus change and stimulus significance. *Psychophysiology, 30*, 231–236.

McFall, M. E., Murburg, M. M., Ko, G. N., & Veith, R. C. (1990). Autonomic responses to stress in Vietnam combat veterans with posttraumatic stress disorder. *Biological Psychiatry, 27*, 1165–1175.

McFall, M. E., Veith, R. C., & Murburg, M. M. (1992). Basal sympathoadrenal function in posttraumatic stress disorder. *Biological Psychiatry, 31*, 1050–1056.

Malloy, P. F., Fairbank, J. A., & Keane, T. M. (1983). Validation of a multimethod assessment of posttraumatic stress disorders in Vietnam veterans. *Journal of Consulting and Clinical Psychology, 51*, 488–494.

Mason, J. W., Giller, E. L., Kosten, T. R., & Harkness, L. (1988). Elevation of urinary norepinephrine/cortisol ratio in posttraumatic stress disorder. *Journal of Nervous and Mental Disease, 176*, 498–502.

Orr, S. P., Claiborn, J. M., Altman, B., Forgue, D. F., deJong, J. B., Pitman, R. K., & Hertz, L. R. (1990). Psychometric profile of posttraumatic stress disorder, anxious, and healthy Vietnam veterans: Correlations with psychophysiological responses. *Journal of Consulting and Clinical Psychology, 58*, 329–335.

Orr, S. P., Pitman, R. K., Lasko, N. B., & Herz, L. R. (1993). Psychophysiological assessment of posttraumatic stress disorder imagery in World War II veterans. *Journal of Abnormal Psychology, 102,* 152–159.

Paige, S. R., Reid, G. M., Allen, M. G., & Newton, J. E. O. (1990). Psychophysiological correlates of posttraumatic stress disorder in Vietnam veterans. *Biological Psychiatry, 27,* 419–425.

Perkins, K. A., Epstein, L. H., Jennings, J. R., & Stiller, R. (1986). The cardiovascular effects of nicotine during stress. *Psychopharmacology, 90,* 373–378.

Perry, B. D., Giller, E. J., & Southwick, S. M. (1987). Altered platelet alpha-2 adrenergic binding sites in posttraumatic stress disorder (letter). *American Journal of Psychiatry, 144,* 1324–1327.

Pitman, R. K., Orr, S. P., Forgue, D. F., de Jong, J. B., & Claiborn, J. M. (1987). Psychophysiologic assessment of posttraumatic stress disorder imagery in Vietnam combat veterans. *Archives of General Psychiatry, 44,* 970–975.

Pitman, R. & Orr, S. (1990). Twenty-four hour urinary cortisol and catecholamine excretion in combat-related posttraumatic stress disorder. *Biological Psychiatry, 7,* 245–247.

Pitman, R., Orr, S., Forgue, D., Altman, B., & deJong, J. (1990). Psychophysiologic responses to combat imagery of Vietnam veterans with posttraumatic stress disorder versus other anxiety disorders. *Journal of Abnormal Psychology, 99,* 49–54.

Prins, A., Kaloupek, D. G., & Keane, T. M. (1995). Psychophysiological evidence for autonomic arousal and startle in traumatized adult populations. In M. J. Friedman, D. S. Charney, & A. Y. Deutch (Eds.), *Neurobiological and clinical consequences of stress: From normal adaptation to PTSD,* pp. 291–314. New York: Raven Press.

Ratliff-Crain, J., O'Keeffe, M. K., & Baum, A. (1989). Cardiovascular reactivity, mood, and task performance in deprived and nondeprived coffee drinkers. *Health Psychology, 8,* 427–447.

Ross, R. J., Ball, W. A., Cohen, M. E., Silver, S. M., Morrison, A. R., & Dinges, D. F. (1989). Habituation of the startle reflex in posttraumatic stress disorder. *Journal of Neuropsychiatry, 1,* 305–307.

Sayette, M. A., Smith, D. W., Breiner, M. J., & Wilson, G. T. (1992). The effect of alcohol on emotional response to a social stressor. *Journal of Studies on Alcohol, 53,* 541–545.

Shalev, A. Y., Orr, S. P., Peri, T., Schreiber, S., & Pitman, R. K. (1992). Physiologic responses to loud tones in Israeli patients with posttraumatic stress disorder. *Archives of General Psychiatry, 49,* 870–874.

Shalev, A. Y., Orr, S. P., & Pitman, R. K. (1993). Psychophysiological assessment of traumatic imagery in Israeli civilian patients with posttraumatic stress disorder. *American Journal of Psychiatry, 150,* 620–624.

Solomon, S. D., Gerrity, E. T., & Muff, A. M. (1992). Efficacy of treatments for posttraumatic stress disorder: An empirical review. *Journal of the American Medical Association, 268,* 633–638.

Southwick, S. M., Krystal, J. H., Morgan, C. A., Johnson, D., Nagy, L. M., Nicolaou, A., Heninger, G. R., & Charney, D. S. (1993). Abnormal noradrenergic function in posttraumatic stress disorder. *Archives of General Psychiatry, 50,* 266–274.

Spinhoven, P., Onstein, E. J., Sterk, P. J., & Le Haen-Versteijnen, D. (1993). Discordance between symptom and physiological criteria for the hyperventilation syndrome. *Journal of Psychosomatic Research, 37,* 281–289.

Storrie, M. C., Doerr, H. O., & Johnson, M. H. (1981). Skin conductance characteristics of depressed subjects before and after therapeutic intervention. *Journal of Nervous and Mental Disease, 69,* 176–179.

Tyrer, P., Lee, I., & Alexander, J. (1980). Awareness of cardiac function in anxious, phobic, and hypochondriacal patients. *Psychological Medicine, 10,* 171–174.

van der Kolk, B. A., Greenberg, M. S., Orr, S. P., & Pitman, R. K. (1989). Endogenous opiates, stress induced analgesia, and posttraumatic stress disorder. *Psychopharmacology Bulletin, 25,* 417–421.

Wenger, M. A. (1948). Studies of autonomic balance in Army Air Force personnel. *Comparative Psychology Monographs 19, 101,* 1–11.

5

Designing and Implementing Epidemiologic Studies

John A. Fairbank, B. Kathleen Jordan, William E. Schlenger

Epidemiology and the Study of Traumatic Stress

Epidemiology was originally the branch of science that focused on the study of "epidemics" of communicable diseases (Last, 1983). Many of the basic research methods of epidemiology were developed during the nineteenth and twentieth centuries in response to the need to understand the etiology of communicable diseases such as influenza, smallpox, tuberculosis, and typhoid fever, and to provide an empirical basis for the development of effective treatment and preventive interventions. Contemporary definitions have broadened, and epidemiology now includes the study of patterns of health and illness in human populations and the factors that influence these patterns (cf. Friedman, 1987; Lilienfeld & Stolley, 1994). Moreover, the focus of epidemiology has evolved to include a wide range of phenomena related to the health of populations, including the mental health of adults and children. Recent examples of major epidemiologic research efforts that focused on mental health and substance abuse include the National Institute of Mental Health (NIMH) Epidemiologic Catchment Area Program (ECA), the National Vietnam Veterans Readjustment Study (NVVRS) sponsored by the Department of Veterans Affairs, NIMH's National Comorbidity Survey (NCS), the National Household Survey on Drug Abuse (NHSDA) funded by the Office of Applied Sciences

(OAS) in the Substance Abuse and Mental Health Services Administration (SAMHSA), and NIMH's ongoing multisite study of Use, Needs, Outcomes, and Costs in Child and Adolescent Populations (UNOCCAP).

The ECA is a prime example of the epidemiologic approach to the study of psychiatric disorder in the general population. Researchers in the ECA assessed specific psychiatric disorders and their correlates among 19,182 community and institutional respondents at five sites ("catchment areas") during the early 1980s. In keeping with other major psychiatric epidemiologic studies, the general purposes of the ECA were (a) to estimate the number of people within a population who have specific psychiatric disorders (prevalence); (b) to estimate the number of new cases of disorders that develop over a specific time frame (incidence); (c) to assess the co-occurrence of other disorders with the disorders of interest (co-morbidity); and (d) to determine the characteristics that differentiate those who have a given disorder from those who don't (risk factors). The NIMH ECA has been an especially productive research effort, disseminating hundreds of scientific papers and reports on the prevalence, incidence, co-morbidity, risk factors, and outcomes for various specific mental disorders among adults in the general population of the United States.

A number of epidemiologic inquiries have specifically examined the prevalence of exposure to extreme events, the prevalence of PTSD, the comorbidity of PTSD with other disorders, and the factors that confer increased risk for exposure to trauma and for development of PTSD (see Davidson & Fairbank [1993], Fairbank et al. [1993], and Fairbank et al. [1995] for reviews of the literature on PTSD epidemiology). Epidemiologic research has provided such estimates for the general adult population of the United States (Kessler et al., in press) and for the adult population of women in the United States (Resnick et al., 1993), as well as for special populations, such as young adults enrolled in a large private-sector health maintenance organization (HMO) (Breslau et al., 1991). Epidemiologic researchers have also focused on populations at risk for PTSD, such as adolescents exposed to a natural disaster (Garrison et al., 1993), children exposed to violence in their homes and communities (Richters & Martinez, 1993), and Vietnam veterans (Kulka et al., 1990).

The utility of epidemiologic research on traumatic stress rests largely in providing data to inform treatment, prevention, and public policy planning. The National Vietnam Veterans Readjustment Study (NVVRS) provides an especially salient example of how epidemiologic data are used for the purpose of furthering clinical, research, and policy action. In the late 1980s and early 1990s, the United States Congress and the Department of Veterans Affairs (DVA) used NVVRS findings on the prevalence of PTSD, its risk factors, and co-morbid conditions to inform policy decisions about the need for integrated and comprehensive treatment services for veterans with PTSD, as well as the need for further research on the psychosocial adjustment of women and minority veterans. Findings from the NVVRS are at least partially responsible for the establishment of a wide range of specialized PTSD treatment programs within the DVA service system and for stimulating DVA and NIMH support for major epidemiologic studies on the psychosocial adjustment of American Indian, Asian American, and Native Hawaiian Vietnam veterans.

Research Designs in PTSD Epidemiologic Studies

Epidemiologic studies of traumatic stress rely heavily on quasi-experimental (Cook & Campbell, 1979) or observational (Lilienfeld & Stolley, 1994) research designs. Traumatic stress epidemiologists have not used experimental designs that would, in principle, entail investigator control over the conditions of exposure and random assignment of research participants to such conditions. For quite apparent ethical and practical reasons, true experimental designs are inappropriate for the study of human psychological trauma. Epidemiologic studies of exposure to trauma and its sequalae thus begin with the understanding that persons are not assigned at random to a specific traumatic condition.

By and large, if you are interested in epidemiologic aspects of psychological trauma, you have two basic design options: Sample the population with regard to symptoms, disorder, and/or functional impairment (case-control design) or sample in terms of exposure to traumatic events (cross-sectional and cohort designs). Case-control, cross-sectional, and cohort designs have been used in epidemiologic studies of traumatic stress. One method of compensating for the absence of experimental control (i.e., random assignment) in traumatic stress epidemiologic research is to attend carefully to the characteristics of the population from which the study samples are selected. Only when the sample that you select accurately represents the population from which it is drawn, can you specify to whom your prevalence and incidence estimates and risk factor analyses apply (Costello & Angold, 1995). Specific methods for controlling for sampling bias are described within the following discussion on research designs in PTSD epidemiologic studies.

Case-control Studies

Case-control studies focus on the etiology and co-morbidity of the disorder rather than on prevalence or on incidence. In case-control studies, comparisons are made between a group of persons who have the disorder under study (e.g., "cases" of PTSD or "cases" of Acute Stress Disorder) and a group that do not (i.e., "controls" or comparison subjects). Cases and controls are compared with respect to risk factors of interest, such as age at time of exposure and family history of psychiatric disorder, to determine if these risk factors occur more frequently among cases than controls. A number of PTSD studies have been published that have used case-control designs. For example, in Keane et al.'s (1985) study of social support factors in PTSD, cases were male Vietnam combat veterans with PTSD and controls were two separate groups: Vietnam combat veterans without PTSD (matched to cases on age, gender, and military service in Vietnam) and Vietnam-era veterans with other psychiatric disorders (matched to cases on age, gender, and presence of a major psychiatric disorder). Brady et al. (1994) employed a case-control design to study the relationship between PTSD and substance use disorders among women enrolled in substance abuse treatment. Cases were women in substance abuse treatment with a diagnosis of PTSD and controls were women in substance abuse treatment without a PTSD diagnosis. In Saigh et al.'s (1995) study of self-efficacy in PTSD, cases were youths exposed to war in Lebanon who met diagnostic criteria for PTSD, and controls were groups of youths without PTSD who were matched on level of exposure to war stress and personal characteristics, such as religious affiliation. Case-control studies such as these have provided considerable insight into a wide range of factors associated with PTSD.

A clear advantage of the case-control design is that it is one of the more feasible ways to study factors related to PTSD. It is generally true that studies using case-control designs require fewer resources than studies employing cross-sectional or cohort designs (described below). Yet, despite the substantial cost and feasibility advantages, case-control designs are not without limitations, particularly in terms of threats to internal validity (e.g., non-equivalent comparison groups) and threats to external validity (e.g., sampling strategies rarely control for selection bias).

A study is externally valid to the extent that it produces unbiased inferences about a target population and findings that are generalizable beyond the subjects in the study (Last, 1983). Probability or random sampling is required to produce such unbiased and generalizable estimates. An example of probability sampling is when subjects are drawn with known selection probabilities from a target population, such as all residents of a specific geographic area affected by a natural disaster. However, PTSD case-control studies have typically employed non-probabilistic, purposive sampling methods (e.g., a nonrandom sample of patients seen for evaluation and for treatment at a specific clinic for PTSD). Such nonrandom sampling methods place severe limitations on the generalizability of findings to larger populations (e.g., the population of all patients with PTSD).

PTSD case-control studies achieve internal validity when the PTSD group and the comparison groups are selected and compared in such a manner that the observed differences between them on the dependent variables under study are, apart from sampling error, attributable only to the hypothesized effect or independent variable under investigation (Last, 1983). A strategy commonly used to improve the comparability of the PTSD and control groups on key external factors (such as level of exposure to an extreme event, comorbid conditions, etc.) is "matching." Matching is a method used to choose controls who are comparable with the cases with respect to extraneous factors (Lasky & Stolley, 1994). In principle, matching may improve the internal validity of case-control studies by controlling for the influence of potential confounding variables. Confounding variables are factors known (or strongly suspected) to be associated with and to influence the disorder or putative risk factors under study (cf. Kleinbaum, Kupper, & Morgenstern, 1982). Norris (1996) addresses the issue of confounding in considerable detail in Chapter 2 of this book.

Cross-sectional Studies

Cross-sectional studies examine the prevalence of and risk factors for exposure to trauma and traumatic stress disorders in defined target populations at a given point in time. A key objective of cross-sectional epidemiologic research is to make precise and unbiased population estimates of exposure to trauma and the psychosocial factors and diagnoses associated with such exposure.

True estimation of population parameters at a given point in time, however, requires the selection of representative samples of the population of inference, be they the U.S. population as a whole, war veterans, survivors of sexual assault, or persons who survive homicidal terrorist activities or political torture. In essence, sample selection lies at the heart of trauma prevalence research because the representativeness of the sample dictates the generalizability and ultimate utility of the findings for informing public policy.

The selection of representative samples of the target population implies the need for probability sampling in which each element in a population has a known (nonzero) probability of being included in the sample (Lee et al., 1989). Epidemiologic studies of traumatic stress have attained probability samples of target populations using a variety of design options, including simple random sampling, systematic sampling, stratified sampling, clustered sampling, multiphase sampling, and multistage clustered sampling designs. In some cases, a census (i.e., every person) exposed to a specific extreme event (e.g., rescue workers who responded to a specific transportation accident) or with certain characteristics (e.g., persons on death row in a particular state) can be assessed for degree of exposure and disorder.

Simple Random Samples

In principle, the most straightforward sampling design is simple random sampling, which requires that each element (e.g., person, medical record, treatment program, census block) has an equal probability of selection and that the list of all population elements be known. In a well known study of the prevalence of and risk factors for PTSD among insured young adults, Breslau and her colleagues (1991) drew a simple random sample from the list of subscribers to a large HMO in Michigan. In the first stage of a study of the relationship between childhood sexual abuse and mental health in adult women, Mullen et al. (1993) selected a random sample from women listed on the electoral rolls in an urban area of New Zealand. Sack and colleagues (1994) examined the current mental health of youths and young adults who survived war in Cambodia by selecting a simple random sample of persons ages 13 to 25 from listings of such youths compiled for two communities in the United States.

Simple random sampling provides a powerful design for making unbiased prevalence estimates. However, simple random sampling is infrequently used because it is expensive, since the proportion of cases is likely to be low in most general population samples, while the cost to access the sample is high because of all the noncases you might assess. For example, if the rate of PTSD in a population is approximately 5 percent, then only one respondent in 20 is likely to be a case. Also, simple random sampling often is not feasible in practice due to the requirement that all elements be known (cf. Levy & Lemeshow, 1980).

Systematic Samples

Another method for obtaining a representative sample is systematic sampling, which is the procedure of selecting according to some simple, systematic rule, such as choosing names from a master list at specified intervals (e.g., every eighth name) or according to order of enrollment into a treatment program (e.g., every fifth patient) (Last, 1983). An example of systematic sampling from the traumatic stress literature is Leo Eitinger's (1973) seminal study of post-war mortality and morbidity among concentration camp survivors. Using a file card registry containing the names of 3,811 Norwegian survivors of concentration camps as a sampling frame, Eitinger (1973) selected the file card of every eighth former prisoner who was living at the time of the study.

A major advantage of systematic random sampling is that it is relatively easy to use and may frequently be implemented by supervised clerical staff once they are trained on the how to implement the sampling procedures. Systematic sampling is particularly appealing as a design option when it would be impossible, extremely difficult, or prohibitively expensive to list all the elements (e.g., persons) in a sample frame prior to drawing the sample. Suppose, for example, an investigator wanted to know the prevalence of PTSD among newly admitted clients to several methadone maintenance treatment programs in a major metropolitan area. To control for seasonality and other variables (e.g., rates of admission and severity of addiction may vary as a function of time of year and the purity and cost of heroin and other opioids on the streets), the investigator may want to sample clients over the course of a calendar year. If 1,000 clients are admitted to each clinic per year, and if power analyses suggest that a sample of roughly 220 clients per clinic are required to answer key research questions, then every fourth new client could be recruited for enrollment into the project (assuming a response rate in the 80–90 percent range).

A drawback to systematic sampling, however, is that the representativeness of the sample is undermined to the extent that other variables are confounded with the chosen sampling scheme. Under some circumstances, systematic sampling may introduce selection biases that compromise the generalizability of findings. This issue is particularly salient when there is reason to believe that selection rules may correspond with patterns of behavior in the target population (e.g., there is a tendency each week for the fourth new client in Methadone Clinic A to be enrolled on Tuesday mornings when a special assessment clinic attracts referrals of more severely impaired patients).

Stratified Samples
When a focus of the study is to estimate prevalence rates of a potentially "rare" event in a population (e.g., cases of PTSD), it is often cost effective to stratify the sample on risk factors for PTSD (e.g., exposure

to potentially traumatic events). Stratified sampling partitions the population into groups or strata (e.g., individuals who report exposure to an extreme event and those who do not) and samples separately from each stratum (Lee et al., 1989). The purpose of stratified sampling is to maximize the proportion of research participants who have positive responses on the dependent variables of interest (e.g., PTSD symptoms and disorder) in order to obtain adequate numbers for analysis. Like simple random samples, stratified samples produce estimates that are neither biased nor spurious, as long as the samples at each stage of stratification are selected with known probability. Given that, it is a relatively straightforward procedure to compute sample weights that take into account the respondents' probability of selection, and therefore allow unbiased estimation of the values of the distribution of a specified variable in a population (Lee et al., 1989).

Dohrenwend et al. (1992) used multistage sampling for stratification to examine the epidemiology of psychiatric disorder in Israel. A sample of 19,000 persons listed on the Israel Population Register was prescreened to obtain a probability sample of 5,000 young adults oversampled on specific sociodemographic characteristics. First stage screening consisted of a brief structured interview with 4,914 persons to distinguish probable psychiatric cases ("positives") from probable non-cases ("negatives"). The brief screening interview included questions on risk factors, symptoms of demoralization, and psychiatric service use (e.g., history of hospitalizations for emotional distress). The second stage consisted of structured clinical interviews with all those who scored positive during screening and an 18% subsample of the negatives, a total of 2,741 of the 4,914 study respondents. Response rates were 94.5% for Stage 1 and 90.7% for Stage 2.

Dohrenwend et al.'s (1992) experience with multistage sampling is consistent with the experience of trauma researchers using even more complex stratification procedures, such as the stratified, multiple frame and multistage sampling strategy used in the NVVRS (cf. Kulka & Schlenger, 1993; Schlenger et al., 1992) and the stratified, multi-stage area probability sampling strategy used in the National Comorbidity Survey (cf. Kessler et al., in press). The lesson learned is that complicated sampling strategies are feasible and cost effective to the extent that investigators avoid investing the bulk of invariably limited project resources (time and money) on the collection of data from a large number of respondents whose experiences are of limited relevance to the research objectives.

Census

If you are willing to accept considerable limits to generalizability, you can use a census design to sample all individuals who have been exposed to a specific event or who have certain characteristics. For example, it is sometimes possible to interview all individuals who have been exposed to a known stressor (e.g., North et al.'s [1994] study of survivors, eyewitnesses, police, and emergency personnel involved in a mass shooting) or who belong to a specific at risk group (e.g., Jordan et al.'s [in press] study of all felons entering a prison over a specified period). You can then make statements about these populations with some certainty. However, generalizability to other populations is limited by the degree of similarity between the population studied and other populations. Although this degree of similarity is usually unknown and unknowable, such data can provide testable hypotheses for other similar studies.

Cohort Studies

The cohort study is a method of epidemiologic research in which subsets of a defined population can be identified who are, have been, or in the future may be exposed, or not exposed, to risk factors believed to be associated with the occurrence of a given disorder (e.g., PTSD) or other outcome (Last, 1983). A distinguishing feature of the cohort design is the inclusion of one or more follow-ups in which the sample is assessed longitudinally for the occurrence of new exposures and disorders (i.e., incidence). Thus, cohort studies of exposure to trauma and PTSD "allow the possibility of investigating the unfolding of psychopathologic processes and testing etiologic hypotheses, pathogenetic pathways of interest, prognostic considerations, lasting treatment effectiveness, patient trajectories, and outcomes of illness" (Mezzich et al., 1994, p. 137).

Data collected in a cohort study consist of information about the exposure status of the individual and whether, after that exposure occurred, the individual developed a given disease or disorder (Lilienfeld & Stolley, 1994). Cohort studies are also commonly referred to as follow-up studies, incidence studies, longitudinal studies, panel studies, and prospective studies. A major advantage of the cohort method over the "slice in time" cross-sectional study is that you can collect information on the incidence of new exposures to traumatic events and the occurrence of new cases of PTSD during the follow-up interval. However, one source of threat to the internal validity of cohort studies may be the non-equivalency of assigned risk of exposure to trauma at baseline and at follow-ups across study groups. Probability sampling is as essential to making unbiased population estimates of PTSD incidence (i.e., number of new cases in a population at risk) in cohort studies as it is to making precise population estimates of PTSD prevalence in studies using cross-sectional designs. It's also important to remember that loss of subjects at follow-up (i.e., selective attrition) may introduce bias in the sample.

Breslau et al. (1995) conducted a longitudinal study of the prevalence and incidence of exposure to traumatic events in a randomly selected sample of youth enrolled in an HMO. She and her colleagues interviewed 1,007 youth at baseline, 979 of whom were reinterviewed at a 3-year follow-up. This design enabled the investigators to report findings on the incidence of exposure to various types of extreme events and PTSD and to relate the emergence of new exposures and cases of disorder to potential risk factors that were assessed prospectively (at baseline).

Other researchers have used various longitudinal approaches to study the psychosocial impact of specific extreme events on populations at risk, including community residents exposed to (a) technological disasters, such as the nuclear reactor accident at Three Mile Island (Davidson & Baum, 1992; Dew & Bromet, 1993) and the collapse of a man-made earthen dam (Green et al., 1994); (b) natural disasters, such as fires (Koopman, Classen, & Spiegel, 1994; McFarlane, 1988), floods (Phifer & Norris, 1989; Steinglass & Gerrity, 1990) and tornados (Steinglass & Gerrity, 1990); or (c) rape (Rothbaum et al., 1992) and other types of crime (Norris & Kaniasty, 1994). Longitudinal approaches have also been used in studies of combat veterans (Solomon, 1989) and former prisoners of war (Ursano et al., 1981). To date, few studies that have used cohort designs have employed sampling methods that controlled for sample selection bias. Despite the limitations that are therefore imposed on generalizability, the findings are nonetheless instructive in terms of identifying relationships among the key variables in the studies.

Key Variables in Epidemiologic Studies of Traumatic Stress

Issues that must be addressed in all epidemiologic studies of traumatic stress are: (1) measurement of exposure; (2) assessment of risk factors; and (3) case identification. By measurement of exposure, we mean: How do you determine whether a given individual has been exposed to an event that fulfills Criterion A of the DSM-IV (American Psychiatric Association, 1994) diagnostic criteria for PTSD, and how much of an exposure the individual has received? By risk factor assessment, we mean: How can you determine what other factors to include in your assessment protocol so that you include those variables likely to confer increased risk for exposure to trauma and for development and maintenance of (as well as recovery from) PTSD and other diagnostic and psychosocial outcomes? By case identification, we mean: How can you tell whether a given individual meets the diagnostic criteria for PTSD, and therefore should be considered to be a "case"?

In each instance, your goal is to increase the internal validity (Cook & Campbell, 1979) of the research. This is important because classification errors in either exposure or case identification reduce the internal validity of case versus noncase comparisons, which are the heart of epidemiologic studies. For example, poor assessment of exposure or case identification may result in real differences between groups going undetected. To the extent that important risk factors are excluded from the study protocol, the potential for explaining the etiology of observed differences between cases and noncases is greatly diminished.

It is redundant to say that anyone who meets the criteria for the diagnosis of PTSD has been exposed to one or more "extreme events." Yet, not everyone who has been exposed to an extreme event develops PTSD. Although exposure to one or more traumatic events is a necessary condition for the development of PTSD in and of itself, such exposure is often insufficient to produce the disorder. Other biological, psychological, and social risk factors may play essential roles in the development of PTSD and functional impairment (cf. Fairbank et al., 1995). As a result, assessment of exposure and other risk factors is an important component of the internal validity of epidemiologic studies of PTSD and is critical to the examination of etiology.

In particular, researchers in the trauma field have struggled with the challenging issues of objective versus subjective evaluations of exposure, the continuous and multidimensional nature of exposure, and the problem of how to develop well-designed measures of exposure to various types of traumatic events. PTSD case identification presents a similarly complicated assessment issue. One of the most important scientific challenges facing epidemiologic studies is the issue of case identification: How does one determine who is a case and who is not?

To enhance internal validity, emphasis is placed on using measures with sound psychometric properties, to identify cases of PTSD, and to assess key constructs, such as exposure to trauma and other risk factors for disorder. Generally, whenever it is feasible to do so, you should attempt to use previously validated measures in your study protocol. Little more than a decade ago, however, there were but a few measures of trauma exposure and PTSD symptomatology available to researchers, and these were relatively untested. As a result, epidemiologic researchers have contributed significantly to the development and evaluation of a rapidly growing compendium of assessment techniques for exposure to trauma and PTSD symptomatology. When the NVVRS was designed in the mid-1980s, for example, the data available on the reliability and validity of existing candidate measures was insufficient to inform the research team on which measures to select for the study. The NVVRS research team therefore launched an extensive case-control validation study to determine the psychometric adequacy of the available measures. Thus, the fact that PTSD is today assessed in various community, service-sector, and at-risk groups using a variety of assessment techniques and measures that have been evaluated in terms of the adequacies of their factor structure, test-retest reliability, specificity, sensitivity, and predictive validity is in part due to the efforts of epidemiologic researchers. For example, there are currently at least four major categories into which existing PTSD case identification methods for use in epidemiologic studies can be divided, based on the underlying approach taken. These categories are: (1) survey interview approaches, (2) semi-structured clinical interview approaches, (3) psychometric approaches, and (4) psychophysiological approaches. Chapter 3 in this book by Solomon, Keane, Kaloupek, and Newman (1996) contains an in-depth discussion of diagnosis and assessment in PTSD research, and chapter 4 by Kaloupek and Bremner (1996) covers physiologic methods and measures to study PTSD.

Designing and Implementing Epidemiologic Studies of PTSD

In this section, we focus primarily on issues related to designing and implementing cross-sectional and cohort studies because, in contrast to case-control studies, they address a greater number of key epidemiologic questions about prevalence and incidence and permit the drawing of inferences about community populations and populations at risk.

An initial step in designing such studies is to define the specific aims and objectives of the research and to identify key research questions and hypotheses. Epidemiologic research hypotheses in the field of traumatic stress are usually framed within the context of questions about rates of disorder (e.g., PTSD) in specific populations and identification of factors that confer increased risk for such disorders (e.g., type, intensity, frequency, duration, and timing of exposure to one or more traumatic events and other biological, psychological, and social risk factors).

Once the research questions have been specified, a subsequent step is to develop a methodology that is consistent with the aims of the study, taking into account issues of sample design and selection, study planning, implementation, and analyses. It is important to keep in mind that any given design solution is not optimal for all questions, and it is therefore imperative to consider the advantages and disadvantages of a range of possible options. Although many of the basic epidemiologic research issues are quite comparable with those described in other chapters of this book, there are at least three points of special importance to keep in mind when designing epidemiologic studies: (a) careful attention must be paid to selecting a sample that characterizes the population of inference; (b) data collection activities are usually labor intensive and expensive given the need to find sufficient numbers of cases in a given sample or subsample, such as cases of PTSD among population subgroups (e.g., minorities, women, adolescents); and (c) data analyses need to take into account the complexity of the research design. Regarding the latter point, the complexity of the research design may dictate the use of sample weights that take into account the respondents' probabilities of selection. In complex sampling designs, the sample weights should also be adjusted for nonresponse (Kessler, Little, & Groves, 1995; Lee et al., 1989).

In recognition of the fact that epidemiologic research requires expertise across a number of scientific disciplines, it is prudent to assemble a research team from appropriate substantive areas with the experience and skills in the technical domains needed to conduct the study successfully. Depending on the complexity of the study, investigators with research funding generally include within the project budget funds to provide direct support for, or consultation from, sampling statisticians, survey methodologists, project managers, and statisticians with experience in analyzing data from studies using complex sampling designs. For example, in our experience, the involvement of a sampling statistician early in the design deliberations is essential to ensuring that the research team understands the range of appropriate and feasible sampling options and can make an informed choice. Sampling statisticians also may provide ongoing expert consultation in other areas as well, such as constructing the sampling frame, and developing sampling weights and adjustments for nonresponse and missing data.

Survey methodologists may provide expert guidance on the implementation of sampling and survey methods, such as procedures for counting, listing, and screening households within a specific community. Survey methodologists also often have considerable experience in procedures for achieving adequate response rates at baseline and at follow-up (for longitudinal studies). In addition, considerable progress has been made over the past decade in the development of statistical analysis methods that have been shown to have direct application to complex and large datasets. Some of these statistical methods are commercially available in software packages, such as SUDAAN (Software for the Statistical Analysis of Correlated Data)(Shah, Barnwell, & Bieler, 1995), and consultation from statisticians familiar with these methods is quite valuable.

If you are interested in designing and conducting epidemiologic studies but have neither grant support nor experienced colleagues in other disciplines available, you face a formidable task, indeed. Clearly, among the first steps in assessing the feasibility of unfunded epidemiologic endeavors should be an evaluation of the potential for developing strong collaborative relationships with colleagues in the requisite scientific disciplines.

Concurrent with development of the sampling design (i.e., simple random sample, systematic sample, stratified sample, census, etc.), the research team usually proceeds with compiling and pretesting the research instruments. You should consider options for assessing risk factor domains, exposure to trauma, PTSD caseness, and co-morbid conditions using methods and measures described in detail in Chapters 3, 4, and 7 of this book. Empirical support for the various methods of data collection should be carefully considered, taking into account feasibility and costs. Potentially viable options to consider include mail surveys, face-to-face surveys, and telephone surveys, including recent technological innovations, such as computer assisted personal interviewing (CAPI), computer assisted telephone interviewing (CATI), and self-administered computerized interviews with prerecorded audio presentation (audioCASI or ACASI). ACASI is a good example of a rapidly developing technology with considerable potential for application to epidemiologic research on sensitive topics, such as one's history of exposure to extreme events. With ACASI, the computer plays a recorded version of question-and-answer choices to the respondent over headphones. The person responds through some data input device, such as a keyboard, or external keypad. The computer then records the response and plays the next appropriate question based on the previous response. An advantage of ACASI technology is the privacy afforded subjects as they are asked about potentially sensitive experiences and behaviors.

Implementing epidemiologic studies is challenging and the time invested in developing a detailed project timeline that indicates which tasks must be implemented in sequence and which may be implemented concurrently is well worth the effort. Innumerable activities require careful planning—with an eye on the clock in order to complete the project on time and within budget (which is always a good idea if one is hopeful of subsequent funding). Examples of tasks that require planned start dates and target completion dates include development and finalization of the study design; construction of the sampling frame and sampling methods; development of assessment measures and procedures; recruitment, training, and supervision of interviewers and other field staff; activities associated with data management, preparation, processing, and analysis; and dissemination of information through final reports, journal articles, and presentations at professional meetings. Finally, epidemiologic studies also require thoughtful attention to issues of project management, quality control, protection of rights of human research participants, and analysis of data and report writing that are described in detail in other chapters of this volume by Smith (1996), Armstrong (1996), Stamm and Bieber (1996), and Green (1996).

References

Armstrong, J. (1996). Emotional issues and ethical aspects of trauma research. In E. B. Carlson (Ed.), *Trauma research methodology*. Lutherville, MD: Sidran Press.

American Psychiatric Association (1994). *Diagnostic and statistical manual of mental disorders* (4th ed.). Washington, D.C.: Author.

Brady, K. T., Kileen, T., Saladin, M. E., Dansky. B., & Becker, S. (1994). Comorbid substance abuse and posttraumatic stress disorder. *American Journal on Addictions, 3,* 160–164.

Breslau, N., Davis, G. C., & Andreski, P. (1995). Risk factors for PTSD-related traumatic events: A prospective analysis. *American Journal of Psychiatry, 152,* 529–535.

Breslau, N., Davis, G. C., Andreski, P., & Peterson, E. (1991). Traumatic events and post-traumatic stress disorder in an urban population of young adults. *Archives of General Psychiatry, 48*, 216–222.

Cook, T. D., & Campbell, D. T. (1979). *Quasi-experimentation.* Boston: Houghton Mifflin Co.

Costello, E. J., & Angold, A. (1995). Developmental epidemiology. In D. Cicchetti & D. J. Cohen (Eds.), *Developmental psychopathology. Volume 1: Theory and methods.* New York: John Wiley.

Davidson, J. R. T., & Fairbank, J. A. (1993). The epidemiology of posttraumatic stress disorder. In J. R. T. Davidson & E. B. Foa (Eds.), *Posttraumatic stress disorder: DSM-IV and beyond.* Washington, D.C.: American Psychiatric Press.

Davidson, L. M., & Baum, A. (1992). Research findings after a nuclear accident: Three Mile Island. In L. S. Austin (Ed.), *Responding to disaster: A guide for mental health professionals.* Washington, D.C.: American Psychiatric Press.

Dew, A. & Bromet, E. J. (1993). Predictors of temporal patterns of psychiatric distress during 10 years following the nuclear accident at Three Mile Island. *Social Psychiatry and Psychiatric Epidemiology, 28*, 49–55.

Dohrenwend, B. P., Levav, I., Shrout, P. E., Schwartz, S., Naveh, G., Link, B., Skodol, A. E., & Stueve, A. (1992). Socioeconomic status and psychiatric disorders: The causation-selection issue. *Science, 255*, 946–952.

Eitinger, L. (1973). A follow-up study of the Norwegian concentration camp survivors' mortality and morbidity. *Israel Annals of Psychiatry and Related Disciplines, 11*, 199–209.

Fairbank, J. A., Schlenger, W. E., Caddell, J. M., & Woods, M. G. (1993). Post-traumatic stress disorder. In P. B. Sutker & H. E. Adams (Eds.), *Comprehensive handbook of psychopathology* (2nd ed.). New York: Plenum.

Fairbank, J. A., Schlenger, W. E., Saigh, P. A., & Davidson, J. R. T. (1995). An epidemiologic profile of post-traumatic stress disorder: Prevalence, comorbidity, and risk factors. In M. J. Friedman, D. S. Charney, & A. Y. Deutch (Eds.), *Neurobiological and clinical consequences of stress: From normal adaptation to PTSD.* New York: Raven Press.

Friedman, G. D. (1987). *Primer of epidemiology* (3rd ed.). New York: McGraw-Hill.

Garrison, C. Z., Weinrich, M. W., Hardin, S. B., Weinrich, S., & Wang, L. (1993). Post-traumatic stress disorder in adolescents after a hurricane. *American Journal of Epidemiology, 138*, 522–530.

Green, B. L. (1996). Writing and submitting manuscripts for publication. In

E. B. Carlson (Ed.), *Trauma research methodology*. Lutherville, MD: Sidran Press.

Green, B. L., Grace, M. C., Vary, M. G., Kramer, T. L., Gleser, G. C., & Leonard, A. C. (1994). Children of disaster in the second decade: A 17- year follow-up of Buffalo Creek survivors. *Journal of the American Academy of Child and Adolescent Psychiatry, 33*, 71–79.

Jordan, B. K., Schlenger, W. E., Fairbank, J. A., & Caddell, J. M. (in press). Prevalence of psychiatric disorders among incarcerated women II. *Archives of General Psychiatry.*

Kaloupek, D. G., & Bremner, J. D. (1996). Psychophysiological measures and methods in trauma research. In E. B. Carlson (Ed.), *Trauma research methodology*. Lutherville, MD: Sidran Press.

Kessler, R. C., Little, R. J. A., & Groves, R. M. (1995). Advances in strategies for minimizing and adjusting for survey nonresponse. *Epidemiologic Reviews: Psychiatric Epidemiology, 17*, 192–204.

Kessler, R. C., Sonnega, A., Bromet, E., Hughes, M., & Nelson, C. B. (in press). Posttraumatic stress disorder in the National Co-morbidity Survey. *Archives of General Psychiatry.*

Klienbaum, D. G., Kupper, L .L., & Morgenstern, H. (1982). *Epidemiologic research: Principles and quantitative methods*. New York: Van Nostrand Reinhold.

Koopman, C., Classen, C., & Spiegel, D. (1994). Predictors of post-traumatic stress symptoms among survivors of the Oakland/Berkeley, California firestorm. *American Journal of Psychiatry, 151*, 888–894.

Kulka, R. A., & Schlenger, W. E. (1993). Survey research and field designs for the study of posttraumatic stress disorder. In J. P. Wilson & B. Raphael (Eds.), *International handbook of traumatic stress syndromes*. New York: Plenum Press.

Kulka, R. A., Schlenger, W. E., Fairbank, J. A., Hough, R. L., Jordan, B. K., Marmar, C. R., & Weiss, D. S. (1990). *Trauma and the Vietnam war generation: Report of findings from the National Vietnam Veterans Readjustment Study*. New York: Brunner/Mazel.

Lasky, T. & Stolley, P. D. (1994). Selection of cases and controls. *Epidemiologic Reviews: Applications of the Case-Control Method, 16*, 6– 17.

Last, J. M. (1983). *A dictionary of epidemiology*. New York: Oxford University Press.

Lee, E. S., Forthofer, R. N., & Lorimor, R. J. (1989). *Analyzing complex survey data*. Newbury Park, CA: Sage.

Levy, P. S., & Lemeshow, S. (1980). *Sampling for health professionals*. Belmont, CA: Lifetime Learning.

Lilienfeld, D. E., & Stolley, P. D. (1994). *Foundations of epidemiology* (3rd ed.). New York: Oxford University Press.

McFarlane, A. C. (1988). The longitudinal course of posttraumatic morbidity: The range of outcomes and their predictors. *Journal of Nervous and Mental Disease, 176*, 30–39.

Mezzich, J. E., Jorge, M. R., & Salloum, I. M. (1994). *Psychiatric epidemiology*. Baltimore: Johns Hopkins University Press.

Mullen, P. E., Martin, J. L., Anderson, J. C., Romans, S. E., & Herbison, G. P. (1993). Childhood sexual abuse and mental health in adult life. *British Journal of Psychiatry, 163*, 721–732.

Norris, F. H. (1996). Designing trauma studies: Basic principles. In E. B. Carlson (Ed.), *Trauma research methodology*. Lutherville, MD: Sidran Press.

Norris, F. H., & Kaniasty, K. (1994). Psychological distress following criminal victimization in the general population: Cross-sectional, longitudinal, and prospective analyses. *Journal of Consulting and Clinical Psychology, 62*, 111–123.

North, C. S., Smith, E. M., & Spitznagel, E. L. (1994). Posttraumatic stress disorder in survivors of a mass shooting. *American Journal of Psychiatry, 151*, 82–88.

Phifer, J. F., & Norris, F. H. (1989). Psychological symptoms in older adults following natural disaster: Nature, timing, duration, and course. *Journal of Gerontology: Social Sciences, 44*, S207–S217.

Resnick, H. S., Kilpatrick, D. G., Dansky, B. S., Saunders, B. E., & Best, C. L. (1993). Prevalence of civilian trauma and PTSD in a representative national sample of women. *Journal of Consulting and Clinical Psychology, 61*, 984–991.

Richters, J. E., & Martinez, P. (1993). The NIMH Community Violence Project: I. Children as victims of and witnesses to violence. *Psychiatry, 56*, 7–21.

Rothbaum, B. O., Foa, E. B., Riggs, D., Murdock, T., & Walsh, W. (1992). A prospective examination of post-traumatic stress disorder in rape victims. *Journal of Traumatic Stress, 5*, 455–475.

Sack, W. H., McSharry, S., Clarke, G. N., Kinney, R., Seeley, J., & Lewinsohn, P. (1994). The Khmer Adolescent Project I. Epidemiologic findings in two generations of Cambodian refugees. *Journal of Nervous and Mental Disease, 182*, 387–395.

Saigh, P. A., Mroueh, M., Zimmerman, B. J., & Fairbank, J. A. (1995). Self-efficacy expectations among traumatized adolescents. *Behaviour Research and Therapy, 33,* 701–704.

Schlenger, W. E., Kulka, R. A., Fairbank, J. A., Hough, R. L., Jordan, B. K., Marmar, C. R., & Weiss, D. S. (1992). The prevalence of post-traumatic stress disorder in the Vietnam generation: A multimethod, multisource assessment of psychiatric disorder. *Journal of Traumatic Stress, 5,* 333–363.

Shah, B. V., Barnwell, B. G., & Bieler, G. S. (1995). *SUDAAN User's Manual, Version 6.4.* Research Triangle Park, N.C.: Research Triangle Institute.

Smith, E. (1996). Coping with the challenges of field research. In E. B. Carlson (Ed.), *Trauma research methodology.* Lutherville, MD: Sidran Press.

Solomon, S., Keane, T., Kaloupek, D., & Newman, E. (1996). Choosing self-report measures and structured interviews. In E. B. Carlson (Ed.), *Trauma research methodology.* Lutherville, MD: Sidran Press.

Solomon, Z. (1989). A 3-year prospective study of post-traumatic stress disorder in Israeli combat veterans. *Journal of Traumatic Stress, 2,* 59–73.

Stamm, B. H. & Bieber, S. L. (1996). Data Analysis: Matching your question of interest to your analysis. In E. B. Carlson (Ed.), *Trauma research methodology.* Lutherville, MD: Sidran Press.

Steinglass, P. & Gerrity, E. (1990). Natural disasters and post-traumatic stress disorder: Short-term versus long-term recovery in two disaster-affected communities. *Journal of Applied Social Psychology, 20,* 1746–1765.

Ursano, R. J., Boydstrom, J. A., & Wheatley, R. D. (1981). Psychiatric illness in U.S. Air Force Vietnam prisoners of war: A five-year follow-up. *American Journal of Psychiatry, 138,* 310–314.

6

Coping with the Challenges of Field Research

Elizabeth M. Smith

The purpose of this chapter is to explore some of the practical issues involved in carrying out traumatic stress research in the community. Most research on disasters and other traumatic events is not readily adaptable to a laboratory or office setting and must be conducted in the field. Events such as disasters usually do not occur in the researcher's territory so it becomes necessary to travel to an unfamiliar area to conduct the investigation. There are a number of practical problems that are encountered in this kind of field research and novice as well as experienced researchers need to be prepared as they enter this relatively new area of scientific study.

Community studies of disaster and other traumas are invaluable in increasing our understanding of the physical, social, and emotional consequences of trauma. These studies can provide estimates of the prevalence of Post Traumatic Stress Disorder (PTSD), as well as other types of disorders in affected populations, identify risk factors for the development of these disorders, and examine the course of responses to traumatic stress.

In order to obtain accurate information about prevalence rates of symptoms and disorders after trauma occurs, it is important to interview survivors in the early aftermath of the event as well as to conduct

*This research was made possible by a grant from the National Institute of Mental Health # MH40025.

additional assessments over time. Retrospective studies can present serious problems caused by forgetting and distortion of memory. As additional life events occur it becomes increasingly difficult to sort out which responses are specifically related to the trauma. Data obtained in the acute phase after a traumatic event are of importance in understanding the immediate consequences of the event and cannot be regained once the brief opportunity to collect them passes.

Designing and conducting these epidemiologic studies of trauma provide a wide variety of challenges, especially when it is necessary to get into the field quickly to study the early effects of the event. Because of our involvement in studies of persons exposed to disaster trauma, both natural as well as human-made, we will use our experiences in conducting these studies to illustrate some of the problems that must be addressed. Important research areas involving traumas from such events as rape, accidents, other forms of violence, and the effects of stress upon rescue workers are not specifically covered in this chapter, but most of the methodological issues discussed here are also applicable to these areas of research.

One of the sources of difficulty in doing this research is the nature of the phenomena under study. Because traumatic events are not predictable it is difficult to plan ahead. In most cases, disasters occur quickly and without warning. You must then design a study as rapidly as possible in order to ensure timely data collection. Timing is often critical in studying these events and logistical concerns never imagined by laboratory researchers can become predominant in a quick response, field-based study of a disaster or trauma (Baum, Solomon, Ursano, Bickman, Blanchard, Green, Keane, Laufer, Norris, Reid, Smith, & Steinglass, 1993).

Even those studies which focus on non-disaster trauma face a number of problems in obtaining access to victims and in approaching them during the aftermath of the trauma. While each event and population has special characteristics, we will address some of the general issues that are common to trauma studies.

In this chapter we will focus on some of the practical problems that are common in these "quick response" disaster studies as well as other studies of trauma: sources of funding, identification of suitable events for study, obtaining access to survivors, approaching potential subjects, selection and training of interviewers, and logistics of collecting data in the field. We will begin by briefly describing our studies as a background for discussion of these issues.

Background

Prospective Follow-up Studies

Our entry into the field of disaster research was prompted by a remarkable set of events which occurred in the St. Louis area beginning in the fall of 1982. First, it was announced that oil which had been mixed with dioxin and sprayed on various sites as long as 10 years earlier was still present in toxic levels. In December, a series of devastating floods swept through the area, causing the evacuation of over 25,000 people from their homes and resulting in an estimated $150 million in property damages. Officials also reported that some of the wells that supplied drinking water in the area had high levels of radioactivity due to seepage from a uranium plant's waste buried in the 1960s. The arrival of spring brought more disasters. Flood waters again covered the area, and a series of tornadoes left a path of destruction.

These disasters occurred just as Washington University was completing the second wave of interviews for the Epidemiologic Catchment Area (ECA) project, which was designed to assess the psychiatric status of the region's population (Robins & Regier, 1991). The instrument developed for the ECA project was the Diagnostic Interview Schedule (DIS) (Robins, Helzer, Croughan, Williams, & Spitzer, 1981), which assesses psychiatric disorders according to DSM-III criteria (American Psychiatric Association, 1980).

To our knowledge this was the first time that an area affected by disaster had, by chance, also been the site of a careful evaluation of psychiatric status just before the disaster occurred. The fact that only some areas of the research site were affected provided another unique advantage—a control group from a similar area, similarly evaluated for psychiatric disorder prior to the disasters.

We were able to return to the respondents who lived in the affected areas in order to learn whether exposure to disaster had had an effect on their psychiatric status. We could judge this effect by comparing changes in their mental health status with changes in the mental health of the unaffected control group.

To identify ECA sample members likely to have experienced these disasters, we received assistance from a variety of governmental agencies, including the Missouri Department of Health, the Environmental Protection Agency, the Missouri Department of Natural Resources, and the Centers for Disease Control. These sources identified areas that had been exposed to the four types of disaster.

We identified 252 ECA respondents whom we believed to have been exposed to these disasters. Most were from a three-county area made up of rural sections and small towns. We selected all of those respondents who were exposed plus a control sample of 200 from the area. To increase the disaster exposed group, an additional 200 residents from dioxin and flood areas were selected at random from areas not involved in the ECA project.

We returned to the field with a new interview shortly before the first anniversary of the disasters and over the next eight months interviewed a total of 547 individuals (373 from the ECA). Follow-up interviews were achieved with 82.5% of the ECA sample and 87% who had not been part of the ECA, for an overall response rate of 84%.

The number of individuals in the ECA sample reporting disaster exposure when we reinterviewed them was much lower than expected on the basis of the information provided by the various public agencies. Only 44 respondents reported personal exposure, and eight of them came from the group we had designated as controls. However, the number of individuals who were indirectly affected through exposure of relatives and friends was much higher than expected.

Forty percent of the total sample were directly affected by one or more disasters, 24% were indirectly affected by exposure of close friends or relatives, and 36% were not exposed (Smith, Robins, Przybeck, Goldring, & Solomon, 1986; Robins, Fishbach, Smith, Cottler, Solomon, & Goldring, 1986).

A new instrument, the Diagnostic Interview Schedule/Disaster Supplement (DIS/DS) (Robins & Smith, 1983), was designed for this project. It provides a comprehensive picture of the disaster experience and is applicable across a wide range of events. The DIS/DS assesses the type of event, type and extent of loss, individual and family risk factors, use of formal and informal support systems, behavioral response to the traumatic event, and 15 DSM-III-R diagnoses selected for their potential relevance to the disaster experience. This interview has been used in all of the disaster studies conducted by the author and her research team, and selected portions of the instrument have been used in other disaster research conducted in this country and abroad.

An offshoot of the ECA Hazards Study described above was the Family Hazards Study, which assessed the effects of disasters on families. This project included all dioxin and/or flood-exposed families from the earlier study who had children under 18 years of age at the time of the disasters as well as additional non-ECA households from similar affected and unaffected areas. A total of 174 families (272 parents and 265 children) were interviewed and the completion rate was 80% (Smith, 1989).

Data were collected over a one-year period beginning approximately three years after the disasters occurred. The timing of three years was not based on any assumptions regarding the optimal interval for follow-up after trauma. Instead, as is often the case, the timing was dictated by the length of time it required us to obtain funding.

Since most disasters occur unexpectedly, opportunities for the kinds of prospective studies just described are rare. It is important for researchers to be alert to the possibilities of obtaining data collected for other purposes prior to the occurrence of a disaster. Examples of possible sources of information are health surveys, studies of special populations such as the elderly, and assessments conducted of pre-school or school-age children.

Following the 1993 floods in the St. Louis area, we collaborated with staff members from a local mental health center in analyzing data on children exposed to the flood. The Center has contracts with a number of schools in the area to conduct annual assessments on all children in kindergarten through 3rd grade to identify learning and behavior problems. Although the data were not as complete as those conducted specifically for research purposes, they provided valuable information on the impact of the flood on these young children (Wilson, Smith, Fox, & Brauks, 1995).

Pilot Studies of Short-term Responses to Disaster

When pre-disaster information is not available, data collected shortly after the event can provide baseline data for longitudinal studies of the mental health consequences of trauma. Since we already had an instrument designed to assess responses to disaster, we began developing methods for rapid entry into the field to obtain data during the acute phase after disaster. We selected three events, each with 25 to 50 survivors available to serve as potential subjects. Interviews were conducted with 106 survivors of these three traumatic events during the acute phase, approximately six weeks after the events occurred. Because of our interest in studying mental health consequences and the expectation that there would be small samples, we selected high-impact events which would be likely to produce symptoms of PTSD and other emotional distress in the majority of those exposed.

The first event studied was the crash of a military jet into the lobby of a hotel in Indianapolis in October 1987 (Smith, North, McCool, & Shea, 1990). There were 10 deaths and several injuries resulting from the crash. Because it occurred in the morning after most guests had departed, employees were the most severely affected group, and all but one who died were employees.

We elected to interview as many of the surviving employees as possible whether or not they were on-site at the time of the crash, since it was expected that even those not present at the time of the crash would be affected. The hotel manager, though cooperative, hesitated to give us the names of employees. He did agree to address and send our letter of invitation describing the study and reply cards to the employees. Forty-six (74%) of the 62 surviving hotel employees responded and were interviewed.

The second disaster, in December 1987, was a shooting spree in Russellville, Arkansas, which left 16 dead and two injured (North, Smith, McCool, & Shea, 1989). Surviving victims and witnesses in some of the four small business establishments where the shootings occurred were contacted in person. A total of 18 (72%) of the eligible subjects were interviewed.

The third event studied was a tornado that cut a path one mile wide and 12 miles long through Madison County, Florida in April 1988, leaving four dead, 17 injured and extensive property damage in its wake (North, Smith, McCool, & Lightcap, 1989). Interviews were attempted with one adult member of each household in the path of the tornado. A total of 42 subjects were interviewed about five weeks after the storm. We were assisted in this study by the director of the local mental health center. He provided a map and tour of the affected area and names of survivors, as well as interviewing space. Help from a well-respected member of this relatively small community was invaluable. As a result, the completion rate was 89%.

Although we had planned to conduct one-year follow-up interviews with the survivors of these three events, funding did not become available until nearly three years later. Follow-up interviews were conducted at that time, with completion rates ranging from 89% to 93% of those initially interviewed.

The hands-on experience of conducting these field studies provided us with the experience necessary to carry out a large-scale longitudinal study of the epidemiology of disaster-related mental health. The study was designed to look at the prevalence of psychiatric symptoms and disorders in the acute phase following the trauma and to examine the course of recovery over time. Six disaster events have been studied and over 600 survivors have been interviewed. Interviews were conducted within three months following the event, and again at one and three years postdisaster. The events and studies are described in the following section.

Quick Response Longitudinal Epidemiologic Studies
First was a mass murder which occurred in October 1991 in Luby's Cafeteria in Killeen, Texas (North, Smith, & Spitznagel, 1994). A total of 24 individuals were killed and many more injured in what has been described as the largest civilian shooting massacre in this country's history. With the cooperation of the local police department, we

were able to identify all of the individuals who were present at the time of the shooting, including customers, employees, and police officers. We also identified persons who were indirectly affected, including off-duty employees and persons in the area, such as police officers and residents of a neighboring apartment building. We were able to interview 136 (85%) of the 160 located subjects, 89% of whom were on site at the time of the shooting.

The Oakland Hills, California firestorm also occurred in October 1991. One of the largest urban fires in this country's history, it caused significant loss of property and lives. Because of the scope of the disaster (i.e., several thousand homes were damaged or destroyed in at least six different neighborhoods), only a small percentage of the affected individuals could be studied. We therefore selected a representative sample. To do this, media reports were used to identify the affected areas. Property tax assessment records for the homes in those areas were obtained from a title company. A random sample was selected from each of the six neighborhoods. This proved to be an effective way of obtaining a sample with varying degrees of exposure since the fires followed such an erratic course. Interviews were conducted with 69 subjects. Although 80% of those who could be contacted agreed to be interviewed, holidays made scheduling difficult and not all of the subjects could be interviewed within the six- to 12-week time frame. At the one-year follow-up, 21 subjects who were originally selected but not interviewed were added, increasing the sample to 90.

Two other mass shootings were studied. Both were on a smaller scale than the Luby's Cafeteria slayings. One occurred in November 1991 at the University of Iowa in Iowa City when a disgruntled graduate student shot and killed seven faculty and staff members. Twenty-three directly- and indirectly-exposed subjects, drawn from the Physics Department where the shootings occurred and from another department at the University were interviewed for the project.

The other shooting occurred in May 1992 in the St. Louis County, Missouri Courthouse. A woman was shot and killed by her estranged husband during the hearing of their divorce case. Five others in the courtroom were also injured before the gunman was wounded and captured. We were able to interview 80 subjects who were in the building at the time of the shootings. Twelve additional subjects declined personal interviews but completed self-administered forms.

Because the event occurred on a day when there was an unusually large volume of court activity, we encountered more than anticipated difficulty in identifying eye witnesses who were not employed in the courthouse. As a result, our sample contained primarily courthouse employees, since other observers quickly left the area.

In both of these shootings, we had to rely on local representatives to assist us in identifying and contacting potential subjects. Therefore, it was difficult to ascertain the number of persons who refused to participate, since only those who agreed to be interviewed were approached by the research team.

The Midwestern flooding that occurred during the summer of 1993 was the subject of our next investigation. In the St. Louis area the Mississippi and Missouri Rivers crested at many feet above flood stage. The flooding was extraordinary and long-lasting, and areas that had not previously flooded were affected as a result of levees breaking. There were 30 flood-related deaths and thousands of homes were destroyed or severely damaged. Records from local emergency management agencies were used to identify flood areas and households were selected at random. The highly mobile nature of the flood plain population, especially in trailer parks and other rental property, made it more difficult in this instance to find many of the affected residents. Interviews were conducted in two areas, one metropolitan and the other rural. A total of 165 subjects were interviewed for a completion rate of 82.5%.

The last event, an earthquake in Northridge, California, occurred in January 1994. Although the earthquake lasted only 10 seconds it caused damages estimated at $30 billion. Hundreds of individuals were injured and 57 were killed. More than 3,000 aftershocks were recorded in the days after the quake, causing increased anxiety for residents of the area. A reverse telephone directory for the area was available and provided a good source for names, addresses, and telephone numbers in the affected area. With information from the news media we selected residential areas in a radius of five miles of the quake's epicenter and drew a random sample from listings in this area. A total of 130 subjects were interviewed over a two-month period.

One-year follow-up interviews have been completed for all six of the disasters with a completion rate of 94%. Three-year follow-up interviews have been conducted at four of the six sites. The three-year response rate is 92%.

As this chapter is being written, preparations are under way to study the April 1995 bombing of the Murrah Federal Building in Oklahoma City, Oklahoma. This was the largest terrorist attack in this country, resulting in 168 deaths and over 500 injuries. The study is being conducted in collaboration with the Oklahoma State Department of Health and the Department of Psychiatry at the University of Oklahoma Health Sciences Center. Approximately 200 survivors will be selected for interview from those who were in the area at the time of the blast.

Studies such as these are costly in terms of money as well as time and effort. In the next section some of the funding sources will be reviewed.

Sources of Funding

As the importance of early assessment in studies of disaster and other traumatic events has been recognized, new mechanisms for funding these projects have become available. Traditional grant proposals submitted to the National Institute of Mental Health (NIMH) require, at a minimum, nine months from the time of submission to the earliest award. This does not count the extensive amount of time involved in preparation of the application or the possibility of having to resubmit it a second, or even third, time in response to reviewers' comments. This lengthy process makes it impossible to get into the field quickly following a particular disaster event. The ECA Hazards and Family Hazards Studies were funded through this process.

NIMH has encouraged grant applicants to focus their research on a particular mental health issue, rather than on a particular event, thereby allowing for review, approval, and funding prior to the disaster. Solomon (1989) observes that although the exact location and timing of a particular disaster cannot be predicted, "the overall occurrence of emergency events is regular and frequent." Funding prior to the event allows you the opportunity to develop instruments, recruit and train interviewers, and design sampling plans.

Several of these grants have been awarded, including one to this author for the longitudinal epidemiologic study described earlier in this chapter. This large-scale study has interviewed over 600 survivors of six different disasters described earlier.

For studies on a somewhat smaller scale, NIMH has earmarked funds for Rapid Assessment Post-Impact of Disaster (RAPID) grants which provide up to $50,000 for one year for salaries, travel, and other expenses. The requirements of the proposal are somewhat less rigorous than those of regular individual research grant proposals: with a page limitation of 10 versus 20 pages; a greater emphasis on methods and practical issues such as identifying a sample appropriate for the research questions to be studied; and obtaining access to these individuals in a timely manner. Peer reviewers are all experienced disaster researchers who are well aware of the problems and limitations imposed by this type of research. The review process is expedited so that an investigator can be in the field within a few months after the event has occurred.

RAPID grants are ideal for new investigators as well as those who are experienced in another field and want to apply methods they have utilized in another area to the study of trauma. They can also provide you with the opportunity for early entry into the field in order to collect some preliminary data while preparing an application for a traditional grant.

Funds are also available for quick-response studies through the rapid response program administered by the Natural Hazards Research Center at the University of Colorado in Boulder. Provided by NIMH and the National Science Foundation, these funds cover travel and data collection expenses but not salaries. The application process is streamlined and requires only a two- or three-page letter describing the purpose of the project, its significance, the methods to be used to achieve the goals, and a proposed budget. The review process is expedited and applicants are notified of approval within a fairly short period of time.

We were fortunate to obtain funding from the rapid response program. This provided us with the opportunity to develop and pilot our methods for collecting data on disaster survivors during the acute phase. (We have described the three pilot studies earlier in the chapter.) Once our proposal was approved, we were able to select events for study which met our criteria and we began work immediately. This pilot data was an important factor in obtaining the funding from NIMH for our longitudinal study.

A final word on funding. A pilot study of disaster need not be very expensive if you have the time and energy to get started and can enlist the help of colleagues or students in data collection. However, a great deal of effort is required to carry out even a small-scale project.

In the next section we will discuss in more detail the selection of disaster events for study.

Identification of a Suitable Event

Certainly the purpose of the study and the research questions to be answered will guide you in the selection of a disaster or trauma event. Raphael et al. (1989) suggest that priority should be given to research that improves the basic understanding of responses to disasters or is geared towards management of disaster situations and the prevention of negative consequences.

Green (1982) points out that defining the populations affected and to be assessed may often be difficult. Unless this is carefully done, the value of any findings may come into serious question. Selection of the group of victims to be studied, the definition of affected populations, and the methods and criteria of case identification may all influence estimates of impairment to a degree. The correct categorization of victims requires careful consideration. Extensive discussion of these issues can be found in Chapter 5 of this volume (Fairbank, Jordan, & Schlenger, 1995).

Green (1982) also notes that the dimensions of the disaster itself may affect the rates of impairment. Disasters with high impact, resulting in deaths, injuries, and high losses are more likely to have greater psychological effect than those with less impact.

The essence of every disaster is its unexpectedness. No two disasters are alike. It is, therefore, very difficult even to give guidelines for selection. The ideal disaster for study would occur in close proximity to the researcher (but not too close) and would involve a readily identifiable and accessible population, all of whom speak English and are willing to be interviewed.

In selecting our disasters we have chosen events which had some specific characteristics previously reported to be linked to the development of symptoms postdisaster in order to maximize the number of subjects with symptoms of PTSD in our sample (Bolin, 1985). These characteristics include a high degree of horror and terror, seeing gruesome images, fear of death, and some degree of anticipation (as opposed to sudden onset).

We have also tried to select disasters characterized by a substantial variation in impact, so that respondents will have experienced different degrees of trauma. This presents a more efficient way of measuring effect than the conventional method of finding a demographically similar non-affected control group.

Obtaining Access to Survivors

Solomon (1989) suggests that gaining access to survivors may be the most difficult problem for any study of disaster or trauma. There are some occasions when you would be able to directly approach potential respondents. In other cases it may be necessary to elicit the cooperation of governmental and/or other agencies in order to obtain objective information about affected areas, as was the case in our ECA Hazards study.

In community settings a number of sources of initial contacts may be available. These include the local newspaper office, health and/or mental health providers, and law enforcement officials. Initial telephone contact with these key individuals (who act as gatekeepers) may also provide valuable assistance for additional sources of information when entering the field.

It can be particularly helpful to make contact with someone who knows the area and to ask that person to serve as a consultant or collaborator on the project. This individual will be familiar with local norms and can guide the researcher as well as help him or her to gain entry into the community. Our experience in studying the tornado in Madison, Florida serves as an excellent example.

A word of caution is indicated regarding establishing relationships with local groups. You need to be careful not to become aligned with special interest or advocacy groups or government agencies. If you are perceived by respondents as being an agent of the government or other organization it could affect cooperation as well as the type of information obtained.

In our ECA Hazards study, for example, we had to rely on the Missouri Department of Health to provide us with information on the areas which had been tested and designated as dioxin sites. Because residents of these areas had been relocated, we were dependent upon the Department of Health to provide us with their names and current addresses. Fortunately the Department of Health had compiled a registry in order to study the health effects of exposure to dioxin. We quickly discovered that there was a great deal of controversy among residents about the possible health effects of dioxin. Most were dissatisfied with the government's handling of the relocation of residents and were suspicious of the government's motives in conducting the health study. Therefore, it was very important that our study not be viewed as a government project and extra effort was made to identify it with Washington University.

What would have happened if the Department of Health had refused us access to their list of names? Although time consuming, it would have been possible to obtain the names of property owners through the property tax records which are available at the tax assessors office in the county courthouse. In Oakland we used a title company to obtain property tax records for the areas affected by the fire. As long as you can specify the area, this method is effective in identifying subjects. Voter registration lists can also be helpful in identifying residents of a particular area.

Once we had the home owners' names two additional tasks would have been necessary: first, locating the new addresses of these individuals and second, determining that they were living in the area at the time dioxin contamination was discovered. Since the focus of our study was the psychological effects of exposure to various hazards, we were interested only in those who were actually living in the area as opposed to those owning property there but residing elsewhere.

Often after a disaster such as a flood, fire, or tornado, individuals will be forced to leave their homes. This can present problems if you want to contact them. This is especially true during the early days after the event. We have found that most individuals have their mail forwarded. Even if they don't have a telephone they can be reached by letter.

If the length of time after the event is months or years, rather than weeks, a number of different methods are available to assist in locating subjects. These include postal searches, Department of Motor Vehicle Records (drivers licenses), city directories, reverse directories, and, in some states, public assistance (welfare) records. Private credit-reporting agencies charge a fee for their service but can be very effective in locating individuals anywhere in the United States.

It is important to obtain future contact information at the time of the baseline interview even if plans for follow-up have not yet been made. The name or names of persons who will always know how to reach the respondent can be invaluable at a later time.

After a disaster, some agencies or businesses may be unwilling to provide names of individuals because of confidentiality. We have encountered this situation in several of our studies with varying results. In some situations they may be unwilling to divulge the names and addresses but will agree to contact the individuals and ask permission to provide this information to you. Or, they may be willing to contact the individuals for you and ask for their participation. This can be a mixed blessing. On the one hand, it can establish your credibility if the contact is made by someone the respondent respects and trusts. On the other hand, if the contact person is not particularly interested in the project or has reservations about it this may be conveyed to potential subjects. In our Indianapolis study of hotel employees this method worked extremely well because the manager was genuinely interested in the project and encouraged his staff to participate. In a few instances we have been unable to carry out a study because of limited cooperation.

When we are going into a community, especially small towns or semi-rural areas (as in the ECA Hazards Study and the Midwestern flood study), we try to notify community leaders of our presence in the area. Letters are sent in advance to the sheriff or police department and to local officials such as the mayor notifying them of the purposes of our study and alerting them to the dates that interviewers will be in the area. The letter, which is signed by the principal investigator, provides a telephone number where the research team can be reached while in the area as well as the investigator's telephone number.

This letter has on several occasions led to some interesting contacts with the press. In one small community, we were met by a cameraman and reporter from the local television station, who had been sent to interview us. We found ourselves featured on the evening news discussing our study and our plans to interview in the area. This turned out to be very helpful because we were immediately recognized by those we contacted to arrange appointments.

Contacts with news media have generally been positive. We usually subscribe to the local newspaper for several weeks immediately after the event in order to become familiar with the area and more specific details of the event. The media can also be helpful by publicizing the study and helping with recruitment. However, there may be some bias in using media-based recruitment. Subjects who volunteer may have special characteristics, such as being particularly upset and wanting to talk about it, or not being affected by the event but enjoying the attention received and perhaps overstating their involvement.

Wortman et al. (1980) offer some practical advice for researchers on establishing sound relationships with agencies who work with victimized populations. They note the importance of the following steps: learning about the organization, identifying key personnel, familiarizing agency staff with the project's purpose and potential benefits, enlisting agency advice and input, and alleviating any potential staff burden caused by the project.

Foa (1994), in discussing her studies of rape victims and the problems involved in obtaining access to rape victims, points out that some agencies may distrust research and researchers and/or lack understanding of the importance of research. They may also be protective of their clients and not want to expose them to the risk of further trauma. She suggests that, whenever possible, researchers allow enough time for the start-up phase so that they can network with community agencies and develop contacts. It can also be helpful to have written notes of agreement that both parties sign following meeting with agencies. When conducting a field study, it is particularly important for you to maintain contact and visibility throughout the project, not just at the beginning.

Giving credit to agencies or others for their efforts in reports and publications is important. Thank-you notes recognizing staff members' assistance and expressing appreciation are also important in developing and maintaining effective working relationships. In a sense, your behavior with agency staff demonstrates your respect for others and willingness to work cooperatively. Developing a trusting relationship is key to the success of any collaboration.

It is also essential to be able to assure the agency that the subjects' rights will be protected in all respects. Reviewing the informed consent form and the human studies protocol with agency staff is an important step. It demonstrates that the subjects' problems and needs remain uppermost in your mind.

An approach which seems sensitive to concerns regarding protection of survivors and yet meets the needs of researchers for access to these survivors was developed after the bombing of the Murrah Federal Building in Oklahoma City. The governor of Oklahoma designated the Department of Psychiatry and Behavioral Sciences at the University of Oklahoma Health Sciences Center as the coordinating body for all research on the bombing. A designated staff member serves as a liaison between researchers seeking to study the bombing and the community. Although the primary goal is to protect survivors, secondary goals are to facilitate research activities, avoid duplication of effort, and ensure that quality data are obtained. All proposed projects are required to submit proof of approval by their own university's Institutional Review Board (Human Studies Committee), as well as a list of the instruments to be used for data collection, and study protocol. When possible, researchers with similar interests or proposals are encouraged to work together rather than having the same instrument administered repeatedly to the same individuals. Survivors who are contacted by researchers are encouraged to contact the university for assurance that they are participating in a legitimate research project.

Approaching Potential Subjects

The success of any project depends not only on the cooperation of agencies and community organizations but also on the cooperation of the survivors themselves.

It is important to approach subject recruitment with great sensitivity because many will have had very traumatizing experiences. Individuals may not want to risk opening up feelings to a stranger or may be reluctant to share their experiences because it is painful. These feelings in potential subjects certainly increase recruitment difficulties.

When recruiting subjects, there is a fine line between coercion and encouragement to participate. On the one hand, you want to maximize the completion rate, get a representative sample, or in small areas, get enough subjects in order to have sufficient numbers for analysis. On the other hand, it is important to respect the rights of potential subjects. They may be especially vulnerable after disaster, and you can be perceived as taking advantage of their misery for your own purposes if you are not careful in your initial approach to subjects.

We have experimented with a variety of approaches and found that a letter explaining the study seems to be the best way of making initial contact. A letter has the following advantages: it is less intrusive than a phone call, it can be read by the individual at his or her convenience, and the letterhead on the stationery legitimizes the researchers and the project. A sample letter is shown below:

Dear _____,

We are writing to you because we are interested in talking with people who have experienced extreme traumatic events. You have survived the _____, an experience few people have had, and you have valuable insights to share.

We are planning to study the event you experienced. The purpose of our work is to learn about how people respond to traumatic events and to understand their special needs. The information you provide can help us to assist those coping with these experiences now as well as in the future. Even if this effort does not help you directly, we expect that the results of this research will extend the limits of human knowledge and directly benefit others.

We will be interviewing in your area soon and would like to arrange an appointment to interview one adult in your household. The interview will require approximately one hour and can be scheduled at your convenience. All information will be confidential, and we will offer $__ as a token of our appreciation of your time. The success of our study depends on the participation of persons whose lives were directly or indirectly affected by this disaster, and therefore, your participation is very important.

Please fill out and return the enclosed stamped, self-addressed postcard to us. If you prefer, you may call our toll-free telephone number between the hours of 9:00 a.m. and 5:00 p.m. and speak to _____ or leave a message on our voice mail. We look forward to hearing from you as soon as possible. Thank you in advance for your contribution to this important study.

Sincerely,

A stamped, self-addressed postcard is enclosed with the letter and respondents are asked to return the card and indicate their interest in participating in the study, their current phone number, and the best time to contact them.

In our experience, slightly less than 50 percent of those who receive letters will return the postcard or telephone to schedule an interview within the first 10 days. Some may call to obtain more information, but many simply do not respond.

Subjects who have not called or returned their postcards are then contacted by telephone. Many of those who are contacted indicate that they have put off sending in their postcard although they are willing to participate. Some are unwilling to commit to an interview, wanting more time or information, and others simply refuse.

When telephoning potential subjects there are several "rules" that need to be followed. First, talk only to the person whom you are targeting to be a subject. Don't leave messages or try to explain the purpose of the call to others; instead try to determine a convenient time to call. Similarly, don't take refusals from persons other than the respondents. Don't telephone before 9:00 a.m. or after 9:00 p.m unless specifically invited to do so. When you do reach a potential subject, make sure that it is a convenient time to talk. Don't leave messages on answering machines unless absolutely necessary; instead call at different times on weekdays as well as weekends.

When subjects decline to participate in a study we try to avoid an absolute refusal and ask if they may be contacted again at a later time to invite their participation. Some who initially refuse may be willing to participate later when they are less upset or have more time, or have found reason to trust the researcher, or perhaps they have learned things from other participants that overcame their initial reluctance.

Although it is important to respect the individual's decision, it can be helpful to inquire about the reason for the refusal. If refusal is based on misconceptions or unrealistic fears it may be possible for you to allay these fears or provide correct information. Sometimes a little extra time or some additional information may be all that is needed to convert a refusal.

Some individuals may prefer a telephone interview rather than one in person or be willing to fill out self-administered forms. Scheduling interviews at the subject's convenience, in terms of both time and place, can also increase cooperation.

Occasionally subjects hesitate or refuse to participate in research studies because they are involved in litigation. This was the case in our ECA Hazards study for those from dioxin areas. We contacted the lawyers representing subjects and explained the study to them. In most cases the lawyers agreed to have their clients participate and some were helpful in reassuring subjects and eliciting their cooperation.

It is important to remember that most survivors of disaster have not been involved in previous research and few have had contact with mental health professionals. You need to show respect and courtesy to subjects. The purpose and importance of the project should be explained to respondents in sufficient detail so that they understand the potential benefits of the study both to society and to themselves. These benefits include the opportunity to talk to a sympathetic listener, the opportunity for intellectual stimulation, the opportunity for financial remuneration, and the possibility of improving intervention techniques. Another advantage from participating in a disaster research study that can be pointed out to potential subjects and key informants is the altruistic nature of research for the purposes of helping other disaster victims in the future (Solomon, 1989).

Our experience has been that subjects find the interview to be a positive experience. Probably the best evidence that participating in a disaster study is a positive (or at least a non-negative) experience for most subjects is the high rate of participation in our follow-up interviews. Over 90 percent of located subjects have participated at one and three years following the disaster.

Although some researchers have used increased monetary incentives in an effort to enhance their completion rate, in most disaster studies the money is not the primary motivation for participation. Making the interview as convenient as possible for the subject and stressing the importance of his or her contribution are usually more powerful incentives.

As is true in many other areas, there is a lack of agreement among researchers regarding the use of monetary incentives. Some feel that it is never appropriate to pay subjects for their participation while others routinely offer payment. Those who argue against incentives believe that paying subjects can introduce subtle bias and may influence subjects' behavior and answers. Large sums of money can be considered coercive and cause people to participate.

Those in favor of financial incentives point out their importance in achieving satisfactory response rates and that compensation shows respect for the subjects' time and effort. We have always felt that it is important to offer monetary incentives to subjects but are careful never to provide an amount that would in itself be large enough to be considered coercive. Subjects would not be likely to participate in the study strictly for the $20 payment.

Selection and Training of Interviewers

Wortman et al. (1980) suggest that high respondent commitment is most likely to be obtained when the research team includes interviewers selected for strong social skills and similarity in background with the respondents.

In selecting interviewers it is important to choose individuals who are mature, flexible, and resourceful. Personal skills are perhaps more important than educational credentials or professional orientation. Almost all of our interviewers possess a bachelor's degree and most have had experience in human services or were in training in psychiatry, psychology, or social work. We have, however, employed individuals with sales or marketing experience, artists, and teachers, among others. While interviewers are selected primarily for their ability to engage subjects, develop rapport, and carry out the interview format, they also need to be comfortable in traveling to new locations and working in unstructured and unsupervised situations outside of a regular office.

The most effective interviewers are those who are sensitive and caring and show genuine interest and concern for others. But they are not therapists when they are interviewing for a research project and they must know that. While they are willing to let subjects talk they must also be able to set limits. A detailed discussion of the difficulties involved in interviewing traumatized subjects in field studies can be found in Derry and Baum (1994).

It is crucial that those in contact with survivors for research purposes have at least adequate basic training and/or clinical skills to interact appropriately with acutely distressed persons and to ensure that those who are in need of attention for mental health problems are recognized and referred.

Training should include techniques for engagement strategies and for interviewing outside of an office situation. Interviewers need to learn the contents of the interview, standard responses to most anticipated questions, and ways to interpret and probe in the course of the interview. Interviewers should also be given careful instruction on safety precautions, ethical considerations of confidentiality and informed consent, and legal considerations around revelations of criminal behavior, particularly child abuse.

You and your interviewers should carefully consider the potential impact of the interview on those subjects who agree to participate. Disaster studies are designed to explore mental health responses to a traumatic event. Answering questions about this kind of experience may be very stressful for some individuals. Even interviews administered long after the event may reactivate symptoms that were in remission. You need to be particularly sensitive to the potential for distress and train interviewers to recognize unusually negative responses. Interviewers should be provided with procedures for dealing with such distress, such as offering a break or to reschedule the interview. Furthermore, interviewers may need to remind respondents of their right to refuse to answer questions which they find upsetting. You also need to insure that access to treatment is available and that interviewers make respondents aware of this opportunity (Solomon, 1989). Interviewers should be given information about referral agencies for persons who appear suicidal or have immediate needs for mental health treatment. Also, interviewers should be instructed to notify the principal investigator of any concerns and to give the principal investigator's telephone number to respondents.

As part of their training, it is important for interviewers to role-play typical and atypical interview situations prior to going into the field and for observations of interviewers to take place during training if at all possible.

It is also important to pay attention to the needs of interviewers which may be overlooked with the focus on traumas of subjects in disaster studies. The interviewer's task requires a careful balance of attitude—needing to distance themselves enough not to be overwhelmed by the intense emotional nature of the interviews they conduct, yet remaining sensitive and open to the human aspects of the experience (North & Smith, 1994). In the field, interviewers may be faced with one person after another with often overwhelming needs that the interviewers can do little to directly address. This can be frustrating and draining. You need to realize the potential for burnout of your interviewers, and potentially of yourself, in the field. Long hours of repeated interviews need to be broken up with opportunities to refresh with time to oneself or with other members of the team for meals, walks, shopping, exploration, or relaxing. In addition, daily debriefing sessions are helpful to allow interviewers to discuss their reactions to the material being reported to them by their interview subjects and to process this intense experience. With skillful debriefing, the resulting experience in the field can be highly stimulating and meaningful as opposed to a negative experience.

Logistics

Location of Interviews
In contrast to most studies, which are conducted in office settings, we have conducted disaster interviews in a variety of locations ranging from homes to hotel lobbies and rooms, cars, parks, restaurants, and other places. Usually we need to go to the subject if we are to get the interview. Even though this may seem more costly in terms of time or mileage, it is important to be ever mindful of the burden imposed by the research and to minimize it in any way possible.

No matter where the interview is conducted, privacy is essential. In hotel lobbies or other public places, attention must be paid to finding a private nook. In subjects' homes, one may have to contend with family members who may be listening in or who may want to sit in on the interview and participate. We have found it necessary to establish a rule that family members be out of earshot if at all possible to avoid potential bias of information. Family members can generally appreciate this if so advised. Often it is helpful for the interviewer to take some time to meet with other family members before or after the interview so that they can share their thoughts.

Other Arrangements
You need to calculate in advance how many interviews can be scheduled and accomplished in a set period of time. Length of interview, scheduling of appointments, and details of interview location and transportation logistics need to be ascertained in advance. Field studies tend to require greater flexibility and more planning than studies conducted in more controlled settings.

Because of the stresses involved in interviewing and being away from home base, we usually send a team of two or more interviewers for four to five days. We alternate teams so that the same interviewers spend a week in office and home before they go out again. Interviewers can usually do a maximum of three two-hour interviews per day. This allows time to revive between interviews.

Conclusion

Field research of traumatic events is demanding, yet extremely rewarding. Because each event has unique aspects, new challenges are presented in each study. In this chapter we have identified some of the problems that you will face if you conduct field research of traumatic events. We have used our experiences to provide examples of both the problems and some possible solutions. We hope that these thoughts will be of help to others and will generate further interest in the fascinating and expanding area of trauma research.

References

American Psychiatric Association. (1980). *Diagnostic and statistical manual of mental disorders* (3rd ed.). Washington, D.C.: American Psychiatric Association.

Baum, A., Solomon, S. D., Ursano, R. J., Bickman, L., Blanchard, E., Green, B. L., Keane, T. M., Laufer, R., Norris, F., Reid, J., Smith, E. M., & Steinglass, P. (1993). Emergency/disaster studies: Practical, conceptual, and methodological issues. In J. P. Wilson & B. Raphael (Eds.), *International handbook of traumatic stress syndromes* (pp. 125–133). New York: Plenum Press.

Bolin, R. (1985). Disaster characteristics and psychosocial impacts. In B. J. Sowder (Ed.), *Disasters and mental health: Selected contemporary perspectives* (pp. 3–28). Rockville, Maryland: National Institute of Mental Health.

Derry, P. & Baum, A. (1994). The role of the experimenter in field studies of distressed populations. *Journal of Traumatic Stress, 7,* 625–635.

Fairbank, J., Jordan, B. K., Schlenger, W. E. (1996). Designing and implementing epidemiologic studies. In E. B. Carlson (Ed.), *Trauma Research Methdology.* Lutherville, MD: Sidran Press.

Foa, E. (1994). Coping with the challenges of field research. Presented at the 10th Annual Meeting of the International Society for Traumatic Stress Studies. Chicago, IL, November, 1994.

Green, B. (1982). Assessing levels of psychological impairment following disaster: Consideration of actual and methodological dimensions. *Journal of Nervous and Mental Disease, 170,* 544–552.

North, C. S., & Smith, E. M. (1994). Quick response disaster study: Sampling methods and practical issues in the field. In T. W. Miller (Ed.), *Stressful life events II.* New York: International Universities Press.

North, C. S., Smith, E. M., McCool, R. E., & Lightcap, P. E. (1989). Acute post-disaster coping and adjustment. *Journal of Traumatic Stress, 2*(3), 353–360.

North, C. S., Smith, E. M., McCool, R. E., & Shea, J. M. (1989). Short-term psychopathology in eyewitnesses to mass murder. *Hospital and Community Psychiatry, 40,* 1293–1295.

North, C. S., Smith, E. M., & Spitznagel, E. L. (1994). Posttraumatic stress disorder in survivors of a mass shooting. *American Journal of Psychiatry, 151,* 82–88.

Raphael, B., Lundin, T., & Weisaeth, L. (1989). A research method for the study of psychological and psychiatric aspects of disaster. *Acta Psychiatrica Scandinavica, 80,* 1–75.

Robins, L. N., Fishbach, R. L., Smith, E. M., Cottler, L. B., Solomon, S. D., & Goldring, E. (1986). Impact of disaster on previously assessed mental health. In J. H. Shore (Ed.), *Disaster stress studies: New methods and findings.* (pp. 22–48). Washington, D.C.: American Psychiatric Press.

Robins, L. N., Helzer, J. E., Croughan, J., Williams, J. B. W., & Spitzer, R. L. (1981). *NIMH Diagnostic Interview Schedule: Version III.* Rockville, MD: National Institute of Mental Health.

Robins, L. N., & Regier, D. A. (1991). *Psychiatric disorders in America: The Epidemiologic Catchment Area Study.* New York: The Free Press.

Robins, L. N., & Smith, E. M. (1983). *The Diagnostic Interview Schedule/Disaster Supplement.* St. Louis: Washington University School of Medicine.

Smith, E. M. (1989). Impact of disaster on children: Dioxin and flood. Final report on grant #MH40025 to the National Institute of Mental Health.

Smith, E. M., North, C. S., McCool, R. E., & Shea, J. M. (1990). Acute post-disaster psychiatric disorders: Identification of persons at risk. *American Journal of Psychiatry, 147,* 202–206.

Smith, E. M., Robins, L. N., Przybeck, T. R., Goldring, E., & Solomon, S. D. (1986). Psychosocial consequences of a disaster. In J. H. Shore (Ed.), *Disaster stress studies: New methods and findings.* Washington, D.C.: American Psychiatric Press.

Solomon, S. D. (1989). Research issues in assessing disaster's effects. In R. Gist & B. Lubin (Eds.), *Psychosocial aspects of disaster*. New York: John Wiley.

Wilson, K., Smith, E. M., Fox, L. W., & Brauks, V. (1995). Effects of flood exposure on young children: Information from an early screening and intervention program. Unpublished manuscript.

Wortman, C. B., Abbey, A., Holland, A. E., Silver, R. L., & Janoff-Bulman, R. (1980). Transitions from the laboratory to the field: Problems and progress. In L. Bickman (Ed.), *Applied social psychology annual*. Beverly Hills, CA: Sage Publications.

7

Special Methods for Trauma Research with Children

Frank W. Putnam

Trauma research with children involves a number of special considerations. The purpose of this chapter is to provide an overview of methods and issues pertinent to trauma research with children. I will divide this chapter into three basic sections: ethical and developmental issues, assessment strategies and techniques, and assessment targets. The first section highlights ethical issues and problems related to developmentally sensitive assessments of children. Here, though I will not devote much space to discussing research design, I will touch on issues related to longitudinal versus cross-sectional designs. The second section surveys standard methods and strategies that are currently available to assess children. The examples of measures provided are not necessarily the "best measures." They are meant to be examples of different kinds of measures that are commonly used. I will not devote much time to an in-depth review of what is available because there is actually very little in the PTSD area that is tailored to children, although this is changing. However, there is sound methodology available from the fields of child development and developmental psychopathology that is relevant to assessing impact and outcome of trauma in children. The final section asks the question, "What should we be assessing in traumatized children?" This section focuses on the importance of careful thinking about what variables might be measured in children to accurately understand their responses to trauma.

Ethical and Developmental Assessment Issues

Ethical Issues

First on the table should be a set of ethical issues that are raised in research with traumatized children. These issues are related to the more general ethical problems associated with research with children. Foremost among these is the legal requirement of mandated reporting. Under the Child Abuse Protection and Treatment Act (CAPTA), the federal government requires all states to enact some form of mandated reporting for suspicion or discovery of child maltreatment (CAPTA, 1992). Each state went out and did its own thing, resulting in 50 different laws (Liss, 1994). As a clinical researcher, you must find out what your state law requires of you. If you have a study in which you are collecting data across state lines, you have to know the mandated reporting laws for each state from which you are sampling. Generally all physicians are covered by state mandated reporting requirements. In most states, clinical psychologists are also mandated reporters. Generally, if you are a licensed health care professional, you are a mandated reporter. However, there is as yet no case law regarding mandated reporting by researchers. This is a complex ethical/legal question that is beyond the scope of this chapter. For a more detailed discussion of ethical issues in maltreatment research with children and adolescents, including a section on mandated reporting ethical/legal issues for researchers, see Putnam, Liss, and Landsverk (in press).

Another ethical concern has to do with guarantees of confidentiality for children. The issue of confidentiality is more complicated for children than it is for adults, who are generally guaranteed confidentiality except in so-called Tarasoff cases (in which the patient may present a risk of harm to others). In many instances, confidentiality, as we understand it from the adult perspective, does not extend to children below age 12. It becomes complicated when you are working with adolescents, particularly early adolescents. It is often unclear exactly what is considered confidential and what is not considered confidential (i.e., that which cannot or should not be withheld from parents). You must come to some agreement within the research team as to the kinds of circumstances under which you would break confidentiality to report dangerous behavior (such as suicidal plans, drug use, unprotected sex, etc.) to parents. This should be part of the informed consent/assent process for the child/adolescent.

A third ethical issue has to do with the fact that there is the legal requirement that the research can only expose children to "minimal risk." The Office of Protection from Research Risks (OPRR) guidelines state that research with children who are not receiving treatment for a serious disease can only include procedures that involve minimal risk. Minimal risk does not mean "no risk." That is a common misunderstanding. Minimal risk is generally construed to be the same kind of risk that riding a bicycle or going swimming entails. Though these seem benign activities, there is in fact some risk involved. Children do get hurt on bicycles and drown while swimming. Generally parents give permission for their children to take part in these sorts of activities. So one must understand the definitions of minimal risk and how your human subjects' Institutional Review Board (IRB) is likely to interpret that requirement. This particularly applies to biological studies in children, such as drug challenge studies.

Lastly, researchers studying children must struggle with the ethical questions of probing of sensitive areas (e.g., asking abused children about the details of their maltreatment). To what extent is it necessary to have clinical coverage available? To what extent can non-clinical researchers be involved in working with traumatic material that might induce clinical decompensation? These are largely unresolved dilemmas that require some forethought on the part of researchers (see Putnam et al., in press).

Developmental Issues in Assessment

It is important for researchers who study children to consider the phenomenology of child development and its impact on the variables under study. This is particularly crucial if one is measuring change over time in traumatized children. Children undergo relatively rapid developmental changes that may have nothing to do with the impact of the traumatic events or may have something to do with the events but are highly confounded by the fact that the child is also undergoing normal physical and cognitive growth (e.g., passage through puberty). In the old days, we metaphorically spoke about child development as a "ladder." The metaphor of the developmental ladder conveys the impression that children grow up in a simple linear fashion, advancing one discrete rung at a time. Early theoretical models of development such as Freudian and Piagetian models were predicated on the notion of a serialized, invariant unfolding of developmental stages.

In actuality, development is not anything like that. It is a much more complicated process. Much as ecologists have moved away from the simplistic idea of a unidimensional "food chain" to the multidimensional concept of a "food web," developmental psychologists have moved away from the idea of a developmental ladder to something along the lines of a developmental web (Bidell & Fischer, 1992). There are a series of basic strands forming the web that involve processes such as affect regulation, physical capacities, and cognitive abilities. These strands intersect and interact at various points in time. In some cases, the strands combine, spawning new developmental processes and capacities that become increasingly complex with time. If one takes cross-sections at various points in time, rough, stage-like phenomena emerge. Thus one can speak in general terms about developmentally salient age/stage issues, but one should understand that there are not crisply demarcated stages in child development like rungs on a ladder.

Pioneering work by developmental psychologists such as Kurt Fisher has shown that a child's capacity in some areas such as affect regulation or ability to think abstractly is very much dependent on the child's mental state at the time of measurement (Fisher & Ayoub, 1994). Children's mental states often change markedly over the course of the day so that the same test may give different "developmental ages" at different times of the day or in different contexts. One may see marked differences in how well a child performs on a given task by manipulating context. This news should come as no surprise to parents.

We are looking at a very complex set of developmental threads that become interlocked and synergistically spawn new processes. As researchers, we are trying to figure out how to assess the effects of trauma while controlling for the complexities of normal development. Early investigators often attempted to study developmental changes with cross-sectional approaches. They would take subjects in a defined age range (e.g., ages 2–15 years), test the children, then divide them into age groups for comparative analyses. Many studies would simply divide the subjects into "older" and "younger" children.

More sophisticated research designs are emerging. Among these is the cross-sequential design (Wohlwill, 1970). In a cross-sequential design, one divides the different aged children into a series of smaller cohorts. A typical example is to divide the children into age groups of two years, (e.g., six and seven year olds, eight and nine year olds, ten and eleven year olds, twelve and thirteen year olds). They represent a series of little cohorts within your sample. That is the "cross" part of the design. The "sequential" part is that you repeatedly assess them at some defined interval such as every year. What you get is a very nice model for separating developmental stage/age effects from other effects of interest.

Using this method, you get both a cross-sectional look, and you get a longitudinal look moving forward in time. For example, if you are especially interested in eight year olds, you have kids who were eight when they came into your study and you have kids who turned eight at different times during your study. Many research studies with children have moved to cross-sequential designs, in which different age subcohorts are assessed and then followed forward in time with repeated measures. There is a terrific increase in statistical power because you have multiple data points on each child, plus, if you wish to increase your sample size for some analyses, you can pool all the eight year olds. When coupled with appropriate statistical techniques, cross-sequential or convergence designs allow one to "accelerate" longitudinal data collection. For example, a cross-sequential design makes it possible to study a nine-year developmental span with only three years of data collection (McArdle, 1994).

In assessing children, one also has to look across multiple developmental domains and multiple contexts. The buzz words for this approach are "multimeasure, multimodal studies." We find that children are extremely context sensitive. If you sample a particular developmental domain in a given child across different contexts, you may see a very different child across these contexts. For example, a child's affect regulation may look very different with peers than it looks in school or with parents. In general, one has to look across multiple contexts with children to determine how well a child is managing, or how impaired a child is in a particular developmental domain.

Accurately assessing children is further complicated by the enormous individual differences that exist among children. This is an inescapable problem, and unfortunately we have very little idea about the range of normative behavior for a given age. As clinicians and as researchers, we often struggle with the problem of where to place a given child. Is this pathological? Is this normal for young children, but pathological for older children? Is it pathological for the child's age only in certain contexts? Or is this just part of the normal spectrum? Often, we do not really know how broad that normal spectrum is. One needs very clean theoretical constructs or experimental variables to cut through the noise of normal developmental variability.

One has to understand that the developmental dynamics of children often produce profound "sleeper effects." It is possible for traumatized children assessed at one point in time to appear virtually asymptomatic and yet when assessed six or 12 months later they may be seriously impaired. Examples include the seminal studies by Judith Cohen and Tony Mannario on sexually abused girls (Mannario, Cohen, Smith, & Moore-Motily, 1991). More than half of the children assessed proximal to the disclosure of abuse were asymptomatic. In fact, girls with penetration abuses were most likely to be asymptomatic when assessed proximal to the trauma. When assessed 12 months later, however, those same girls were the most disturbed of the children. So there can be profound effects of trauma that emerge only over time. The upshot of this is that you need to assess multiple domains at multiple time points and to build in controls for normal developmental change.

Another challenge in studying traumatized children is the very limited availability of standardized measures in children. There are very few child measures that have been systematically normed below age eight. You also find terrific age discontinuity in the normative samples for different child measures. If you are seeking to measure affect regulation or cognitive ability, typically what you find is either that your measure is not normed at all or that you have one measure that is normed for ages two to four years and another measure that is normed from five to seven years, and a third measure that is normed from ages six to nine for boys only. There is a lot of developmental discontinuity in terms of the scales and measures that are available. It is a challenge to identify the developmentally salient constructs and find instruments that validly measure those constructs across the enormous changes in cognitive and motor capacities that occur. It is very difficult to find measures that are valid and reliable across that degree of developmental change. You often end up having to use a series of overlapping scales and hope that there is acceptable developmental continuity in the construct that those scales purport to measure. A good example would be depression—measuring depression in four year olds versus measuring depression in nine year olds versus measuring depression in late adolescence. Are you really measuring the same thing? I think not!

There are also enormous gender-related differences in children. Girls, by and large, are ahead of boys in acquisition of many social skills, toilet training, some physical skills, and cognitive capacities. You always have to be aware of the fact that you have gender-related differences and that these are also often developmental age/stage related. On some tests, seven-year-old girls can be very different from seven-year-old boys. Although adults often think of young children in asexual, gender-neutral ways, one can never ignore gender effects when working with children.

There are also large cultural differences that are expressed developmentally. One cannot go into certain populations and expect to see "average" American children. Younger children are particularly influenced by their parents and home environment. For example, there are significant differences in toilet training between whites and blacks, with African-American children typically being toilet trained at much earlier ages than white children. You have to be sensitive to ethnic and cultural child rearing customs as they interact with developmental capacities. There are also significant racial differences in physical maturation. In a current study, we are looking at, among other things, physical development in abused children. We find significant differences between blacks and whites in terms of the age of appearance of secondary sex characteristics. Unfortunately, many of the "norms" that we operate on (e.g., Tanner staging norms) are based on middle-class whites samples, and do not necessarily apply to other racial, cultural, or ethnic groups.

Another problem that you have to be aware of is the fact that you are often dependent on parent-completed measures. Typically there are significant discrepancies in behavior ratings by children and parents of the child's behavior. In general, parents are fairly reasonable reporters of what we call "externalizing" symptoms and behaviors, such as aggression, sexual behaviors, and conduct problems. Children are generally very poor reporters of these behaviors in themselves. On the other hand, parents are generally poor reporters of "internalizing" behaviors, such as depression, anxiety, hopelessness, and fear, whereas children are much better reporters of these problems. You may have large discrepancies if you are seeking to measure something such as depression with parent reports. You need to include a self-report measure because parents are generally poor reporters of depression in their children. But if you want to look at aggression, it is best to use a parent measure because children are very poor reporters of their own aggression or violence. In some studies, the degree of discrepancy between the parent and child report may be the variable of interest. For example, the Richters and Martinez study of children's exposure to community violence found important discrepancies between parents' and children's reports both of levels of violence witnessed by the child and of the child's anxieties (Martinez & Richters, 1993; Richters & Martinez, 1993).

We have serious problems with the validity of psychiatric diagnoses in children. The DSM-III-R and DSM-IV do not work well for children (Richters & Cicchetti, 1993; Wakefield, 1992). There have been unsuccessful pleas for a child version. The DSM operates on the misguided, adultomorphic principle that whenever possible, the adult disorder criteria should be blindly applied to children without any consideration for the child's age/stage or environmental context (Richters & Cicchetti, 1993; Wakefield, 1992). As a result, you find that many very disturbed children do not make DSM criteria for disorders which they in fact have, and some children may not actually have mental disorders for which they meet DSM criteria, such as conduct disorder (Richters & Cicchetti, 1993). If you are relying solely on

DSM diagnoses as your outcome variable, you are not going to get very meaningful results. We need a developmentally sensitive child and adolescent diagnostic system.

There are few data on the developmental continuity of child disorders into adulthood. Does depression in childhood translate into depression in adulthood? You would think that we would know something about this, but in fact we know very little. With a few notable exceptions, there are almost no studies in which we have followed emotionally or behaviorally disturbed children into adulthood and looked at the continuity of child and adult diagnoses. There are reasons to suspect that a lot of problems that are apparent in childhood do not necessarily translate into the "same" adult disorders. Consequently one must be wary about extrapolations that the existence of a given disorder in childhood presages the same disorder in adulthood.

Strategies and Techniques for Assessing Children and Adolescents

Now that we have identified a series of issues in the assessment of children, let us focus on the strategies and methods of assessing children. There are a variety of different kinds of methods, some of which have already been mentioned, such as the use of parent reports and child self ratings. By about age eight or nine years and beyond, one can frequently get good results with a self-rating scale. Even younger children can perform satisfactorily using "thermometer scales," where they color in a bar to indicate "how much" or "how high" something is (e.g., a pain rating). There are some fairly good self-report measures for children. Some are analogous to accepted adult measures. For example, for depression you can use the Child Depression Inventory (CDI) developed by Marika Kovacs (1981), which is related to the Beck Depression Inventory. The CDI is a reasonable measure of clinical depression in children.

There are a host of parent report measures. Perhaps the most widely known and used is one the Child Behavioral Checklist (CBCL) (Achenbach & Edelbrock, 1983). The CBCL has its own psychometric problems in terms of middle-class norms and the generalizability of its factor structure across racial and ethnic groups. But you will find hundreds, perhaps even thousands, of CBCL-based studies in the literature.

I like to use teacher ratings. Teachers are usually good observers and they have extensive experience with children of the same age as the index child. They have a terrific comparison group available in the form of the other children in the class. They see the index child repeatedly and they see him or her in the standardized context of school. With that context in mind, one can often use teacher reports as good measures of deviant behavior. You can have the teacher compare the child against other children in the same class. Good examples of teacher report measures include: the Teacher-Child Rating Scale (TCRS) (Hightower, Spinell, & Lotyczewski, 1986) and the teacher version of the CBCL (Achenbach & Edelbrock, 1986).

Another technique that has been used in assessing children is what we call "peer nominations." Peer nominations make use of the fact that children are very good observers of each other's behavior, particularly abnormal or deviant behavior. Peers are also extremely important influences on older children and adolescents and represent an important domain to sample. An example of peer nominations would be to ask the children to rank the kids in their class in terms of who misbehaves the most. Obviously there are tricky ethical and methodological issues associated with having kids rate each other, but peer nomination strategies have been used with good success.

Structured psychiatric diagnostic interviews are predicated on the DSM and have all of the inherent problems of the DSM approach to child psychopathology. There are a variety of DSM child diagnostic interviews out there. All of them have reasonable reliability for DSM-based disorders. None of them is particularly good for detecting posttraumatic stress disorder (PTSD) (McNally, 1991; Putnam, in press). There are, however, a number of structured interviews available for assessing PTSD symptoms in children including the 20-item Post-Traumatic Stress Disorder Reaction Index (PTSD-RI) (Pynoos, Frederick, Nader, Arroyo, Steinberg, Eth, Nunex, & Fairbanks, 1987); Children's Posttraumatic Stress Disorder Inventory (CPTSDI) by Saigh (1991); and the Children's Impact of Traumatic Events Scale - Revised (CITES) (Wolfe, Gentile, & Wolfe, 1989). The PTSD-RI is the most widely used measure and can be completed by the parents as a checklist or administered to children (McNally, 1991).

One largely unacknowledged problem with structured diagnostic interviews is that younger children often do not have the faintest idea what they are being asked. In most cases, structured diagnostic interviews are not recommended for children below the age of nine years. For example, see Schwab-Stone and colleagues' test-retest study of the Diagnostic Interview Schedule for Children (DISC), which found that children were particularly unreliable in reporting time factors such as the onset and duration of symptoms (Schwab-Stone, Fallon, Brigs, & Crowther, 1994). These types of problems occur with all structured interview studies of younger children. I think that researchers often end up having to use a structured psychiatric diagnostic interview because everybody is financially tied to the DSM. It has become the tail that wags the dog. If you want to get your study funded you have to generate DSM diagnoses as an outcome variable. Yet most researchers who seriously consider the problems of child assessment do not think that DSM-based, structured diagnostic interviews are a valid place to start, especially with younger children.

Another assessment model that can be used with children uses standardized behavioral situations. You set up a scripted behavioral situation and record (e.g., videotape for later blinded rating) how the child reacts in that situation. We have a measure we call the "Strange Man Situation" in our child abuse study. We are interested in how abused and nonabused comparison girls react to a standardized interaction with an unfamiliar male, who is scripted to respond neutrally to their interactions. It turns out that there are some significant behavioral differences between abused girls and control children. In fact we find very large differences in terms of certain "sexualized" behaviors emitted by the children. We also find some very interesting developmental curves as to how these differences in behaviors change over time in the two groups.

A second example of a provocative type of behavioral situation comes from the work of Pamela Cole and colleagues (Cole, Zahn-Waxler, & Smith, 1994). She uses a "disappointment task," where the child is brought in and told "you will get a prize, if you do well on this puzzle." A tray of potential prizes is set before the child who is asked to rank the prizes from the most desirable to the least desirable. The prizes are removed and the child does the nominal task. The experimenter says something to the effect of, "You have done well and earned a prize and here it is." The child is then presented with the prize that he or she had ranked as the least desirable. The experimenter then moves on to another subject, seemingly oblivious to any response that the child might show. Behind a one-way mirror, the child's emotional response to this disappointment is videotaped with the experimenter in the room and again after the experimenter steps out for a moment. The videotape is later coded by raters who are blind to the child's diagnosis and other relevant variables. Cole found important gender differences in how children handle such a disappointment task. Standardized behavioral situations offer very rich assessment paradigms. However, it is difficult to get valid data from them unless you have your constructs carefully defined and your scoring system well operationalized.

Projective assessments are also a source of important information about the child's perception and thinking. Measures such as the Thematic Apperception Test (TAT) or Draw-a-Person can be very useful ways of getting at what one would call unconscious processes or thematic assessments with a child. For example, Pistole and Ornduff (1994) used the TAT to study sexual preoccupations and guilt in sexually abused girls. Unfortunately interpretation of the results of projective tests are difficult because many lack systematic·scoring systems and adequate norms, reliability, and validity. This is particularly true for some of the art-based tests used in the trauma field. Nevertheless, projective test results can help generate hypotheses which can be investigated with more rigorous methods.

Computer-administered interviews are catching the attention of child and adolescent researchers. Computers have been used in clinic settings to administer the CBCL (Sawyer, Sarris, & Baghurst, 1991) and to ask adolescents about sensitive issues (e.g., sex and drug use) (Paperny, Aono, Lehman, Hammas, & Risser, 1990). Computer-assisted interviews, questionnaires, and rating scales appear to work best in the 9-to-15-year-old range. Several studies indicate that children and adolescents reveal more sensitive information to computers than to face-to-face interviewers. Computers can be programmed to have culturally-sensitive voices and use culturally-relevant graphic images. They provide privacy and they eliminate the interviewer's reactions, which can bias results by eliciting socially desirable responses to sensitive questions. Computers present the information consistently from subject to subject and record data in easily analyzable formats. And of particular import is the fact that they can be made novel and stimulating —even fun. As yet, computer-assisted interviewing has not been applied to research with traumatized children, but the success of this format with sensitive subjects, such as sexual behavior and drug use, indicate this methodology should be considered in future research.

Finally, I would suggest that there are uses for physical examinations and a variety of biological tests. One can certainly get some very interesting data that enriches our understanding of the effects of trauma and suggests new areas for routine assessment and targeted treatment interventions (DeBellis & Putnam, 1994). The first place to start is by looking at growth and development. Physical examinations, Tanner staging, and plasma hormone measures are relatively easy to obtain. It turns out that it is not that difficult to get blood out of kids. Most children do not mind it as much as you and I (or your IRB) seem to think. If you choose not to draw blood, there are a variety of salivary measures (e.g., cortisol, testosterone, adrenal androgens) that are available (Malamud & Tabak, 1993). You can also get urine samples, although you may find, as we did, that adolescents are more reluctant to collect their pee in a jug for a day then they are to have an IV in for four hours. There are also interesting opportunities for motor activity monitors and heart rate variability monitors. So there is a variety of relatively noninvasive things that one can do to investigate biological variables and activity.

There are various types of biological and pharmacological probes to test the integrity and regulation of major biological systems. For example, corticotrophin releasing hormone (CRH) infusion studies look at the hypothalamic-pituitary-adrenal (HPA) axis. We have done such challenge studies with traumatized children and found them extremely important in understanding biobehavioral regulation disturbances

(De Bellis, Burke, Trickett, & Putnam, in press; De Bellis, Chrousos, Dorn, Burke, Helmers, Kling, Trickett, & Putnam, 1994a; De Bellis, Lefter, Trickett, & Putnam, 1994b). We find that most children tolerate them very well. In fact, the most difficult thing about some of these procedures (such as the CRH infusion study) is the child must sit or lie relatively still with an IV for three or four hours. They get bored. They are not distressed. They are bored! We provide video tapes, television, and computer games to entertain them.

What Should be Assessed in Traumatized Children?

What should we be assessing if we are conducting research with traumatized children? We need to look at a number of areas related to the effects of trauma. The first domain would be a set of what I call trauma-related symptoms and problem behaviors. Foremost among these would be conduct problems including aggression, hyperactivity, oppositional behavior, delinquency, hyper-sexuality, and substance abuse. There are data that demonstrate that trauma in children is not always manifested by the more classic PTSD symptoms, but is often expressed indirectly in forms such as conduct disorders, disruptive behavior, aggression, risk taking, or suicidality (Putnam, in press).

One should also look at what I call bio-behavioral disturbances of regulation. Sleep disturbances, particularly in children, may be very sensitive indicators of trauma, as are problems with bowel and bladder control. In pre-adolescents, we see a lot of difficulties that one would call "secondary" enuresis and encopresis. The secondary refers to that fact that the child had previously achieved control of bowel and bladder regulation and after the trauma loses that control. Secondary enuresis with sexual abuse is a very frequent occurrence. Appetite, activity level, and age-appropriate affect regulation are also important areas to probe for trauma effects. For example, one could use a disappointment-type task to look at the child's ability to socially mask disappointment or to regulate anger in socially appropriate ways.

Of course, PTSD symptoms also need to be assessed. Including symptoms of hyperarousal, avoidant symptoms, reexperiencing symptoms, and dissociation. In terms of the hyperarousal symptoms in traumatized children there some assessment methods that are promising. For example, it is possible to put activity monitors on children and measure their motor activity. There are a number of validated hyperactivity scales that can be used and at least one study has assessed hyperstartle responses in traumatized children (Ornitz & Pynoos, 1989). The PTSD avoidant and reexperiencing symptoms are not inquired about by many standard child behavioral/psychopathological measures. However, there are now a number of newly developed PTSD scales and interviews for children and adolescents that are worth investigating (McNally, 1991). There are valid dissociation scales available for children (Putnam, Helmers, & Trickett, 1993). A newly developed self-report measure for adolescents, the Adolescent Dissociative Experiences Scale (A-DES) is now being validated and should be published in the near future.

One would also want to assess attention, memory, and cognition in traumatized children, particularly looking at a variety of different domains of memory such as implicit, explicit, and autobiographical memory. IQ and other forms of intelligence should also be assessed. Assessing concentration with continuous performance tasks (CPTs) may be useful. A CPT is a test where a child sits down in front of a computer screen that is rapidly presenting a series of stimuli and selectively responds to specific, intermittently presented cues. For example, one kind of response is required if an "A" is followed by an "X." Another kind of response is supposed to occur if there is no "X" following the "A." There may be long sequences of irrelevant letters between the designated target stimuli. CPT tasks provide quantitative measures of attention, concentration, and impulsivity in terms of the number of correct and incorrect responses and response delay times.

School is an extremely important context for kids and measures of school performance and behavior may prove useful in understanding responses to trauma. As discussed above, you can use teacher ratings to gather data. Grades, however, have not proved to be very useful (Trickett, McBride-Chang, & Putnam, 1994). All of the comparison group studies to date suggest that you just do not see evidence of trauma impacting on grades. I think that this says something about the subjective nature of grades and the difficulties in comparing grades across different teachers. In our recent study comparing the school performance and behavior of sexually abused girls with matched control girls, we found profound impacts in many areas of school behavior in the classroom and with peers (Trickett et al., 1994). But there was no significant difference in grades. If you can compare your children on standardized achievement tests you are indeed fortunate. However, many school systems give different forms of achievement tests, so that studies that cross county and state school systems are not likely to be able to include standardized academic test scores. National standardized testing, such as the Scholastic Achievement Tests (SATs), will likely miss many traumatized children, who are underrepresented among college-bound SAT test takers.

As described above, peer relationships are particularly important for teenagers and can be assessed both with peers and by using various self-report social support measures. We find dramatic differences in peer relationships patterns between our sexually abused and control children. For example, we find extremely interesting developmental differences in terms of when children in the two groups acquire friends and what kinds of friends they acquire. Prior to puberty our sexually abused girls are basically friendless. They have significantly fewer female and male friends. Around ages 12–13 years, the sexually abused girls suddenly acquire significantly more boyfriends than the control girls. These boyfriends are often several years older than the girls. That is, 13-year-old girls are going out with 15- to 17-year-old guys. This is not always a wholesome situation. This difference in dating patterns probably has something to do with the higher rates of negative outcomes such as early pregnancy, substance abuse, and school dropout that are common in sexually abused girls. It is important to investigate social contexts and functioning because they have such important ripple effects on long-term social and occupational attainment.

Then there is the question of assessing family environment. Family environment is an extremely important area in understanding the impact of traumatic experiences, particularly if one is assessing moderating variables and coping resources available to children. One may want to assess peers and siblings as well as the index child. There are a variety of different family measures, some of which can be given to both the parents and the child, so that you can look at response discrepancies. For example, the Family Environment Scale (FES) by Moos and Moos (1981). If you want to look at child rearing attitudes, measures such as the Block-Q sort are useful (Block, Block, & Morrison, 1982). But one has to pay careful attention to cultural and ethnic differences in family and child rearing styles to avoid misinterpretation of results in culturally mixed samples.

As I indicated, there are all sorts of family coping issues and styles that are relevant to children's responses to trauma and you have to be sensitive to the family environment. For example, numerous studies have identified the presence of a grandmother in the home as being an extremely important protective factor for children exposed to poverty. Presence of a grandmother in the home makes for a very different childhood environment. You need to consider the extent to which the family's coping processes are active in support of the traumatized child and to what extent are they impediments to the child's response to the trauma. To what extent do the family's coping processes serve as models to the children? To what extent do children and adolescents model their coping responses to trauma on the coping responses of their parents, their siblings, or other significant people? At least one study suggests that the intensity of children's reaction to stress or trauma is best correlated with the degree of discrepancy between the coping responses of the parents (Handford, Mayes, Mattison, Humphrey, Bagnato, Bixler, & Kales, 1986). In short, you are not looking at a simple process here, you are looking at a set of very complex and interactive processes. There are also additional factors such as extra-familial supports or impediments to the child's coping (e.g., teachers, coaches, and peer responses) that account for some of the variance and should be considered.

As discussed above, it is important to consider developmental age/stage as it affects coping responses to trauma. For example, children and adolescents typically show different patterns of coping with grief and loss. One has to be sensitive to these developmental differences in coping strategies. Then there are what I would call "coping process issues." I will provide two examples of what I mean by this. First, consider the classic Kubler-Ross model of processing death, that is, the sequence of denial, anger, bargaining, depression, and acceptance. A cross-sectional evaluation, depending on where you happen to cut into that type of process, yields a very different view of the child so that a child might appear to be angry at one time and depressed at another. Thus if a researcher does not consider whether these different views of the child reflect an ongoing coping process, he or she might misinterpret the results.

A second example of the importance of coping process issues is talking to oneself. If you look at children who talk to themselves when stressed, you find that at the time that the child is maximally talking to him/herself while working on a task, they are often performing poorly. You might conclude that excess talking to oneself is associated with poorer outcomes, because it appears to be in a cross-sectional analysis. However, in a longitudinal analysis, you find that children who are having trouble and talk to themselves ultimately do much better than children who are having trouble but do not talk to themselves (Diaz & Berk, 1992). So talking to oneself would be seen negatively if assessed at one moment in time and more positively if viewed over time. In short, it is important to attend to possible developmental progressions in the response to trauma in order to accurately understand children's coping.

Conclusion

In conclusion, I would stress again the complexities of normal development and the necessity of taking a longitudinal perspective in seeking to understand the impact of traumatic events on children and adolescents. In this brief overview, I have tried to highlight the unique ethical and methodological problems facing child researchers and the need to use a multimeasure, multimodal approach to these questions. Unfortunately there is very little research on the effects of trauma on children, particularly the long-term effects. I hope that some of you accept this challenge to enrich our knowledge and to add to our clinical understanding of the effects of trauma on children and adolescents.

References

Achenbach, T. M. & Edelbrock, C. (1986). *Manual for the teacher's report form and teacher version of the child behavior profile*. Burlington, VT: University Associates in Psychiatry.

Achenbach, T. M. & Edelbrock, C. S. (1983). *Manual for the Child Behavioral Checklist*. Burlington, VT: Queen City Printers.

Bidell, T. R. & Fischer, K. W. (1992). Beyond the stage debate: Action, structure, and variability in Piagetian theory and research. In R. Sternberg & C. Berg (Eds.), *Intellectual development* (pp. 100–140). New York: Cambridge University Press.

Block, J. H., Block, J., & Morrison, A. (1982). Parental agreement-disagreement on child-rearing orientations and gender-related personality correlates in children. *Child Development, 56*, 965–974.

CAPTA (1992). Child Abuse Prevention and Treatment and Adoption Reform Act, 42 U.S.C.A. 5101 et seq.: P.L. 102–295.

Cole, P. M., Zahn-Waxler, C., & Smith, K. D. (1994). Expressive control during a disappointment: Variations related to preschoolers' behavior problems. *Developmental Psychology, 30*, 835–846.

De Bellis, M. D., Burke, L., Trickett, P. K., & Putnam, F. W. (in press). Antinuclear antibodies and thyroid function in sexually abused girls. *Journal of Traumatic Stress*.

De Bellis, M. D., Chrousos, G. P., Dorn, L. D., Burke, L., Helmers, K., Kling, M. A., Trickett, P. K., & Putnam, F. W. (1994a). Hypothalamic-pituitary-adrenal axis dysregulation in sexually abused girls. *Journal of Clinical Endocrinology and Metabolism, 78*, 249–255.

De Bellis, M. D., Lefter, L., Trickett, P. K., & Putnam, F. W. (1994b). Urinary catecholamine excretion in sexually abused girls. *Journal of the American Academy of Child and Adolescent Psychiatry*. In press.

De Bellis, M. D., & Putnam, F. W. (1994). The psychobiology of childhood maltreatment. *Child and Adolescent Psychiatric Clinics of North America, 3*, 1–16.

Diaz, R. M. & Berk, L. E. (Eds.). (1992). *Private speech: From social interaction to self-regulation*. Hillsdale, NJ: Erlbaum.

Fisher, K. W. & Ayoub, C. (1994). Affective splitting and dissociation in normal and maltreated children: Developmental pathways for self in relationships. In D. Cicchetti & S. Toth (Eds.), *Rochester symposium on developmental psychopathology, volume 5: Disorders and dysfunctions of the self* (pp. 149–222). Rochester, NY: University of Rochester Press.

Handford, H. A., Mayes, S. D., Mattison, R. E., Humphrey, F. J., Bagnato, S., Bixler, E. O., & Kales, J. D. (1986). Child and parent reactions to the Three Mile Island nuclear accident. *Journal of the American Academy of Child Psychiatry*, *25*, 346–356.

Hightower, A. D., Spinell, A., & Lotyczewski, B. S. (1986). The Teacher-Child Rating Scale: A brief objective measure of elementary children's school problem behaviors and competencies. *School Psychology Review*, *15*, 383–409.

Kovacs, M. (1981). Rating scales to assess depression in school-age children. *Acta Paedopsychiatrica*, *46*, 305–315.

Liss, M. B. (1994). Child abuse: Is there a mandate for researchers to report? *Ethics and Behavior*, *4*, 133–146.

Malamud, D. & Tabak, L. (Eds.). (1993). *Saliva as a diagnostic fluid.* New York: New York Academy of Sciences.

Mannario, A. P., Cohen, J. A., Smith, J. A., & Moore-Motily, S. (1991). Six and twelve month follow-up of sexually abused girls. *Journal of Interpersonal Violence*, *6*, 494–511.

Martinez, P. & Richters, J. E. (1993). The NIMH community violence project: II. Children's distress symptoms assocated with violence exposure. *Psychiatry*, *56*, 22–36.

McArdle, J. J. (1994). Structural factor analysis experiments with incomplete data. *Multivariate Behavioral Research*, *29*, 409–454.

McNally, R. J. (1991). Assessment of posttraumatic stress disorder in children. *Psychological Assessment*, *3*, 531–537.

Moos, R. H., & Moos, B. S. (1981). *Family Environment Scale manual.* Palo Alto, CA: Consulting Psychologists Press, Inc.

Ornitz, E. M. & Pynoos, R. S. (1989). Startle modulation in children with posttraumatic stress disorder. *American Journal of Psychiatry*, *146*, 866–870.

Paperny, D. M., Aono, J. Y., Lehman, R. M., Hammas, S. L., & Risser, J. (1990). Computer-assisted detection and intervention in adolescent high-risk health behaviors. *Journal of Pediatrics*, *116*, 456–462.

Pistole, D. R. & Ornduff, S. R. (1994). TAT assessment of sexually abused girls: An analysis of manifest content. *Journal of Personality Assessment*, *63*, 211–222.

Putnam, F. W. (in press). Posttraumatic stress disorder in children and adolescents. In L. Dickstein, M. B. Riba, & J. M. Oldham (Eds.), *American Psychiatry Press Review of Psychiatry, Volume 15.* Washington, D.C.: American Psychiatric Press.

Putnam, F. W., Helmers, K., & Trickett, P. K. (1993). Development, reliability and validity of a child dissociation scale. *Child Abuse and Neglect, 17*, 731–741.

Putnam, F. W., Liss, M. B., & Landsverk, J. (in press). Ethical issues in maltreatment research with children and adolescents. In K. Hoagwood & P. Jensen (Eds.), *Ethical issues in research with children and adolescents with mental disorders*. Hillsdale, NJ: Lawrence Erlbaum.

Pynoos, R., Frederick, C., Nader, K., Arroyo, W., Steinberg, A., Eth, S., Nunex, F., & Fairbanks, L. (1987). Life threat and posttraumatic stress in school-age children. *Archives of General Psychiatry, 44*, 1057–1063.

Richters, J. E. & Cicchetti, D. (1993). Mark Twain meets DSM-III-R. *Development and Psychopathology, 5*, 5–30.

Richters, J. E. & Martinez, P. (1993). The NIMH community violence project: I. Children as victims of and witness to violence. *Psychiatry, 56*, 7–21.

Saigh, P. A. (1991). The development and validation of the Children's Posttraumatic Stress Disorder Inventory. *International Journal of Special Education, 4*, 75–84.

Sawyer, M. G., Sarris, A., & Baghurst, P. (1991). The use of computer interviews to administer the Child Behavior Checklist in a child psychiatry service. *Journal of the American Academy of Child and Adolescent Psychiatry, 30*, 674–681.

Schwab-Stone, M., Fallon, T., Brigs, M., & Crowther, B. (1994). Reliablity of diagnostic reporting for children aged 6–11 years: A test-retest study of the Diagnostic Interview Schedule for Children - Revised. *American Journal of Psychiatry, 151*, 1048–1054.

Trickett, P. K., McBride-Chang, C., & Putnam, F. W. (1994). The classroom performance and behavior of sexually abused females. *Development and Psychopathology, 6*, 183–194.

Wakefield, J. C. (1992). Disorder as harmful dysfunction: A conceptual critique of DSM-III-R's definition of mental disorder. *Psychological Review, 99*, 232–247.

Wohlwill, J. F. (1970). Methodological and research strategy in the study of developmental change. In L. R. Goulet & P. B. Balters (Eds.), *Life-span developmental psychology*. New York: Academic Press.

Wolfe, V. V., Gentile, C., & Wolfe, D. A. (1989). The impact of sexual abuse on children: A PTSD formulation. *Behavior Therapy, 20*, 215–228.

8

Emotional Issues and Ethical Aspects of Trauma Research

Judith G. Armstrong

Becoming a trauma researcher often means facing a tangle of emotional and ethical issues that are difficult to think about and talk about with one's research supervisors. Examining and discussing feelings and morality are not usually part of research methodology courses. It may be easy for you to conclude that such issues are too private, too subjective, and too unscientific for discussions of research design.

The fact that this chapter is included in a book on trauma research methodology indicates that feelings and ethics play an important part in our research. In the opening sentence I write about "becoming" a trauma researcher, rather than just "doing" trauma research. Your research will be an expression of who you are because there is a profound connection between a researcher's personality and his or her research. You may have observed that the scholarly interests of your professors often parallel, or in some way balance, their personalities. For example, a shy, analytic teacher may specialize in numerical analysis of data or an outstandingly logical professor may become fascinated with organizing the varieties of thought disorder.

This personal link between researchers and their research also means that we can be changed by what we learn about our topic and ourselves while doing our research. The research process is much more personal, exciting, grueling, distressing, and risky than the picture one gets from the usual dry format in which we write our articles.

I can think of no research area where emotions and ethics are more important than in traumatology, especially when we study the catastrophic affective reactions people have to social catastrophes such as national and family violence, where the ethical strictures of a social group seem to be shattered. It is natural to have strong emotions and be morally outraged while investigating such situations. Does this mean that we are doomed to be biased as we do such research? To some degree, bias is inevitable in all research. Since we can never escape from who we are, we can never be completely free of our own subjectivity.

One way that we can limit and control this natural subjectivity is by our training in the research methodologies discussed in the previous chapters. The uniting purpose of each of the research tools described in this book is our need to construct a standard, reliable, and practical methodology, one that will act as a clear lens through which we all can view trauma, enriched by our personal insights, but undistorted by our personal needs and biases.

Since researchers' subjective reactions to their research have often been treated as irrelevant at best and prejudiced at worst, I am sure that it is easy for you to conclude that your feelings and judgments here ought to be discouraged, if not eliminated. Only then can your work be truly scientific. Yet personal needs do not disappear when we become researchers, nor do they vanish even when we utilize the best of methodologies. While being driven and overwhelmed by feelings and judgments is surely not conducive to clear and balanced work, ignoring our personal reactions to our research is no guarantee that we will not be biased. Denying our inevitable emotional and moral concerns is likely to mean that they work to influence us on an implicit level, removed from our ability to reflect on them in a rational manner. Moreover, denial of our reactions to the suffering of others is likely to blunt our perceptiveness, empathy, and respect for our research participants. How then can we balance our desire to work objectively with the reality of our subjectivity?

It is important that our subjective responses to studying the catastrophic reactions of others be part of our research methodology. Without a means for anticipating and discussing our personal reactions, we may turn away from the study of trauma as too unsettling, depriving the new and growing field of traumatology of much needed knowledge.

Emotional Issues in Trauma Research

Contagion of Trauma

You may find, as you begin your research, that trauma can be catching. For example, you may see people cry as they respond to your questions about their trauma and this may evoke in you sympathetic feelings of sadness and anxiety. You may not be fully aware of being vicariously traumatized when you are in the midst of your work, so you need to be alert to indirect cues that may only become apparent when others comment on changes in your behavior or when you notice that your leisure activities have become invaded by unpleasant associations to your trauma study. One of the ways that you can put your theoretical and clinical readings about trauma to practical use is to apply them to understanding your own reactions to the traumas of others. For example, you can use your readings about traumatic overarousal to help determine whether you are experiencing some emotional flooding from your research. Even if you are simply manipulating test scores or biological data, the fact that you are analyzing the effects of human suffering remains an underlying theme of your research. Leakage of this traumatic material into the researcher's waking and sleeping life is a common phenomenon. Researchers often experience an inability to stop thinking about their material, even in their sleep. More difficult to detect are diffuse reactions that may be wholly emotional or physical, rather than ideational. For example, irritability, exhaustion, inability to relax and enjoy yourself, or physical symptoms of stress may be signals of traumatic overload experienced at an implicit, unconscious level. Such reactions can be enormously helpful in educating yourself about the realities of trauma, but they will not help you develop and survive as an objective researcher unless you can obtain some distance from them. If you suspect that you are experiencing trauma contagion, it is often helpful to make notes of your ongoing reactions. Keeping a research response diary will help you to more clearly determine the triggers of your overarousal. You then need to make a plan to control your contagion reactions through a mixture of identifying, soothing, and distancing procedures.

Identifying procedures involve examining whether there are aspects of your research environment that are particularly stressful. For example, do you feel safe when you are conducting your research? Perhaps you are interviewing people who live in neighborhoods that are plagued by violence. You may need to find a more secure setting in which to do your study (e.g., a room in a public library in the area) and also learn some practical self-defense skills. Or, as you think about the reasons for your fearfulness you may realize that it comes from incorrect assumptions that you have made (e.g., that immigrants or mentally disturbed people are violent people). If it is hard to specify the source your distress it is probably a sign that you need to get further training or supervision to clarify the problem. For example, you may be unsure about how to deal with the reactions of your participants to your study and your sense of being unsafe has more to do with your feelings of helplessness and confusion than with any actual danger.

Soothing activities involve acknowledging that a certain amount of contagious trauma is inevitable and, therefore, planning supportive activities that will help you defuse. This can be as simple as scheduling a half hour break at the end of the day when you can relax and make a transition from work to home. Your strategy might include modifying your data collection procedures. For example, you might alternate data gathering with your traumatized group and your control group, to modulate the amount of painful material you face at one time.

Distancing, as the word suggests, means putting some space between yourself and your research material. The most useful distancing technique is development of a clear theoretical grounding in your area of study. Intellectual understanding forms a stable framework that will help you better tolerate your emotional reactions. Readings, discussions with teachers and peers, and professional conferences not only provide you with social support, they also give you intellectual tools that can be used to gain a better awareness and understanding of your own reactions to your research. For example, one researcher was distressed to find himself getting increasingly hostile towards his research participants, a highly traumatized group of patients who seemed to demand an inordinate amount of emotional support from him in order to complete their measures. Supervision helped him to understand that his anger stemmed from an overidentification with his participants, which had caused him to place unrealistic demands on himself and them. He was viewing them as helpless "victims" and himself as their "rescuer." With the reasons for his anger and guilt clarified, the researcher could now respond to his participants' complaints with a calm warmth that expressed his concern, while keeping them on task.

Once you have begun to identify and control trauma contagion it can become a strength. Your experience can feed back into your work, making you a better researcher. For example, if you are being traumatically flooded by the research material, what about your research participants? You may decide to monitor their reactions by asking then how they are doing as you proceed. Or you may decide to build rest periods into your study by alternating stressful and neutral tasks. Periods of rest and support can also be components of your standardized procedure.

Denial of Trauma

Trauma consists of two alternating poles of experience: flooding by, and denial of, the traumatic experience. It is quite likely that people who completely deny trauma will not be attracted to trauma research unless they have a need to reinforce their denial by developing research that attacks the validity of these experiences.

A milder version of denial that can easily affect trauma researchers, however, is the tendency to overly distance themselves from the people or the data that they are studying. At first glance this might not seem to be a serious problem. Research, with its structure, intellectuality, and ability to transform raw experience into numbers and categories, is well suited to people who prefer to cope with painful material through distancing. Problems occur when researchers become too distanced from their research. Just as distancing in a trauma scene narrows people's range of vision, so distancing in research can narrow our field of inquiry. We run the risk of becoming overly compartmentalized and overly rigid in our thinking. Our theoretical system may not be used to help us understand trauma, but rather to protect ourselves from traumatic experiences. This is bound to limit the research questions we ask, the behaviors we notice, and the conclusions we are able to draw from our studies.

For example, let us consider a researcher who is studying the reactions of emergency room trauma teams to the stress of the work. The researcher is sometimes horrified at the callous indifference shown by medical staff to the suffering of their patients, and at other times, impressed by the cool objectivity with which they view fatal injuries and family bereavement. What if this researcher empathetically put herself in the place of her participants for a time and considered the daily onslaught of painful responsibility with which they must deal? She might begin to wonder whether the contrasting reactions of callousness and intellectuality that she has noted are actually two expressions of the underlying phenomenon, the numbing effects of severe secondary trauma. This hypothesis would allow the researcher to expand the line of inquiry and increase the scope and usefulness of this study (e.g., the researcher might decide to collect data on staff turnover, somatic complaints, and other indirect signs of severe stress).

Arousal of Trauma

If your contagion responses are particularly vivid and do not decrease with your identifying, soothing, and supportive efforts, then you need to seriously examine whether your research activities have triggered issues within you. It is not unusual for trauma research to reawaken a past trauma and this does not necessarily signal that you are emotionally unsuited to research in the field. In fact, your personal insights into the experience of actually being traumatized may enable you to develop a particularly sensitive and original approach to important questions in the field.

Even when past traumatic reactions appear to have been resolved through treatment or other life experiences, doing trauma research often reopens these issues. While this is unsettling, it can also give the researcher an opportunity to take a look at old injuries in a new way and further grow. Traumatic reactions can range from miserable life experiences such as being the butt of sadistic teasing in childhood, to severe losses such as the death of a parent, to traumatic life experiences such as childhood abuse. When doing research, it is extremely important to have an appreciation of the role that these past traumas play in one's present life, including understanding the connection between one's past trauma and one's present desire to do research in the field. This self-awareness will help insure that your research remains objective and balanced, free from the biases, constraints, and obsessions of your own life battles.

For example, a graduate student with a background of childhood incest and anorexia treats a patient with a similar history. Struck by the parallel between their lives, and wondering if the correlation between incest and eating disorder is more than a coincidence, the student decides to study the connection of childhood sexual abuse and eating disorders. While her life history and clinical experience may have sensitized this researcher to an important issue, she must pay careful attention to maintaining her scientific neutrality in her research project. She needs to consider the objectivity and variety of her measures to insure that she is not looking so hard for the expected correlation that she overidentifies abuse and eating disorder and overlooks other important variables. She should carefully consider appropriate control groups to determine whether, for example, an eating disorder is more highly associated with incest than with other family dysfunction variables. In other words, she must plan to consider various hypotheses, hypotheses that differ from her present understanding of her own life history and that of her patient.

Keeping notes of ongoing reactions can help identify where trauma research meets personal trauma, and pinpoint research phenomena that may have been exaggerated, overlooked, or misinterpreted. Regularly scheduled consultations with supervisors and fellow researchers and use of therapy can help maintain the boundaries between the personal and the professional in your research.

Even those whose lives have been untouched by trauma may find that their research opens up a number of profoundly unsettling issues. Facing the trauma of others encourages us to struggle with a variety of philosophical problems—problems that are not simply academic, but speak to the purpose of life. How can people find meaning and hope when they are living in a destructive and chaotic world? Is the presence of evil inevitable in the world, and in ourselves? How can we ever be certain that we know the truth about traumatic events? These are questions that our scientific training does not give us powerful enough tools to answer. The more sheltered our lives have been, the more unprepared we may be face these questions, much less answer them. Yet looking for answers to such questions is one of the ways that doing research in trauma can lead to personal as well as professional growth. Moreover, these philosophical questions help direct our attention to the ethical implications of doing trauma research.

Ethical Aspects of Trauma Research

We turn now to some general ethical issues that you are likely to encounter when researching trauma, regardless of the specifics of your study. I will begin by discussing ethics and your research participants and then turn to ethics and your research setting. Each discussion will be subdivided into surface and underlying ethical aspects. Surface ethical aspects are dangerous if you ignore them, but they are straightforward problems that are clearly visible to everyone from a distance, so that you can prepare for them. While surface aspects can be complex and sometimes contradictory, they are generally set forth in detailed legal and bureaucratic documents. What you need to think about and do will be reasonably clear. Underlying ethical aspects are like jagged reefs hidden beneath the water. Unless you are given a map, you can run aground without knowing how or why. Underlying ethical/social elements of your research are not easily articulated, they are not codified in written form, but they are important for you to deal with if you are to guide your research to safe harbor.

Ethics and Research Participants
Surface aspects. In thinking about the ethical implications of your study it is important to keep in mind that your research is part of a larger context, the lives of your research participants. All of the ethical

points discussed here speak to the need for you to be concerned about the well-being of these participants, especially if your study inquires into their painful experiences and memories.

Most professional organizations have developed documents offering ethical guidelines for research with human subjects. Central to these guidelines is the importance of insuring that your research participants are making a free and educated choice about whether or not they will take part in your research. This is one point where morality meets practicality. Informed consents are both legal and ethical requirements. Thus, writing informed consent forms will be an essential step in getting your research going. Basic information in these consents includes:

1. a description of the study's purposes and procedures, written in language that is understandable to your participants or their legally authorized representatives (e.g., to parents, if you are studying children);
2. a description of the benefits and risks of participating in your study, as well as any alternative procedures available to your participants. Note that risks include emotional pain and embarrassment and not just physical injury;
3. even if your study contains minimal risks (no more than everyday discomfort), you should describe whom to contact should your participants have questions or concerns about their reactions to the research;
4. a description of the extent and limits of confidentiality of your records for identifying participants;
5. a statement that participation is voluntary and the choice of whether or not to take part in your study will involve no penalty or loss of benefits to them;
6. a statement that participants may withdraw at any point from the study without any negative consequences to them; and
7. the name, address, phone number, and institutional affiliation of the principal investigator.

Following informed consent requirements may indeed become a moral challenge because it requires you to override the personal need to complete your research as quickly as possible with the largest sample. You must balance these professional aspirations with your ethical understanding that first, you must do no harm. The informed consent procedure helps you make a bridge between research and reality by encouraging you to think about the social implications of your findings and spell them out in common sense terms.

Trauma research is especially prone to the complexities of confidentiality and its limits. Imagine finding out from a research participant that he or she, or a family member, is abusing a child. Under law, you will need to report that information to child protective services. Obviously, thinking about your options after the problem arises is no safe or sane way to conduct research. It will be important for you to learn the state and federal laws that apply to confidentiality in your area of research. If you are asking questions regarding any acts with criminal implications it is crucial that you to obtain information about the limits of confidentiality and requirements for reporting the suspected crimes to the appropriate social agencies.

It is helpful to keep in mind that while informed consent is a significant ethical consideration in any research, it is especially important for people whose sense of control over themselves and their lives has been compromised by trauma. In fact, you will also need to give some thought to the way that you approach your participants so that you don't inadvertently exploit their sense of dyscontrol or need for external validation. A discussion of the risks and benefits stated in your consent form can help you and your participants balance the positives and negatives of their becoming involved in the study and support their sense of having a free choice in the matter.

Trauma research is not inevitably upsetting to participants. Discussion of traumatic experience can be cathartic and can help people come to terms with painful reality. Moreover, the issue of risks and benefits also applies to evaluating the impact of your research on society in general. Often traumatized people feel that any discomforts they might have while participating in a study would be more than outweighed by their knowledge that they have contributed to research that will benefit others. They feel strengthened by the sense that they have taken steps to turn a life tragedy into something positive.

Underlying aspects. One major ethical problem you will face is not addressed by existing informed consent procedures, regardless of your research topic and design. This is the possibility that the process of studying people may, in itself, change them.

Let us say that you are examining childhood physical abuse in the general population. In your informed consent and your verbal instructions to your participants you indicate that you are examining the nature and incidence of early physical abuse experiences. It is possible that a number of your respondents may not have labelled these experiences as upsetting, much less abusive. Even if you study publicly acknowledged disasters such as war or industrial accidents, your participants may reconsider their judgments about their experiences based not only on their reactions to your questions, but also on their understanding of why they are being studied. The fact of being studied sometimes lends an aura of seriousness and importance to an experience someone has been trying to ignore or devalue. If your research offers new labels like "abuse," "trauma," "PTSD," or even established labels like "fatigue, " "depression," "stress," and "anger," you may cause your respondents to attend to, and possibly reorganize, their life experiences in a new way. If you use an interview for gathering data, you may discover that your subjects spontaneously tell you that they had never recognized the importance, or extent, of certain events in their lives. Even questionnaires are not immune to this phenomenon. These instruments may also focus on, and organize material in, ways that are new to your respondents and which may arouse their interest. They may evaluate their experiences as more or less important, depending on their interpretation of your study. These new interpretations could then cause them to make different life decisions (e.g., to engage in treatment, or in a lawsuit; to put energy into, or terminate, a relationship).

Thus, the very fact of being studied may have impact on your participants' behavior in ways that can influence them and influence your findings. The fact that the process of being observed and examined can contribute to error in research is certainly not unique to trauma studies. However, the phenomenon is likely to be of special importance when we are studying a topic that is a new one, and therefore, more likely to stimulate people to take a fresh look at their lives. As a trauma researcher, you should give extra thought to the labels that your questions present to make them as neutral as possible. For example, asking someone to explain how they were "punished" rather than how they were "abused" is a less judgmental and less biasing questioning technique. In general, describing behaviors, rather than summarizing them with suggestive labels, minimizes these error effects on your research. You may also decide to obtain post-study data from your participants on their reactions to your research so that you can identify and track the role of any unintended influences of the research on your participants.

Ethics and Your Research Institution

Surface aspects. Before you begin your research, you will need to obtain official approval from the university Institutional Review Board (IRB) that your research satisfies present day ethical standards. If you are doing your research in a setting other than your university, you must obtain approval from the IRBs of both institutions. IRBs are charged with educating you and guiding you through the ethical and procedural issues and pitfalls that your research presents. IRB policies are complex and obtaining IRB approval can be a daunting experience in which bureaucratic formulations and contradictory information at times seem to overwhelm ethical concerns.

In finding your way through this, it is important to understand that the IRB has two roles. The first is to protect your research participants. Thus, the Board concerns itself with issues such as informed consent discussed in the previous section. However, the second role of the IRB is to protect the institution and its members, including you. In our increasingly litigious society, we have a practical concern to avoid inadvertently breaking laws in the process of doing our research and to take steps to avoid being sued by participants who perceive themselves to be harmed or exploited by our research. Understanding that both you and the institutions that are supporting your research are vulnerable to painful and costly legal procedures may make it easier for you to tolerate the detailed instructions of your IRB.

Rather than approaching IRB procedures as a hurdle, you can view the IRB itself as a complex, sophisticated ethical and legal counselor.

Find out who is on the IRB and whether your department has any liaison to this group. Talk to at least one member of the IRB before your proposal comes up for approval, with the idea of utilizing him or her as a resource to IRB policy and procedure. Using the IRB early on in the development of your study means that you won't have last-minute problems with your research design.

Underlying aspects. The IRB may have particular concerns about your research because it is in the field of trauma. While it is natural for the Board to pay close attention to studies that deal with painful and unsettling experiences, it may well be that the most unsettled responses to your research will not come from your participants, but from the IRB itself. Like sexuality and suicide, trauma has long been a "forbidden" subject in our society and in others as well. There has long been a tendency for people to believe that examining forbidden topics can lead to personal and social chaos. The corollary of this is the opposite tendency to assume that the forbidden topic doesn't exist, or if it does, that it isn't very important (e.g., that its magnitude is exaggerated or that people are misreporting the data).

As part of your interaction with the IRB, you may need to counter assumptions like these by informing yourself and the Board about the incidence and significance of trauma and the effects of questioning people about traumatic experiences. You should be able to tell the Board what previous and ongoing studies have to say about the risks and benefits of your research procedures. In other words, in order to facilitate your IRB approval, you need to educate the IRB about your field of study. This will insure that your IRB makes informed decisions about the ethical guidelines governing your work.

Conclusion

The researcher has been often viewed as a neutral stimulus, one whose unemotionality and adherence to standardized behavior insures that research will be conducted in an unbiased fashion. Trauma research strains this model because strong feelings and value issues, both on the part of the researcher and the participant, are important components of the study of human adversity. The purpose of this chapter has been to give you an overview of ways to use your emotional and moral responses in a controlled, flexible, and informed fashion so that they become tools to enrich your research. The inevitability of emotional responses during research means that it will be important for you to develop basic empathy and self awareness skills. It will also be important to think through your value priorities as you weigh research risks and benefits and make decisions about how to handle the challenges that participants will present.

Just as your emotional reactions to your research will enrich your work, so your struggles to clarify the ethical aspects of your study will inform your research. In particular, dealing with these dilemmas can help you clarify the most important question you can ask yourself about your research: why, given the potential risks of my study, is this project worth doing?

Suggested Readings

The following are suggested readings that discuss major points in this article in greater detail.

Derry, P. & Baum, A. (1994). The role of the experimenter in field studies of distressed populations. *Journal of Traumatic Stress, 7* (4), 625-635.

Federal Register. (1991). *Part II: Federal policy for the protection of human subjects: Notices and rules* (46CRF56, No.117).

Sommer, J. F., Williams, M. B., Stamm, B. H. & Harris, C. J. (1994). Ethics in research, practice and training for traumatic stress. In *Handbook of post-traumatic stress*. Westport, CT: Greenwood Press.

U.S. Department of Health, Education and Welfare. (1979). *The Belmont report: Ethical principles and guidelines for the protection of human subjects of research* (Federal Register Document No. 79-12065). Washington, D.C.: U.S. Government Printing Office.

9

Data Analysis: Matching Your Question of Interest to Your Analysis

B. Hudnall Stamm, Stephen L. Bieber

In our combined 30 years of statistical consulting, probably the most frequently asked and bothersome question is, "How can I analyze my data?" In fact, many of the people we see are quite distressed by this question. And to some extent, as one of us has previously argued, this is as it should be. As a researcher, you have a responsibility to the research itself and to those who will consume the research. Research may be used as the basis of a treatment plan or for the development of public policy (Sommer, Williams, Stamm & Harris, 1994). Generally, researchers are cognizant of the potential uses of research and are aware of the potential impact on clinical work and public policy. However, awareness alone does not reduce the distress nor does it help you think clearly about analyzing your data.

Determining the most appropriate analysis for a particular research problem is perhaps one of the most difficult parts of the research process (Bieber, 1988; Bieber & Smith, 1986). For trauma researchers, this problem is intensified by the very nature of our work. Trauma, as we know it, is not an invariant construct across people nor even across time within the same person. Moreover, intervening variables may have

An earlier version of this chapter was presented at the Eighth Annual Meeting of the International Society for Traumatic Stress Studies, Los Angeles, CA, October 6, 1992.

moderating effects on the basic structure of the traumatic experience and therefore on the complexity of the data. This, of course, may lead to large, complex data sets and to the use of complex multivariate techniques. Thus, for traumatologists, decisions about an analysis strategy —whether univariate, bi-bivariate, or multivariate—can be particularly challenging.

What follows may appear to be a cookbook approach to solving the analysis dilemma, but it is more than that. We also recognize that while we have found the following organization to be successful and helpful, it is certainly not completely unique and naturally flows from the most basic principles of research. However you use it, we hope it will help you think more clearly about your research and that it will lead you to better analysis decisions.

The "Question of Interest"

Overview

At the base of any research process is the "Question of Interest" which contains two pieces of information vital to selecting an analysis strategy: (a) the nature of the variables being used to answer the "Question of Interest" and (b) the nature of the question itself (Bieber, 1988). Understanding the implications of the "Question of Interest," in the context of the subjects and design, should lead the data analysis process in a particular direction.

Grasping the nature of the variables can be confusing, particularly since there is sometimes disagreement among researchers about variable definitions. However, at a most basic level, variables can be categorized in one of two ways: (a) as discrete variables or (b) as continuous variables. We will discuss both of these types of variables in Part A below.

Although potentially as complex as the nature of the variables, the nature of the question can also be categorized in one of two general ways: (a) as an interdependency question that asks "what is the relationship of one or more variables with one or more other variables?" (as in Pearson correlation or canonical correlation); or (b) as a dependency question that asks "how do one or more variables depend on one or more other variables?" (as in ANOVA or MANOVA). We will discuss the nature of the question in Part B below.

Analysis procedures tend to be designed to accommodate one of the two aforementioned questions in conjunction with some combination of the two types of variables. This chapter will focus on identifying the nature of the variables and the nature of the question. We have simplified the concepts for the sake of clarity, and this chapter by no means covers all the potential analysis techniques nor even special applications of common techniques. However, we hope that it will assist you in working through the complexity of assessing what type of analysis most closely addresses your "Question of Interest."

Part A: The Nature of the Variables

Although there are several levels of variables—nominal, ordinal, interval, and ratio—variables can generally be classified as discrete or continuous. Discrete variables have few levels while continuous variables have many levels. Just how many levels denote few or many is a topic that is not clear in the behavioral sciences. However, we believe it is inappropriate to set strict criteria for a specific number of levels because of the individual needs of researchers and because of the diversity in the field. Instead, we will discuss the concepts germane to few levels and many levels to help you make your decisions about the nature of your variables.

Discrete Variables
Overview. Discrete variables also are known as qualitative, non-numeric, or non-metric variables. Discrete variables are variables with few levels. The clearest example is the dichotomous variable, which follows Boolean logic—that is, the presence of one condition implies the absence of the other. In other cases there can be more than two categories to a discrete variable. Moreover, in some cases, the order of the categories is meaningful.

If discrete variables are classification variables and reflect only differences in kind, they are nominal. If they reflect differences in degree with a specific order of classification implied, they are ordinal. In either case, the non-numeric characteristic of discrete variables prohibits the use of mathematical (numeric) calculations. Therefore, measures of central tendency must be made using the mode (for nominal variables) or the median (for ordinal variables). Distributions generated with discrete variables are non-normal; that is, they are not unimodal and symmetric. The distribution that is generated from discrete numbers can be described in terms of separate units, with no intermediate values between points (Hurlbert, 1994; Hogg & Craig, 1978).

The independent variable in an Analysis of Variance is a discrete variable. For example, you may decide to study the effect of Cognitive Therapy on PTSD. You could divide your subjects into two groups, one that receives the treatment of Cognitive Therapy, and one group that does not receive therapy. It is impossible to be in both groups. Thus the independent variable, Cognitive Therapy, becomes a discrete variable with two levels.

When very few categories exist, ordinal data generally are treated as discrete variables. An example of this is a three-category scale: "Yes, no, or sometimes." Suppose I ask all the patients who come into my clinic to fill out a checklist of symptoms. I might ask them to classify their responses as "No, I do not have this symptom," "Yes, I have this symptom," or "Sometimes I have this symptom." Sometimes is between Yes and No but it is not clear exactly where it fits—is it mostly yes or mostly no? Thus, it is difficult to understand the intervals between the categories.

At other times, an observant reader will notice that ordinal variables may be treated as continuous variables. In these cases, the researcher usually argues that you can tell the difference between the categories in some systematic way. For example, it may be possible to assume some sort of meaningful interval on a 4-point Likert Scale. However, researchers differ in how they approach such interpretations.

Discrete Variable Definition. As the previous paragraph indicates, defining discrete variables can be difficult. At the simplest level, a discrete variable is "one with no possible intermediate values between two adjacent points" (Hurlbert, 1994, p. 551). Guilford offers specific guidelines to determine a variable's nature. A discrete variable must be

(a) well-defined, (b) mutually exclusive, and (c) exhaustive (Guilford, 1970). These variables may be a reflection of a naturally-occurring grouping such as sex. At other times they are contrived by the researcher, as in treatment and control groups. Sometimes discrete variables are imposed theoretical constructs based on the researcher's knowledge about the subjects. For example, a researcher might label one variable as "people with a PTSD diagnosis" and another variable as "people without a PTSD diagnosis."

Naturally-occurring grouping variables generally follow the above prescribed guidelines of well-defined, mutually exclusive, and exhaustive. For example, biological sex (with rare exceptions) yields only two categories—male or female. Thus the categories are well-defined. Further, in most cases, subjects are either male or female; therefore, the categories are mutually exclusive. With only two biological categories for sex, researchers can safely assume the categories are exhaustive.

Discrete Variable Definition: Well-Defined.

In naturally-occurring grouping variables or in researcher-contrived categorizations such as treatment and no treatment, definitions may be clear. Unfortunately, when variables are theoretical constructions and not naturally-occurring grouping variables, meeting the criteria of well-defined, mutually exclusive, and exhaustive is more difficult. Problems of variable definition abound in trauma research. For example, if you are categorizing subjects' stressful experiences, how do you define a stressful experience versus a traumatic experience? Is it the event itself, the person's reaction to the event, or the combination of the two? Which events qualify for being truly traumatic? What if an event, such as an earthquake, seemingly qualifies but the person appears fine? Is this person doing well or is he or she repressing? The answer to these questions lies in the definition of the variable, but arriving at the definition itself is problematic.

Discrete Variable Definition: Mutually Exclusive.

A classic dilemma of mutual exclusivity can be seen in the issues surrounding dual diagnosis. If a person has a history of trauma and suffers from symptoms of depression, do you diagnose the individual as depressed or as someone with PTSD? At least some of the DSM-IV symptoms apply to both diagnoses, which makes it difficult to separate the diagnoses. Theoretical constructs also affect mutually exclusive categorization. Take, for instance, relaxation training and cognitive behavioral therapy as possible treatments for intrusive images. Are these techniques truly separate or do they have overlapping elements? Consider how the mutually exclusive requirement can be at risk. Depending on your theoretical perspective, you can view these techniques as truly separate treatments and thus consider them discrete variables. On the other hand, if you believe they have overlapping elements, then they do not meet the mutually exclusive criteria. Another scenario in which the mutually exclusive requirement cannot be met is when different levels of a medication are administered. Consider treating trauma-related depression with fluoxetine. The first group might get n mg per day and the second n/2, mg while the third group gets none. In this case, the treatment groups are not mutually exclusive but are differing levels of the same variable.

Discrete Variable Definition: Exhaustive.
Meeting the criteria of exhaustiveness is perhaps the most difficult. Sometimes it is impossible to consider or even to know about all competing options. For example, a researcher may not be aware of all extant treatments for a particular symptom. In practice, the researcher's financial resources, skill, and theoretical orientation limit the exhaustive criteria.

Continuous Variables
Overview. Continuous variables are also called quantitative, numeric, or metric variables, and they have many levels. Age is an example of a continuous variable. For instance, the moment of birth might represent the transition from 0 days old to 1 day old. Thereafter, each day adds an equal interval of time to one's age. By the time a person has accumulated 36,500 days, they would be 100 years old! In this case, the order and the unit between the measures is meaningful. In some cases, such as with age, there is a clear beginning point.

If continuous variables reflect equal interval, ordered categories, and differences in amount, we call them interval variables. When they have equal interval, ordered categories with a true zero point, and reflect a measurable difference in amount, they are called ratio variables. In either case, continuous variables are quantitative variables and permit mathematical calculations. It is possible to add and subtract with interval variables; ratio variables allow the use of addition, subtraction, multiplication, and division. Therefore, measures of central tendency may be made by taking a numeric average known as a mean. Moreover, continuous variables generate normal distributions; that is, they are unimodal (one hump) and symmetric (if you fold it in the middle, the two sides will match). These distributions illustrate the continuous variable, "one with an infinite number of values between adjacent scale values" (Hurlbert, 1994, p. 550). Most observations, or points, of the data collect around a central point and the tails of the distribution approach 0, but never touch it (Hogg & Craig, 1978). Because of these properties, it is possible to use parametric statistics such as t-tests and correlations on these data.

When a variable has an inherent numerical coding scheme it is likely to be a continuous variable. Again, take age for example. Generally, it is simplest to ask a subject's age based on days, months, or years, depending on the range of interest. Actual annual income is another variable that has an inherent coding scheme.

While some continuous variables are simple to define and use, others are less easy to defend as continuous. Consider the example described in the section under discrete variables. Remember that some ordinal variables may be treated as continuous variables? In these cases, the researcher believes that you can tell the difference between the categories in some systematic way; that it is possible to assume some kind of meaningful interval on a 4-point Likert Scale. However, others argue that with so few points 1, 2, 3, and 4 are actually discrete categories.

Continuous Variable Definition. As previously stated, a continuous variable is "one with an infinite number of values between adjacent scale values" (Hurlbert, 1994, p. 550). While there are naturally occurring continuous variables, many variables in the behavioral sciences are contrived, like scale scores on a psychological test. In reality, variables that are used as continuous variables are actually multiple ordered categories. To determine when a variable meets the criteria for continuousness, two questions can be asked. The first is, "Does the variable have an equal interval definable order?" The second and more important criterion is, "Does the distribution of the variable allow for a reasonable estimation of unsampled points?"

Continuous Variable Definition: Equal Interval Definable Order.

Many scales in trauma research have equal interval ordered categories. Consider this example. You present PTSD patients with a line anchored with 1 (not stressful) on the left and 100 (extremely stressful) on the right. You ask each subject to draw a slash bisecting the line at the point they believe represents their stress level. You then take a ruler marked with the 1-100 scale and measure the distance from point 1 to the subject's slash mark. Say, for example, that your first subject drew a line about 3/4 of the way from left to right. You could measure the response to be 74.3. This is an interval type of continuous measure.

Sometimes the continuous number has a definable order with equal intervals and a meaningful 0—the 0 means the subject has exactly none of the quantity being measured (Guilford, 1970). Consider the following dependent variable in a Regression Analysis. You decide to study the effect of an SSRI like fluoxetine on urinary free cortisols in PTSD patients. For each subject, your measurement of urinary free cortisols could range from 0—that is, no urinary free cortisols—to some potentially infinite amount. The 0 represents the complete absence of urinary free cortisols and each subject's score is free to range on a continuum. This qualifies as a ratio type of continuous variable.

Continuous Variable Definition: Estimation of Unsampled Points.

Because continuous numbers have "an infinite number of values between adjacent scale values" (Hurlbert, 1994), it is possible to estimate unobserved points. This principle underlies the estimate of the regression line. Consider a woman with an eating disorder. You could chart her daily weight gains and losses over a period of two months. You could draw a line through the middle of the data, and, based on the trajectory of that line, make a reasonable estimate of her weight change one week in the future. Likewise, many users of psychological tests argue that their scales can allow for the estimation of unsampled points and thus meet the criteria for a continuous variable.

Summation of Nature of the Variables

Generally, variables can be defined as either discrete (few levels) or continuous (many levels). Discrete variables are non-metric measures of categories (nominal) or ordered categories (ordinal) and should be (a) well defined, (b) mutually exclusive, and (c) exhaustive. Continuous variables are metric measures of differences in amount that (a) have an Equal Interval Definable Order and (b) have a distribution that can allow for the estimation of unsampled points. The better the variable meets the criteria set forth for each specific type of variable, the less error will be introduced into the analysis and the better the chance the researcher has in seeing any effect that is present in the data.

Table 1 summarizes all the information that has been discussed in Part A. The top three lines of the table indicate the discrepancies between the strict definitions of continuous and discrete variables as contrasted with their common usage. The next line of the table shows the names of the specific types of variables: Nominal Ordinal, Interval, and Ratio. The next set of boxes shows the definitions of the variables (the Organizing Heuristic) as was given in the text of Part A. The Quality of Measurement line enhances the definitions given by describing the characteristics of each level of measurements. The next line gives summary examples of the levels of measurements, while the Actual Data Type line represents the mathematical qualities of the levels of measurements. The bottom line shows how the data are commonly used.

Part B: The Nature of the Question

As was implied in the introduction, the Question of Interest is the pivotal point of any research process. The Question of Interest drives the analysis. In simple research projects, the Question of Interest may stand alone as the sole focus of the research. In more complex projects,

Table 1. Summary of the Nature of the Variables

	Nominal	Ordinal	Interval	Ratio
I Actual	← Discrete — few levels →		← Continuous — many levels →	
II Use	← Discrete →	← Continuous →		
III Name	Nominal	Ordinal	Interval	Ratio
IV Organizing Heuristic	classification	ordered classification	equal interval ordered classification	true zero equal interval ordered classification
V Quality of Measurement	difference in kind	difference in degree	difference in amount	measurable difference amount
VI Examples	sex ethnic group DSM diagnosis colors	development stage letter grade good, better, best Likert Scale	IQ Score GPA scale of 1–10 Likert Scale	weight reaction time days post event percent liking income
VII Actual Data Type	qualitative frequencies	qualitative frequencies	quantitative metric values	quantitative metric values
VIII Commonly Used Data Type	← qualitative frequencies →		← quantitative metric values →	

it may be necessary to ask multiple questions or sub-questions to fully answer the Question of Interest. The clearer the questions are at the beginning of the process, the easier you will find the analysis. Regardless of how many parts the question must have to be clear, they generally come in one of two types: (a) Interdependency Questions and (b) Dependency Questions.

Interdependency Questions

Overview. Questions of interdependency address whether or not things go together without asking how they do this. In its most general form, an interdependency or relatedness question asks about the shared variance, or the overlap, between variables without asking about how those variables go together. You probably recognize this question as a correlation question. A great deal of work in all of the behavioral sciences is done with questions of interdependency.

Interdependency questions can be asked of two variables at a time or of more than two variables at a time. In either situation, the basic nature of the question stays the same.

By definition interdependency questions address whether or not variables are related to each other. Mathematically, this can be defined as shared variance between variables. The definition can be illustrated in the following question: What is the relationship of one or more variables with one or more other variables? It is important to note that there is no implied nature of the variable in this definition. In its general form, this question can be asked equally of discrete or continuous variables.

Interdependency Question Definition: Simple Interdependency. When you address variables two at a time—pair by pair—you are asking a simple interdependency question. In its most basic form, this question is: What is the relationship between one variable and one other variable? There is one general mathematical formula for analyses of simple interdependency, but the exact formula for the simple interdependency analysis depends on the nature of the variables of which the question is being asked. There are specific mathematical formulation

Table 2. Simple Interdependency

Question: What is the relationship of one variable to one
other variable?

	discrete	*continuous*
discrete	Yule's Q	Eta
	Tetrachoric	Point Biserial
	Gamma	Point Multiserial
	Tau b, c	Sommer's D
	Sommer's D	
continuous		Pearson's r

variations for pairs of discrete variables, pairs of continuous variables, and for pairs when one variable is a continuous variable and one is a discrete variable. Table 2 suggests some of the possible statistics that use the different formulas appropriate to the nature of the variables.

Consider the interdependency of two discrete variables: you could use a Yule's Q test. In this case, perhaps you were interested in the relationship between PTSD diagnosis (yes or no) and Combat Duty (yes or no). If you were examining the relationship between two continuous variables, say scores on a stress scale (range 0-100) and age, you could use the familiar Pearson's Correlation.

Sometimes it is important to examine the relationship between one discrete and one continuous variable. A common measure of interdependency for mixed variables is eta. Maybe you have noticed that eta is often reported along with an Analysis of Variance, another test that uses a mix of discrete and continuous variables. While the Analysis of Variance is not a measure of interdependency, eta is. Drawing from the examples above, perhaps you are interested in the relationship between the discrete PTSD diagnosis and the continuous stress scale score. Eta would give you a measure of the relationship between these two variables.

Interdependency Question Definition: Multiple Interdependency. When you address groups (more than two) of variables, you are asking a multiple interdependency question. In its most basic form, this question is: What is the relationship between one or more variables to multiple other variables? As with simple interdependency, there is one general mathematical formula for analyses of multiple interdependency. The exact formula, of course, depends on the nature of the variables of which the question is being asked. There are specific mathematical formulation variations for groups of discrete variables and groups of continuous variables. Table 3 suggests some of the statistics that use the different formulas. While there are possible analyses for groups of mixed variables, these raise interesting philosophical questions that are beyond the scope of this paper.

If you address the interdependency of groups of discrete variables, you could use some form of a Log-Linear analysis in which the variables are not specified as independent or dependent. For example, maybe you would like to address the relationship between having a PTSD diagnosis (yes or no), Combat Duty (yes or no), and Sex (male or female). When you address the relationship between one continuous variable and a group of continuous variables, you would use a Multiple Regression. An example of this might be the relationship between the level of perceived stress (range 0–100) and a collection of physiological measures such as heart rate, galvanic skin response, and respiration. Taking this same analysis one step further, if you wanted to consider the relationship between a group of self report scores on one side and a group of physiological scores on the other, you could use a Canonical Correlation.

Dependency Questions

Overview. Questions of dependency are asked to determine how variables depend on each other. It is tempting to treat questions of dependency as causal questions. However, given the complexity of most of the questions we ask, it is usually impossible to determine whether variables are in a causal relationship. Nevertheless, the question in its dependency form is relevant and interesting. Understanding depen-

Table 3. Multiple Interdependency

Question: What is the relationship of one or more variables to multiple other variables?

	discrete	continuous
discrete	Contingency Tables Log-Linear Analysis	
continuous		Multiple Correlation Canonical Correlation

dency relationships allows the researcher to predict future events relating to the dependency.

Dependency Question Definition. By definition, the dependency question addresses how variables depend on each other. Mathematically this can be defined as shared variance, but with the important addition that the dependency of the variables is defined. In its most general form, the dependency question asks: How do one or more variables depend on one or more other variables? As in the interdependency question, there is no implied nature of the variable in the definition. In its general form, the question can be asked of discrete and continuous variables.

Dependency Question Definition: Simple Dependency. When you address a single dependent variable (DV) along with one or more other independent variables (IV), you are asking a simple dependency question. In its most basic form, it can be stated as: How does one variable (Dependent or Response Variable) depend on one or more other variables (Independent or Grouping Variable)?

As you probably suspected, there is one general mathematical formula for this type of analyses. Just as it was for the interdependency analyses, the specific formula you select is a reflection of the nature of the variables. Table 4 contains suggestions for different formulas.

In the simple dependency question, a single DV is assessed with one or more independent or grouping variables. This is the classic ANOVA or regression model. For example, one might ask how scores on the PK scale of the MMPI depend on sex (male or female) and PTSD diagnosis (yes or no). In this case, the DV is continuous (PK scale scores) and the IVs are discrete (sex and PTSD diagnosis) and the appropriate analysis is a standard 2x2 ANOVA.

Suppose the question was posed in relation to a hurricane: "How does PTSD level depend on length of stay in temporary housing and loss of property?" This could be analyzed with a traditional regression, in which all of the variables are continuous. The DV might be the PK scale and the IVs could be days in temporary housing and property loss in dollars.

It is also possible to ask these questions with all discrete variables. For example, you might think that PTSD diagnosis (yes or no) depended on previous traumatic experiences (yes or no) and current traumatic experiences (yes or no). This analysis could be done with a Log Linear analysis. We invite you to remember that we also suggested a Log Linear Analysis for interdependency analysis of discrete variables. Is this a contradiction? No, in the interdependency analysis, there were no specified DVs and IVs as there are in this dependency example. There are multiple other options for this type of analysis, including some that allow you to mix discrete and continuous IVs. Table 4 shows other options for analysis of simple dependency questions.

Dependency Question Definition: Multiple Dependency. The multiple dependency question differs in only one way from the simple dependency question. It has multiple dependent (response) variables. A multiple dependency question asks: How do multiple variables (Dependent or Response Variables) depend on one or more other variables (Independent or Grouping Variables)? As you would expect, there is one basic mathematical formula that is adapted to the nature of the variables used as IVs and DVs.

The designation of multiple dependency is determined by the presence of more than one dependent variable and not by the total number of variables. It is conceivably possible to have a single independent

Table 4. Simple Dependency

Question: How does one variable (DV) depend on one or more other variables (IVS)?

	IV		
	discrete	*continuous*	*mixed*
discrete DV	Contingency Tables Logit Analysis Log-Linear Analysis	Discriminant Analysis	Logistic Analysis Logistic Discriminant Analysis
continuous DV	Analysis of Variance	Regression Analysis Time Series Analysis	Analysis of Covariance Indicator Variable Analysis

variable in a multiple dependency design. For example, suppose the question is, "How do scores on the Impact of Events Scale (IES) and the PK scale depend on sex of the victim?" This could be analyzed as two simple dependency questions, one with the DV of the IES and the IV of sex (male or female) and the other with the PK scale as the DV and sex as the IV. However, this is not a nice, clean set of analyses. The alternative is to analyze it as one Question of Interest in a multiple dependency question. There are several analyses that could be used. For example, you could chose a Discriminant analysis or a MANOVA. Using the multiple dependency analysis strategy enhances a global interpretation of the results and is often the preferred method because of the interpretability. Table 5 contains suggestions for other multiple dependency analyses.

Another type of multiple dependency question comes from a situation in which a single measure is taken repeatedly from the same subjects. Although there are simple dependency analyses for repeated measures, the more precise way to assess change over time is through multiple dependency analyses such as a Trend Analysis or Repeated

Table 5.   Multiple Dependency

Question: How do multiple variables (DVs) depend on one or more other variables (IVs)?*

	IV		
	discrete	*continuous*	*mixed*
discrete DV	Logit Analysis Log-Linear Analysis		
continuous DV	Discriminant Analysis MANCOVA Trend Analysis Repeated Measures Analysis	Multiple (variate) Regression	MANCOVA

* There are some analyses which are pure inter-relationships and have no identifiable dependent nor independent variables. Examples of such would be Multidimensional Scaling, Factor Analysis, and Cluster Analysis.

Measures Analysis. The advantage comes from the fact that scores gathered from the same subjects at multiple points in time are not independent from one another since they came from the same person. Thus, it is appropriate to consider the same variable, measured at multiple points in time, as one would multiple variables from the same person.

Matching Your Analysis to the Nature of Your Variables and the Nature of Your Questions

By now, it should be apparent that Tables 2–5 can be used to guide you in your selection of an analysis technique. To find a suggested analysis, simply match the table to your question and then identify the nature of your variables. The analyses in the cell that lines up with your variables will provide suggestions for your data analysis.

While these tables do not cover the total number of statistical techniques nor the unique applications of them, they do point to classes of analyses that should enable the researcher to know where to search for a special application when one is needed. More importantly, by learning to identify and articulate clearly one's questions and variables, a great deal of the battle has been won.

Addressing the Nature of the Variables and the Nature of the Questions from a Process Approach

In sum, good research has an identifiable thread running through the Question of Interest that ties it to the nature of the variables and to the nature of the question. The earlier the thread is identified, the sturdier the research has a chance to become. Make a plan, follow it, adjust it where needed, but do not lose sight of the plan.

In order to avoid losing one's way, we advocate writing an analysis plan before the data collection. This plan contains each of the study's questions in simple word forms, along with their variables, and the anticipated analysis. After the data have been collected and encoded, the researcher simply goes down the list, accomplishing the prescribed analysis, and recording the answer. In most cases, some additional analyses will present themselves after the fact (a posteriori). Being clear-minded about the planned (a priori) research questions and analyses will enhance the researcher's ability to spot important bits of information that are apparent a posteriori.

It is our belief that good planning and a knowledge of one's field leads to good decisions about data analysis and its interpretation. We hope that the process we propose here has value to you and that it can help you keep your research project on course and your data-analysis-induced-stress at a minimum.

References

Bieber, S. L. (1988). Multiple regression and its alternatives. *Social Sciences Journal, 25* (1), 1–19.

Bieber, S. L., & Smith, D. V. (1986). Multivariate analyses of sensory data: A comparison of methods. *Chemical Senses, 11* (1), 19–47.

Guilford, J. P. (1970). *Fundamental statistics in psychology and education*, 4th ed. New York: McGraw-Hill.

Hogg, R. V., & Craig, A. T. (1978). *Introduction to mathematical statistics*, 4th ed. New York: Macmillan.

Hurlbert, R. T. (1994). *Comprehending behavioral statistics*. Belmont, CA: Wadsworth.

Sommer, J. F., Williams, M. B., Stamm, B. H., & Harris, C. J. (1994). The development of ethical principles for posttraumatic research, practice, training, and publication. In M. B. Williams & J. F. Sommer (Eds.). *Handbook of posttraumatic therapy*. Westport, CT: Greenwood Press.

10

Submitting and Presenting Conference Papers

Eve B. Carlson

Active researchers will want to attend conferences and present their work. Most successful researchers would agree that while publications are important, the social networking that occurs at conferences is enormously important for developing one's career. Knowing other researchers personally facilitates collaboration and makes it possible for you to call on colleagues for assistance in planning, conducting, and understanding the results of your research. Discussions of critical issues in fields often occur in the corridors and restaurants at conferences. Such discussions are very helpful in clarifying one's own thinking and in being aware of progress in your field, often years ahead of when that progress will be reflected in published literature. Presenting at conferences tends to put you in the middle of these intellectual interactions in a way that isn't likely to happen if you simply attend a conference as a member of the audience. Presenting your work also ensures that colleagues will be aware of your research and interests. The dizzying expansion of the literature makes it harder and harder for people to be aware of others' work, especially the work of those who are new to the field. If other researchers meet you personally, they will be more aware of your work and more likely to contact you when seeking colleagues for research collaboration, to review journal articles, to write book chapters, and to present at other conferences.

Novice researchers almost always feel unsure and intimidated about the prospect of submitting a paper to a conference. The information and advice in this chapter is meant to demystify the process and thereby make it less daunting. I will discuss choosing a conference, the different kinds of presentations one can make at conferences, and guidelines for the contents of abstracts or summaries submitted to conferences. Embedded in the guidelines for contents of abstracts are my recommendations for the contents of presentations. The content of a good conference abstract and a good presentation are basically the same. In terms of the presentation itself, I'll present some general guidelines for organization and clarity, suggestions for preparing and delivering an oral presentation, and suggestions for effective use of visual aids.

Choosing a Conference and a Presentation Format

Choosing a Conference

There are myriad conferences to choose from when you want to present your research. They range from small, local meetings to large, international ones. Important characteristics to consider include how much it will cost to register for the conference, stay in the hotel, and travel to the conference; the intended audience for the conference (e.g., clinicians, researchers, social service providers); the likelihood that your paper will be accepted; the quality and interests of the other presenters at the conference; the possibility of pre-conference workshops that would be valuable to you; and the value to you of the overall conference agenda and goals.

There are some limitations for presenters set by the conferences themselves. Most conferences only accept submissions from members of the sponsoring organization, though you can participate as an invited presenter in a symposium organized by a member. As a student, you can join many organizations at very low cost. Some memberships are limited by discipline, however. For instance, only M.D.s or medical students can join the American Psychiatric Association.

Advantages to very large conferences (such as the American Psychological Society, the American Psychological Association, and the American Psychiatric Association) are the great variety of fields represented at the conferences and the kinds of people you'll meet. Also, very large, national conferences typically have some kind of employment advertising and interviewing, which may be of interest to you. On the other hand, large conferences can be anonymous, impersonal, and somewhat overwhelming to novice researchers. Often sessions are held at several hotels and one spends a lot of time traveling about to sessions of interest. There may also be relatively few sessions in your specific area of interest and you may meet few people with whom you have much common intellectual ground. These large, national conferences are probably the most competitive conferences in terms of getting your submission accepted because of the large number of submissions.

Smaller conferences include regional conferences, such as the Midwestern Psychological Association. The advantages and disadvantages associated with very broad-focused conferences also apply to regional conferences, but they have the advantages of being closer to home, smaller (usually held at only one hotel), and typically more friendly and less competitive. Some of these conferences have very little if any trauma research being presented, which could be an advantage or a disadvantage, depending on your point of view. One disadvantage is that the most prominent researchers in the field may not go to regional conferences because they are already going to several large, national conferences and to specialty conferences.

Specialty conferences are typically national or international conferences that focus on a particular area of interest. There is one conference solely devoted to the study of trauma: the annual meeting of the International Society for Traumatic Stress Studies. Other specialty conferences focus on specific populations (e.g., children), specific types of trauma (e.g., child abuse), or related phenomena (e.g., dissociation). The advantages of specialty conferences are that you can share your research with a great number of people with the same interests and you can make contacts with and learn from more experienced researchers in your field. These conferences are often less formal than the larger, national conferences and there are often more structured opportunities to interact with other conferencegoers (e.g., receptions, interest group meetings).

Presentation Options

Conference presentations can take several forms and one typically specifies the format desired when submitting a paper. The most common formats are poster presentations, paper presentations, and symposia presentations. Poster presentations are generally more likely to be accepted than are the other two types. Submitting a poster is a good idea if your study is limited in scope and unlikely to be accepted as a paper presentation. They also have the obvious advantage of eliminating the intimidating task of "giving" a conference paper. This might be a good option if you want to "get your feet wet" as a conference presenter. The disadvantage of poster presentations is that they usually get less exposure at a conference, so you will not be able to share your findings with as many people.

Paper presentations usually involve submitting a paper that you would like to present orally. Most conferences group together three or four papers on the same general topic into a single paper session. Your paper is often more likely to be accepted if it relates well to the theme of the meeting or the goals of the conference.

Increasingly, conference organizers are favoring pre-arranged symposia in the selection process. For this type of presentation, three or four people with similar interests submit their papers together, often complete with a symposium chair and a discussant. This is an attractive format, but a difficult one for students or novice researchers to participate in because researchers generally put together symposia with colleagues they already know. The best way to become one of those "already known" colleagues is to attend conferences, connect with people with similar interests, and discuss the possibilities for symposia at the same conference the following year. Collect real and email addresses and write to people who express interest in forming a symposium. Since there is always a dearth of people willing to take on organizational and administrative tasks, you may find that others are willing to join the symposium if you are willing to handle the paperwork.

Writing and Submitting a Paper to a Conference

The Review Process

Whether you have decided on a poster presentation or a paper presentation, your preparation of an abstract for review will be similar. For simplicity's sake, I will use the term "paper" below to refer to both posters and orally presented papers. For most conferences, many more papers are submitted than can be included in the conference. Program committees are charged with reviewing these submissions and rating them so that the papers for the conference can be chosen. Often, a submission is given a low rating, though the study or paper it describes is valuable. This occurs because the author doesn't do a good job of conveying the content of the paper or study. As an assistant program chair of a conference for several years, I read hundreds of conference abstracts of varying quality. From this vantage point, I have some suggestions about how to write an effective conference abstract.

Writing the Abstract

A conference "Call for Papers" will be available from a sponsoring organization nine or 10 months before the date of the conference. Generally, submissions are due six or seven months before the conference. The "Call for Papers" will specify what form the submission should take. Most conferences ask for abstracts or summaries of the paper to be presented. The recommendations below apply to both abstracts and summaries, though I have referred only to abstracts below to simplify the writing. If you are submitting an abstract, you will need to cover each suggested point in one or two sentences. If you are submitting a summary, expand each section as much as possible without exceeding the page limits given.

A good abstract or summary should convince the reader of the importance of the research. To do this, you need to convey a lot of information in very few words. Some conferences have limits on the lengths abstracts as stringent as 100 words, while others allow a few pages to describe the proposed paper. The first rule of thumb is to follow closely any guidelines for submissions that appear on the "Call for Papers" for the conference. Never exceed the limits on length, but always include as much information as possible within those limits. With so many important points to make, it should never be the case that your submission is significantly shorter than the limit set in the "Call for Papers."

If the "Call for Papers" does not provide any specific guidelines about the content of your submission, I suggest you include as many of the following elements in your abstract as you have room for. Some of these criteria apply better to some topics than others. For example, the purpose of a study in some cases may be obvious. When space is very limited, you will have to use your judgment to decide when something is important enough to include in the abstract. I have marked the elements that I consider essential to any abstract, no matter how brief, with an asterisk. Some of the elements that are most useful, but most often missing, in abstracts include the rationale for exploring the topic and the conclusions or expected applications of the ideas.

*Topic. A brief statement of the topic of the study is necessary to orient the reader of the abstract.

Rationale. You need to explain your rationale for undertaking the study. Why was your study needed? Why was it potentially valuable? It isn't necessary that your reader (or the reviewer) agree with your rationale, but it is necessary for the reader to understand what you think the rationale is. Don't force readers to try to figure the rationale out for themselves. Some may attribute a rationale that you don't intend and some may misunderstand your points because they don't really understand your purpose in exploring the topic. Worse yet, a reader may be left wondering why you bothered to do the study at all. It is frequently assumed, but rarely true, that the rationale for a study is truly obvious.

Conceptual framework. If you have room in an abstract or summary, it's helpful to readers if you put your ideas into a theoretical context. Every new idea builds on previous work and you should make it clear what "starting points" you used for your work. If you give no starting point, the reader may mistakenly assume you have a particular theoretical orientation or may wonder whether there is a sound basis for your research questions.

Research hypothesis. The primary research hypothesis is an important element that is frequently left out of abstracts. You should specifically state your main research question before describing methods and results. Don't try to list all of your research hypotheses in an abstract; just cover the most important ones.

Subjects. It's important to provide some information about subjects in even the shortest abstract. You should describe the number of subjects, the population or diagnostic group of the subjects, and any other relevant characteristics, such as ages or gender. Give only essential information here: don't use up space with excessive detail.

Design. Specify the design of the study (e.g., experimental, naturalistic, single subject), the data gathering procedures, methods, complete names of any measures used, and specifics about name and dosage of any drugs used in the study. If the study design was experimental, describe control groups (i.e., no treatment) or comparison groups (i.e., other treatments). If psychological measures likely to be unfamiliar to reviewers or readers are used as an integral part of the study (e.g., a newly-developed or little-known scale or questionnaire), you may want to include a sentence describing the measure.

Results. It's important to describe the results of your study, specifying what statistical tests were used and findings of the tests, including values of the test statistics, degrees of freedom, and statistical significance levels. In my experience, a common reason for not accepting a research abstract is that the abstract does not describe the results of the study. In some cases, the results are described in such general terms that reviewers suspect that the data has not yet been collected. Most program committees consider only research papers that are complete at the time they are submitted. This policy is necessary since only completed research can be evaluated in terms of its importance to the field.

Generalizability. It is helpful to many readers if you describe how generally or specifically the findings can be applied. Do they have a broad application or are there limited ways in which the findings might be useful? If you don't explain the generalizability explicitly, readers may misunderstand how broadly you think the ideas can be applied.

Conclusions, implications, applications. Don't forget to include the conclusions you have come to after considering your findings. Are there important implications or applications for your findings for treatment or research? You can never assume that the conclusions, implications, or applications are obvious. Many who read conference abstracts are new to the field and may not be able to come to a conclusion based on your results or may not see implications or applications that you have in mind. It's best to make them explicit.

Pre-reviewing Your Abstract

Many conferences publish the abstracts *as submitted* as part of the conference proceedings or materials. When this is the case, your abstract will be widely read and it is especially important that it is well-written and visually pleasing. A sloppy, poorly typed abstract will give colleagues a poor impression of your work. I suggest that you ask one or two colleagues to review your abstract before you submit it. This is such a brief bit of reading that you should have no trouble convincing someone to help you. Try to find "pre-reviewers" who regularly present at conferences and who have written abstracts that are clear and complete. Give them any instructions from the "Call for Papers" guidelines and ask them to give you honest feedback about the weaknesses in your abstract. This process may well help you catch problems in the abstract *before* you submit it.

Making Effective Conference Presentations

If your research is of high quality, you may well have the ambivalent experience of receiving a letter of acceptance for your poster or conference paper. Many have found that the joy of this victory is quickly followed by anguish about the very frightening prospect of presenting one's work to an audience.

Poster Presentations

If you have opted for a poster presentation, you will benefit from being able to carefully prepare the content of your entire presentation in advance. The only demand on you during the poster session will be to coherently answer questions about your findings and discuss the relevant issues with interested persons. Most people find this process to be rewarding and not too stressful as poster session conversations are typically informal and friendly.

To make the information on your poster most accessible to passersby, you must keep the content simple and make the text easily readable. In general, you should follow the content guidelines offered above to prepare your poster. Remember that poster session attendees will only want to spend a limited amount of time reading each poster. It's very important to have an abstract that's brief (100-150 words) and to clearly label the sections of the paper (typically, Introduction, Method, Results, Discussion). You should present and report results of only your *major* research questions. Discussion and findings of two or three hypotheses are probably the maximum amount you can cover well in a poster session. Find out in advance how much space will be available for your poster and, using guidelines for visibility described below, limit your text to fit the size of the space assigned to you.

To make sure your poster can be easily read, you should enlarge the text so that it can be read from a distance of five or six feet. People are comfortable standing at this distance from posters and may skip yours if they can't make out the text easily as they pass by. Needless to say, this size print is much larger than normal print. You can achieve this using a large font size or by having the text enlarged after it is printed. I have found that it increases readability to print the entire text in boldface. Don't use all capital letters, though: while all caps are very visible, they are very difficult to read. Using a large size font is very easy on Macintosh computers. If you're unfamiliar with Macintosh computers, it may be worth the time to get help to convert your text and print the poster out since the results are so nice. Alternatively, most universities have machines that will turn text on a standard sheet of paper into a poster two feet by three feet in size. Get feedback from colleagues on the content of the poster and its readability before you print your final version.

On the day of the session, you should arrive at least 15 minutes early to your poster session so that you'll have time to set up your poster. You might want to bring extra thumbtacks and photocopies of your poster if you want to give them to interested persons. Be sure to include your complete address and phone number so that people can contact you later.

Paper Presentations

If you have opted for an oral presentation of a paper, you will be faced with a more daunting task than the poster session. All of us have seen conference presentations that were interesting and well-presented, but we have also endured the tedium of boring, disorganized, and uninspired presentations. Most of those who present at conferences are understandably anxious that their "performance" fall into the first category, but many aren't sure how to make that happen.

As a conference presenter, I have first-hand experience with the stresses of speaking to an audience of professionals. This can be particularly unnerving when one is at the beginning of one's career, unsure of oneself intellectually, intimidated by an august audience, or all three. In addition to struggling personally with the task of making conference presentations, I have also spent a great deal of time teaching the elements of effective presentations. In undergraduate psychology courses I teach, I always assign oral presentations. When I began teaching, I quickly discovered that many students gave abysmal presentations if left to their own devices. I determined that presentation skills, like any other academic skill, needed to be taught explicitly. Through listening to and evaluating hundreds of oral presentations, I have identified many common impediments to successful presentations and have developed presentation guidelines for those who are new to this task. The guidelines may also be useful to those who would simply like to give better presentations. I frequently consult them when preparing for my own research presentations to make sure I don't forget to follow my own advice! Making effective presentations is never easy, but there are many steps you can take that are sure to improve your performance.

Planning Your Presentation

Organization. Make sure the content of your presentation is well-organized so that it will be easy for the audience to follow the flow of ideas. Remember, while your audience may be knowledgeable about your topic in general, they won't be familiar with the new points you'll be making in your presentation. A logical, orderly presentation will help them follow your train of thought. You should follow any content guidelines provided in the conference "Call for Papers" or use content guidelines such as those provided above.

Scope. Avoid trying to cover too much in your presentation. The 15 or 20 minutes typically allotted for a conference presentation greatly limits how much material you can cover. If you are presenting a paper that you have written for publication, you will probably have to cut out much of the content for your presentation. Since people cannot process as much information when listening as they can when reading, you can coherently explain far less in a conference talk than you could read aloud in the same amount of time.

Explain your terms. Include explanations of terms or ideas that will be unfamiliar to your audience. Don't make too many assumptions about the sophistication of your audience! I have rarely seen presentations that err on the side of simplicity, but have frequently seen speakers lose the audience by presenting complicated, unfamiliar ideas too quickly. Also, avoid jargon and acronyms that are not *extremely* well known. You're probably safe with "DSM" and "PTSD," but even "WAIS-R" or "SCID" would be unfamiliar to many conferencegoers. You probably already know how frustrating it is to listen to a talk focused on an acronym when you don't know what it means!

By the same token, don't describe results on the "WAK-Q" without explaining exactly what the WAK-Q measures and how it is administered. This information is frequently left out of presentations, probably on the assumption that audience members already know the content and procedures for the measures used. I think this is frequently not true, however, and audience members may be confused. Worse yet, they may make the unfortunate assumption that the content and procedures of measures don't really matter.

Practice, Practice, Practice

Many neophyte presenters mistakenly assume that oral presentation skills are a talent that one either has or doesn't have. While it's true that there are a few very gifted speakers who are able to speak well extemporaneously, most people become good speakers by practicing. There is no shame in practicing a presentation before you give it. It's not true that having good ideas or being knowledgeable about your subject matter will be enough to ensure a successful presentation. I have seen very bright, well-regarded professionals who clearly hadn't practiced their presentations and who embarrassed themselves because of it.

Rehearse. Practice your presentation in front of a colleague or a wall or audiotape or videotape the presentation. If you practice in front of a colleague, make sure it is someone who is knowledgeable enough about conference presentations to give you helpful advice and that the person is willing to give you critical feedback. Having a well-meaning friend tell you that your presentation is "fine" when it's not will be to your disadvantage.

An audiotape or videotape is the most helpful for pinpointing problems with the presentation. When you listen to or watch your tape, be alert for unclear explanations, overdependence on notes or text, stumbling, frequent "ums" or "uhs," low voice volume, overly rapid rate of speech, mumbling, or a monotonous tone. Also note whether you appear to be interested in your topic and energetic. If your anxiety is impairing your performance, you should continue practicing until you can present in a relaxed manner. With a videotape, it will also be possible to notice excessive movements of your body or hands. Some animation is appropriate for a presentation, but constant or excessive movement can be distracting.

It is usually necessary to go through the entire presentation at least three times in order to know the material well enough to deliver it from notes (see Presenting Cues below). It is crucial to practice the presentation aloud (instead of in your head) since problems with timing, difficulty explaining points, and leaps of logic are likely to surface only when practice the presentation aloud.

Timing. If you don't already have details about the timing of your paper presentation about a month before the conference, find out from the paper session or symposium chair (or the conference administrators if you can't locate the former) exactly how long you will have to make your presentation. Don't assume that this information will automatically be provided to you. I have been in symposia where the decision about how much time each person had was made in the last moments before the session started! Conference presentations are typically 15 or 20 minutes long. Often, five minutes are allowed in addition for questions, and it is important to know whether your question period is to occur at the end of your presentation or at the end of the whole session.

It is very helpful to have some idea how much time is left as you progress through the talk. Many session chairs will slip you a note with a "two-minute warning" of the end of your allotted time. It's fine to ask for this before the session begins, but even more helpful if you provide notecards (or slips of paper) with big numbers on them. A five-minute warning and a two-minute warning are probably sufficient and not too disruptive. Session chairs may have their own unique systems for warnings, so it's important to ask about this. I was quite surprised during one conference presentation when the session chair slipped a note onto the podium that simply read "STOP!" If the chair seems vague or inattentive, you can offer to time all of the presentations and let people know how much time they have left. It a terrible thing when you're the last person to speak after the first three people all go over their allotted time. Similarly, it is *very bad* form to go several minutes over your allotted time, even if no one tries to stop you. If all else fails, ask the person next to you to give you a two-minute warning or time yourself.

Time your presentation and cut your material until you can comfortably finish in the time allotted. This is such a simple concept, but one of the most heinously violated of the rules. How many times have you seen a conference presenter look aghast when the chair slips them the note that says "five minutes left"? Time and again I have watched and listened with pity as presenters fritter away the first five or 10 minutes of a 15-minute presentation, elaborating on non-essential details. These presenters inevitably end up speeding through their most important points, flipping through slides, results, and conclusions at a rate that the audience simply can't comfortably follow.

Ideally, you should know how far along you ought to be at the five-minute and two-minute warnings. If you should find yourself short of time when you get a warning, *do not* begin racing through your material. It is better to skip points or slides that are non-essential than to speed up and lose your audience. You might even want to plan what to skip if you run out of time toward the end. Also, avoid stopping very abruptly if you run out of time. Try to summarize and come to a graceful end, but don't take longer than a minute to do it!

Presentation Cues. You'll want to rehearse until you can deliver your presentation smoothly from slides, overhead transparencies, an outline, or notes. It is important to avoid long pauses, stumbling over words, or excessive "uhs" as these are very distracting to your listeners. It may not be possible to detect these without using a tape recorder or enlisting the help of a friend who is willing to be critical. *Never* read your presentation word-for-word from a prepared text. This kind of presentation is torture to listen to. (See Expressing Interest below.)

Several common problems that can crop up during a presentation include losing one's place in presentation text, not being able to reconstruct an idea from a notecard cue, not being able to read one's text in a darkened room, and not being able to look at the audience often enough when following a text. Eliminating the written text eliminates all of these complications. One technique suggested by a friend that I have since adopted provides an almost foolproof way to keep organized during the presentation. The "work from the slides" method uses material on slides as the cues to the presentation, rather than a written text. Instead, the slides are designed to take you through the whole presentation and cue you to make your important points. Another advantage of this method is that it encourages listing of points on the slides (as cues to you). Audiences find these lists extremely helpful when they are taking notes, or just trying to follow your train of thought.

Checking Equipment. There are innumerable technical difficulties that can be distracting for you and the audience during your presentation. My worst technical nightmare occurred despite my careful planning of the content of my presentation. The podium faced the audience in such a way that my back was to my slides whenever I looked at my text or the audience. To complicate matters, the microphone was designed for rock stars and wouldn't amplify my voice unless my lips were actually touching it. I'm sure it was quite amusing for the audience to watch me spin in circles while trying to look cool and composed. During the presentation no one could figure out how to work the room lights. They dimmed and flashed dramatically at random intervals during my talk as a well-meaning volunteer tried every switch on the huge panel. The slide projector worked, but I kept advancing slides when I wanted to focus them because I couldn't see the buttons in the dark. The pointer was a huge cylinder that weighed several pounds, and was attached to a cord. It barely reached far enough to point at the screen, flashed on and off when I tried to use it, and ungracefully rolled off the slanted podium every time I put it down. The podium light worked sporadically, leaving my text in total darkness at crucial moments.

I have since learned my lesson and now try to anticipate problems. I have even purchased a pocket-sized portable pointer that has proved invaluable and makes me terribly popular with other presenters who borrow it. I suggest you go to the assigned room at least 15 minutes prior to the session start time and check on the technical equipment you will be using. Don't let yourself get waylaid during these precious minutes by people waiting for the session who want to chat. Check on as many of the following as possible. Can you see your slides without turning your back on the audience? If not, can the lectern be shifted or can you use a portable microphone and not stand behind the lectern? Does the microphone work? Do you know how to dim the lights if you need to? Is there someone assigned to dim the lights for you? If not, whom can you ask to do this? Can your slides/overheads be easily read from the back of the room? Can you control the slide projector from the lectern or should you find a volunteer to change slides or overheads? Do you know how to focus slides from the lectern, even in the dark? If you plan to use a text or notecards, is there a working lectern light so you can see them in the dark? If you need a pointer, is there one available and do you know how to work it? This is also a good time to clarify what notice you'll be given about time running out (See Timing above).

Making a Dynamic Delivery

Audibility. Speak loudly enough that everyone in the audience can hear you. For most presentations you will use a microphone, but the audience won't be able to hear you unless you speak clearly and directly into the microphone. If you have a small voice, it is wise to ask if those in the back can hear you and modify accordingly. If you have a tendency to mumble or slur your words, practice with a tape recorder until your words are clear and distinct. Sometimes you must put your mouth right up against the microphone to be heard. This is hard to do, but you should do it if necessary. It's very frustrating for the audience if they can't hear you and after a few attempts to get you to speak up, they may well give up.

Remember to keep your head up and look at your audience. It is much easier for your audience to hear what you are saying if they can see your mouth move as you speak. This will also help your voice carry to the audience.

Pacing. A common problem with presentations is that they are delivered too quickly. You must work very hard to speak slowly. Most people cannot process complex ideas quickly, so they must be presented at a much slower rate than conversational speech. Unfortunately, many speakers inadvertently speed up their delivery because of nervousness, making it extremely difficult for the audience to follow. We have all heard presentations delivered at a rapid-fire pace that defies comprehension. Be aware of your rate of speech during your presentation. If you notice that you are speaking too quickly, take a deep breath and slow down. Another reason why reading from a text is taboo is that it almost always results in speaking too quickly.

Expressing Interest. It is very important that you appear to be interested in what you are presenting. How are you going to convince anyone else to be interested if you don't look and sound interested? Surely no one would intentionally want to look or sound uninterested in their own presentation, but this often occurs. Sometimes, it is the result of nervousness. For example, I have seen anxious presenters read papers word for word so that they will not get lost or otherwise "mess up" the presentation. But, as mentioned above, reading a presentation inevitably leads to a delivery that is droning and too rapid. If you are tempted to read your talk, tape record yourself reading it and listening critically to the result. Presentations that were read have been among the very worst I have witnessed.

You can use your voice and facial expression to help motivate your audience's interest. If you listen to really good speakers, you'll notice that they frequently change the tone and pitch of their voices. These modulations have the effect of expressing the speaker's interest in the content of his or her presentation. You can similarly modulate your voice, using it to emphasize key points and to show curiosity about your research questions and excitement about your findings. While you don't want to gush or bubble, a little bit of enthusiasm can help enliven a presentation.

Visual Aids. Use visual aids like slides or overhead transparencies to highlight unfamiliar terms, lists, or outlines of complex material. This will make it easier for your audience to follow your presentation and take notes. As described above, it may also provide a structure to help you keep your presentation on track. I recommend using slides rather than overheads in presentations for several reasons. Slides are much easier to handle during a presentation. Moving to the next slide is almost always less distracting than putting up the next overhead. Overheads almost always need adjustment (straightening) and almost always require an assistant who is extremely well-versed in the presentation. Such an assistant is seldom available and presenters using overheads often must rely on saintly volunteers who have no idea what is on the overheads. Further, slides are certain to stay in order if you put them in the projector correctly. Overheads, however, are easy to mix up as you take each off the projector to put the next one on, especially since the assistant doing this task is typically is unfamiliar with the structure and content of the presentation. My impression is that slides are perceived as more professional than overheads. Most college and university libraries can make slides from your printed text and figures for you at a relatively moderate cost. New technologies for printing slides directly from a computer are also increasingly available at university and college libraries or media centers.

Be sure that your visual aids and handouts do not overload your listeners. Flashing a slide with 50 numbers on it will only confuse your audience. Take the time to pare down your visual aids to the bare minimum so that your audience will be able to read the slide and listen to what you are saying about it. Limit yourself to a few columns and a few rows per slide. Don't worry about having too little information on a slide or overhead. Wouldn't you rather see a slide that is easy to process than one with much more information than you can process?

Also, be sure to use very large print on your slides or overheads and test them to be sure that they will be readable from the back of a long room. Print must be three or four times the size of regular print to be readable on slides or overheads. Typing the text in bold print also increases readability. For Macintosh users this is quite easy. I have found that the New York font in 24 point size, bold face, capital letters is quite readable on slides and overheads. If the computer you use cannot print in larger fonts, consider using a Macintosh in a campus computer lab if one is available. The ability to print text sideways on a page is also useful for making slides since text that is wider than it is long is best suited for the shape of slides and projector screens.

If you must use overheads and don't have access to computers to make large, bold type faces, it is best to hand letter overheads with a thick marker. Don't worry about appearing unsophisticated! Your audience will be grateful that they can read the overheads. Don't worry that the words will be too big. There is no such thing as a slide or overhead that is too easy to read.

In some cases, it is also useful to distribute tables or graphs that are important to the presentation, but make sure that it is *truly* necessary and useful for the audience to have the table or figure in hand. I have frequently seen presenters spend a great deal of time and cause considerable distraction in passing around handouts, only to make only passing reference (or no reference at all!) to what was on the handout. A conference presentation is not like a dissertation oral defense: audience members want to get a general idea of your hypotheses, methods, and findings, not an exhaustive account of the details. Also, as any teacher knows, audiences will tend to focus on and read anything they have in their hands rather than listen to what a speaker is saying. I think this reflects the fact that for most people it is much easier to process complex information visually rather than orally. Be aware that audience members may well become glued to your handout if you pass one out.

Relax. Do whatever you can to relax while presenting. For many, this is the hardest task of all. Most people are anxious about speaking in front of an audience. When I first began attending conferences, I thought that experienced presenters didn't get anxious about presenting, because they always looked cool and composed up at the podium. But when I began presenting at conferences, I was surprised to discover that at close range (at the presenter's table), one can detect signs of anxiety in even the most experienced presenters. Somehow, it was a comfort to me as a beginner to observe even the biggest of the "big shots" perspiring profusely and trembling before and during presentations. It may be discouraging to think that you will never be free of anxiety while presenting, but you can still aspire to look cool and composed to the audience. While this may seem like a trivial distinction, I think it's actually quite important. One can easily focus on the content and ideas of a presenter who appears relaxed, but signs of anxiety are terribly distracting. I can recall many, many presentations where the presenter's visible anxiety began to make the audience feel anxious. Also, as described above, anxiety frequently has a very detrimental effect on the pace and tone of a presentation.

One way to become more at ease is to practice until you know the presentation inside out. If you have any experience with relaxation or meditation techniques, this may be a good time to use them. Oddly enough, the more relaxed you look, the more polished your presentation will appear.

Since you are unlikely to ever be free from anxiety while presenting, you might try using your anxiety to your advantage. Experienced speakers do not view their nervousness as an impediment, but as a sign that they are getting the shot of adrenaline they need to make their talk dynamic. In this way your anxiety can be used to lend energy and intensity to your voice and your presentation. Expressing your ideas with high energy in your talk will actually help keep your audience interested.

Conclusion

These suggestions should help you prepare for a conference presentation so that you can approach the talk with confidence. Your first few talks will probably not be flawless, though, so try to convince yourself that a less-than-perfect presentation will not be the end of the world. It may be some comfort to know that even the very best presenters have given talks that didn't go well. What's important is that you take the time and make the effort beforehand to prepare your presentation. Most audience members are extremely sympathetic to presenters who come prepared and make an honest effort to present clearly.

11

Writing and Submitting Manuscripts for Publication

Bonnie L. Green

The preceding chapters have dealt primarily with the development and conduct of research in the area of traumatic stress. The previous chapter by Dr. Carlson has addressed how to submit an abstract to a conference and present a paper. The final stage of any research project—disseminating it more widely via publication in a professional journal—is the topic of the current chapter. I will address this phase by first discussing the elements of a good journal article. This discussion is based on publication guidelines from the American Psychological Association. Then, I will suggest a number of considerations to keep in mind when choosing a journal to which to submit your manuscript. Finally, I will go over the review process that your paper is likely to undergo when you submit it for publication, using the *Journal of Traumatic Stress* as an example. I will describe how the reviews are conducted at the *Journal of Traumatic Stress* (*JTS*), and on what basis various editorial decisions are made.

Elements of a Good Paper

No matter how good your research study is with regard to its planning and execution, it is of little use to others unless your thinking about it, and your methodology, can be appropriately communicated to your reader. An article describing your study will not be accepted for publication unless it is well-written, clear, and seen to make a significant contribution to the literature. While there are real differences between studies with regard to their potential contribution, reviewers' perceptions about the value of your study are also dependent upon your ability to conceptualize it and to understand and communicate its significance. Thus, the write-up is extremely important. And if you are like me, you may ultimately understand how all of the elements of the study and its findings fit together and make a contribution only through the process of writing a manuscript for publication. Some researchers find this process to be extremely frustrating and painful, while others find it stimulating and challenging. Whichever camp you fall into, however, there are certain elements that need to be addressed in any paper, and I will briefly review these. In my review, I rely heavily on the *Publication Manual of the American Psychological Association* (4th ed.) (1994), and I strongly recommend that you consult that source as you prepare your manuscript. The manual includes chapters on organizing a paper, what each section should look like, expression and presentation of ideas, guidelines for reducing linguistic bias, how to decide about authorship of articles, ethical issues with human subjects, and many other issues related to the conduct and reporting of research. It is an excellent resource.

Journal Instructions and Transmission

An important and fairly easy general guideline for submitting a paper to a particular journal is to follow that journal's directions for manuscript preparation and submission. Every journal has in each issue a page or section entitled "Instructions to Contributors." You need to look over this section carefully and be sure that you are submitting the paper in the style of that journal. If you do not follow its style, the editor may simply send it back and say, "It is not in our style; do it over." At the very least, you will have to revise the article to their specific style for publication, and having it in the journal's style creates a more positive impression with the editor and the reviewers. Guidelines include length restrictions, typing instructions, number of copies that need to be submitted, etc. They also usually include a statement of the types of articles that the journal publishes, so you will know whether your manuscript is appropriate to that journal.

I also encourage you to write a letter accompanying your manuscript. The letter should say something like, "My co-authors and I are submitting the enclosed paper, entitled 'XYZ,' to be considered for publication in Such and So Journal." Be certain to include your name, address, phone number and fax, electronic ("e-mail") address, and alternative addresses and numbers if you will be unable to be reached over the next six months at the original location. It is important that the editorial office be able to contact you. The title page should also include this information for the corresponding author. If the journal practices blind review, the only identifying information should be on the title page and/or in the author notes. Some journals require a transmittal letter, in some cases stating that the article is not submitted elsewhere, and/or that copyright is transferred if the article is accepted. *JTS* deals with copyright only after the article has been accepted; however, it is a good idea to state that it has not been published elsewhere. If you have published other articles based on the same study, and it is not completely obvious from the manuscript how they differ, you should write a section in the transmittal letter explaining the differences. In this way, the editor will be able to determine whether the new manuscript is sufficiently different from past papers to warrant publication.

Abstract

The most important thing to remember about an abstract is that it may be the only thing that most readers are going to know about your research. They will flip through the journal and read the abstracts, and unless your research is specifically in their area, or something that really catches their imagination when they read the abstract, they will not read the article, and your abstract will be the only communication of your work. This also may happen when people learn about articles from indexing sources. All they may see is the abstract, and they may refer to the paper from the abstract alone. Or they may decide whether to obtain a copy of the entire article based on the abstract. Thus, while writers often write their abstracts as an afterthought, I think it is important to remember that the abstract is all that most people will see. For this reason, abstracts need to be complete, describing all important aspects of a study, concise, and comprehensible to an audience who may not be familiar with particular instruments or statistical procedures. Abstracts should include your conclusions and the usefulness of the information. It is very challenging to accomplish this in the limited number of words allotted, but it is worth the trouble.

The APA *Publication Manual* limits abstracts to 120 words and most journals have a similar length limit. If abstracts are more that 120 words, the abstracting services will reduce them to this length. If your abstract is no more than 120 words, then your original abstract will be the one used by the abstracting services and you won't have to worry about others shortening your abstract in ways that reduce its clarity and effectiveness.

Introduction

It is easier to specify the important elements of an empirical study in detail than it is to specify the important elements of a theoretical or conceptual paper, so I will review these first. With regard to an introduction, you need to define the nature of the problem. You have conducted the study because there was something the field needed to know that the study was designed to assess. Thus, the introduction needs to 1) introduce the problem, 2) clearly state the goals and hypotheses of the study and the rationale for doing it at this particular time, and 3) cover the background and the specific literature related to your question. Avoid very general statements about the area that have myriad references associated with them but do not really home in on the literature that provides the background for your study question. Be clear about why you are doing this study and why you are doing it now, as well as how it fits into the overall flow of information in this particular area. As with all aspects of a paper, it needs to be clear and easily readable.

Method

It is important to remember the purposes of the method section. I believe there are two major ones: First, someone should be able to replicate your study precisely based on what you tell them and this requires complete information. The second purpose is to allow first the reviewers, and later the other readers, to evaluate the rigor of your methods and the validity of your conclusions. This assessment is based in part on the extent to which you have a reasonable and appropriate design. However, that can't be determined unless you supply all of the important details, which include 1) your recruitment of participants, i.e., how you identified potential participants, whether you advertised the study, whether you paid people for their participation, etc.; 2) a complete description of your final sample, including information about age, gender, how they differed from non-participants, and any other relevant characteristics; 3) a clear and careful description of the instruments used; and 4) the procedures used for the study.

The detail needed to describe instruments depends to some degree on the familiarity of the readers of the particular journal with the measures. For example, the readers of *JTS* would likely need less information about the Impact of Event Scale than they would need about the Rorschach. The information provided also depends to some extent upon the availability of the references to the instrument in the literature. The more familiar the instrument to the audience, and the more available the information from other sources, the less description is needed in the article. Conversely, if you are using a new instrument, particularly one that you are developing, a great deal of information needs to be provided. Unless the instrument is extremely familiar to the journal audience, some reliability and validity data should be provided. And you always need to describe the content of scales that will be reported on and discussed. These suggestions mean that if you rewrite the article for another journal, you must reassess the method section to see which descriptions could be reduced and which might need to be expanded. Also, remember that it is important to avoid jargon. Use only terms that would be familiar to all of the readers of the journal or explain your use of specific terms.

The procedure needs to be spelled out clearly and succinctly: specifically, what did you tell participants about the nature of the study? what were any specific instructions for instruments? were participants debriefed? what was the time frame for data collection (including timing in relation to any target events)?

Any information about piloting of the instruments or study procedures should also be covered in the method section. Preliminary analyses related to instruments are usually included in this section, while data reduction analyses might be more appropriate for the beginning of the results section. Reviewers and editors may vary with regard to where they believe preliminary analyses fit best, but they should always be included.

Results

It is very important to proceed in an orderly and logical way through the results of your study, from the more general to the more specific. This includes an overview of your sample(s) (i.e., how do your samples compare to other clinical and non-clinical samples on the same instruments?). This requires means and standard deviations or ranges for all of the main study instruments. Readers need to have a sense about whether your group is in the normal range or in the impaired range, and so on.

Appropriate and efficient use of tables includes having neither too many nor too few. Sometimes we get articles which include 10 or 12 tables and most of them really aren't necessary. You don't need a table if you can easily and concisely summarize the information in the text. You need tables for more complex information—information that people need to make reference to as they go through your results section. Be certain to refer to your tables by number in the text, and avoid redundancy between the tables and the text. Tables should be carefully titled, clearly labeled, and easily interpreted without the text.

Most editors urge writers to minimize figures as well. There are certain things that are much easier to see in a figure, for example, certain interactions or longitudinal data. However, group-related means or proportions look more, or less, different on a figure depending on how much you spread out your y axis, so they may not be particularly informative. Certainly you do not need tables and figures for the same information.

In the text, be certain to report values for all inferential statistics, including the magnitude or value, the degrees of freedom and the significance level. The possible exception to this is non-significant findings, and editors and journals differ in this regard. Some require all statistics to be reported, even if they are nonsignificant. I personally find that confusing and like to see only significant statistical results reported. As long as the actual data are reported (e.g., means and standard deviations, correlations, etc.), the reader can judge whether your lack of findings is a result of lack of power or whether there really was nothing going on. If a test statistic is not significant, the writer should just state that the groups were not significantly different or that the two variables were not significantly related.

Another important thing to remember is to summarize what you found, particularly if you have complex findings. Your audience varies in its knowledge of statistics. Even for those who are quite knowledgeable, important points may be difficult to take in with a complicated data set, so it is important to highlight the main findings. This can be done at the end of the results section or along the way, depending upon the complexity of your analyses. Also, be sure to use the same terms for your variables throughout the paper. While this seems obvious, it is not always done. Using consistent terms makes the paper much easier to read and follow.

Discussion

The important elements of a discussion section include whether or not you found what you were looking for (were your hypotheses supported?) and how your findings fit with, and contribute to, the existing empirical literature (do your findings coincide with what other investigators are finding, or are they different?). This is more difficult if your findings are in a new area, but you need to relate your data to other studies to the extent possible. This may take some creativity and breadth if you are entering a new area and your study is more exploratory.

How do your findings fit with your conceptualization of your work? You may not have a theory per se that you are using, but you certainly have an overview of how you are thinking about your work and how your findings fit in with your and others' conceptualizations. This includes relationships among variables, levels of variables, nature and direction of changes, etc. You need to help the reader make sense of your findings. If you have findings that are unexpected in some way, you need to try to explain those, but be sure to minimize pure speculation.

This entails carefully thinking and sorting through the likely possibilities (but not pages and pages of "it could be this, it could be that," etc.). Don't ramble! State everything as clearly and concisely as possible.

It is important to be clear about the strengths and weaknesses of your study. Think of the reviewers (and the readers) of the article in this regard. They will know what the weaknesses are. If you are not clear about this as well, it will appear as if you don't understand these problems, or that you are trying to cover them up. Even a study that has significant problems associated with it can sometimes make a contribution, depending on how well and thoughtfully it is put forward, and how clear the authors are about the extent to which their findings will generalize, or not generalize, to other settings, or under what circumstances their findings might apply. Mention the strengths of the study as well; however, be sure not to overdo it. Use a neutral, non-aggrandizing tone throughout the paper. In our field, it is rare for an article to be the definitive study, but authors sometimes claim to have answered a question once and for all, which does not go over very well with reviewers (or editors!). Be clear about what your findings mean. You have to answer the "So what?" question. Why should your reader be interested in what you found? What are the implications for clinical practice? This is particularly important if you are submitting your work to a journal like *JTS* whose readership is predominantly clinicians. What are the implications for future research?

If you want a great model for writing up a research study, look at any article by Fran Norris. She does very complex studies with complex analyses but she walks the reader carefully through what the problem is, why she is studying it, and how she is studying it. She summarizes the complex findings as she goes along. She then discusses the strengths and weaknesses of her study, its contributions, and the implications for clinical practice. Her work is an excellent model to follow.

References
Find out the referencing style of the journal to which you are submitting and use it precisely. References should be used judiciously. At this point, almost all journals restrict the number of pages or words for articles, and you do not need to refer to every study that has anything to

do with your paper. Sometimes you can just use examples, particularly when you are making general points.

Appendices

These are usually discouraged but sometimes are appropriate for brief material that is new. Again, please look at the American Psychological Association guidelines. They have some very good suggestions.

General Guidelines

As noted earlier, it is more difficult to specify the important elements of a conceptual paper. Conceptual/theoretical papers, as well as review papers, are more difficult to write because there is no formula (introduction, method, results, discussion) to follow, so the organization has to come from the writer. This is challenging, but needs to be seen as an important aspect of what makes the paper useful. It must be well-organized and coherent, as well as clear and readable. Even if the paper has an excellent idea or contribution, and the reviewers think that there might be something there, it is not likely to be accepted if it is not clear and well organized. Unless it is well-written it will not be useful to the readers. Obviously, the paper must make an original contribution, even if this is primarily a new way of looking at old information.

There are a number of points that apply to both empirical and theoretical or review articles. One of these is avoiding gender bias and ethnic bias. The APA *Publication Manual* has an excellent section on this issue. Another somewhat common problem is the use of language that sounds political rather than scientific. This mistake undermines everything in the article and is a real turn-off for reviewers. You also need to remember that writing an article for a journal is very different from writing a dissertation or thesis or from doing a presentation. Dissertations and theses are much longer, and include much more explanation of why you did everything you did. Articles are much more condensed. A "cut and pasted" thesis or dissertation almost never makes a good article. You have to develop a different mindset. There is obviously useful information in a thesis, but writing an article for publication really requires starting over. Similarly, presentations tend to be more informal, so the language used is often inappropriate for a publication.

Also, in presentations, there is usually less need to go into all of the specific details of the design and results. People are more open to "taking your word for it" because you are trying to get across some basic information in a limited time frame.

Another general point involves knowing your audience, that is, who are the readers of your targeted journal? This determines to what extent you may need to elaborate on a point. If you are submitting an article to *JTS*, for example, you don't need two pages about the diagnosis of PTSD. You can assume that readers are familiar with the diagnosis. But if you are writing for a more general journal where the readers may not be that familiar with PTSD, you may need a paragraph explaining the diagnosis.

Always get someone else to read the paper and make editorial suggestions. If this is one of your first papers, and even if it is not, you need to get a colleague to look over it. If the paper is co-authored by individuals who are used to writing articles for publication, their feedback may suffice. If not, ask a colleague with experience at publishing research to read it over and give you honest feedback. If you cannot find such a person who is willing, give it to a colleague who does mental heath work. While everyone may not know all of the statistical procedures, etc., the overall coherence and integrity of the paper, along with its readability, can be evaluated by someone who is not an expert on the topic. Do not write off misunderstanding as a problem with the reader. Reviewers will likely have the same problems. Regardless of the value of the study itself, readability and clarity are extremely important to how the article comes across. No matter how good the research is, if it is not well-communicated, it will not be highly rated.

Choosing a Journal

How do you go about figuring out the journal to which you will submit? Again, you need to ask colleagues for suggestions. You need to think about what audience you are trying to reach, which relates to assessing the level of information in your article. If you are into a new area that relates to general mental health practice, you might want to submit to a journal that is more general. If you are working on, for example, subtle aspects of differential diagnosis within the trauma field, it would make more sense to aim for a journal where the readers are interested in that level of complexity or subtlety. One good way of considering potential journals is, as you gather the literature together for the article that you are writing, to observe where those articles are published. The journals publishing the literature that you are citing are most likely to be interested in the type of work that you are reporting on. You also need to make a realistic appraisal of the contribution of your article relative to other kinds of research going on in the field: What's the quality of your design? What's the scope of your study? While we would all like to be published in the very best and most widely-read journals, it is also very discouraging to be rejected. So you need to find journals that publish articles like yours, since you have a much better chance of getting your articles accepted in such a journal. Of course your article needs to fit the particular journal format, and again, you can find that information in "Instructions to Contributors."

Journal of Traumatic Stress

Since the topic of this book is research in traumatic stress, I think it would be helpful to share some specific information about the *Journal of Traumatic Stress*. This information may help you to decide about the appropriateness of *JTS* for an article that you are writing and will also give you a sense about how articles are reviewed. *JTS* was founded by Charles Figley and is published by Plenum Publishing Corporation in New York. We are in our eighth volume, so it is a relatively new journal. We are indexed by most of the major services, so an article that you write for *JTS* will be picked up, via your designated key words, in all of these indices. They include *Psychological Abstracts, Index Medicus, Current Contents, Health Instrument File, Research Alert,* and *Social Sciences Citation Index*.

In 1993 we received 179 manuscripts. I sent 10 of those back because they obviously were not appropriate for *JTS* for one reason or another, so 169 were reviewed. About one-third of those came from

outside of the United States. Approximately two-thirds were new submissions, with the other one-third being re-submissions of articles that
had been previously reviewed.

The rejection rate for *JTS* in 1993 was about 80%; that is, we accepted (with minor revisions) only about 20% of the articles submitted. I have been doing this for almost three years and I don't think I
have taken an article yet without at least minor revisions. Another
40% were rejected outright, without encouragement to resubmit. The
final 40% comprised the middle group where there was promise of a
potential contribution. These authors were invited to make major revisions to the article and resubmit it. The article was reviewed again
without any guarantee that it would be accepted, although the acceptance rate for revised articles, as you might expect, is much higher than
for new articles. The decision rate was similar in and out of the United
States.

The editorial board for the *Journal of Traumatic Stress* in 1994 consisted of 45 members, most of whom are members of ISTSS. I try to
balance this board particularly by their topical expertise but also by
gender, discipline, and geographic region. We use an additional 150
people who are not on the editorial board as ad hoc reviewers, and
these people are acknowledged once a year in the fourth issue of the
volume. So there are many people reviewing manuscripts for *JTS*, as
there are for any journal.

Our formats include regular articles (empirical, theoretical, reviews)
of 30 double-spaced manuscript pages or less, brief reports (cases, program descriptions, preliminary data in new areas or on a new measure,
replications) of 10 pages or less, and commentaries (which are usually
responses to earlier articles, but may also be brief essays) of four pages
or less. Our commentaries are reviewed, and if they are accepted, with
or without revisions, the original author gets a chance to reply to them.
Finally, we publish media reviews (books and tapes), which are so-
licited by our book review editor.

The review process is blind, so the reviewers technically cannot identify the author. However, it is sometimes possible to figure it out from
the manuscript, especially if authors write, "In our previous studies
(Jones, Jones, and Jones)." It's up to the author to blind the manuscript

internally, but we take all external identification off of the manuscript. If the author's name is on every page, we return the manuscript.

I assign three reviewers to almost every manuscript. I rarely make a decision with fewer than two reviewers. We try hard to get three reviews, particularly if there is disagreement regarding recommendations. If papers are reviewed again following revisions, I try to have them reviewed by a subset (usually two) of the original reviewers. Occasionally, I will add a fourth person who is new. However, I try to avoid that unless there is a specific reason, because if a new person gets involved, new issues can come up, and generally I try to focus on the original criticisms. I attempt to put together a group of reviewers who can address different aspects of the article under review. So, for example, an epidemiological study or general population study may be reviewed by a clinician who sees patients with the problems being studied, as well as someone who has done similar studies and is familiar with the sampling, data analysis techniques, and so forth, that apply to that type of study. If it is an article with complex statistics, I would assure that I have someone who could evaluate their use.

When we request an evaluation from reviewers, we send them a letter, our evaluation and author feedback forms, and the manuscript. If it is a revision, they get back the original reviews and my first decision letter, along with the usual forms, so they know specifically what was asked to be done for the revision. The authors are asked to write a cover letter to the revised version stating very specifically how they revised the manuscript, and that letter goes back to the reviewers as well.

We have managed to turn around new manuscripts in approximately four and one-half months. Of course, manuscripts don't come in at a steady rate. They come in sporadically. For example, we receive an influx after the end of the academic year. We try to turn revisions around in two or three months. We ask our reviewers to complete their reviews in a timely fashion by sending them reminders and later calling them (depending on whether they are on the editorial board and how well we know them).

It is important to point out, and this is true for all journals, that the reviewers are advisory to the editor. The reviewers don't vote about whether a manuscript gets accepted or not, so it is possible, for example, that two reviewers think that the manuscript should be accepted and one reviewer thinks that it should be turned down, and it would be turned down. It is also possible to be turned down even if each reviewer recommended some form of revision or acceptance, although that is unusual. The editor is obviously swayed by the reviews, and if he or she chooses the reviewers well, they will be people who are thorough and have opinions that are worth listening to. But the reviewers remain advisory to the editor, and it is ultimately the editor who makes the decision. This is because only the editor has access to all of the potential problems raised by the reviewers; and the editor is in the best position to know what is already in the pipeline of the journal. He or she also knows the full range in the quality of submissions to the journal and so judges the manuscript against all of the other manuscripts submitted.

I write fairly lengthy feedback letters to authors invited to revise and resubmit, specifying exactly what changes need to be made (this is also true for "accepted with revisions"). I write shorter letters for rejection, just trying to give authors an overall sense of the reasons. We also send the specific comments of each of the reviewers to the authors, regardless of the decision. Some editors write something like "Look at the comments of the reviewers and make the revisions accordingly." I attempt to integrate that information for the authors, being clear about what I think is more important and less important. In addition to the decision letter and the reviewer feedback, the author sometimes receives checklists or guidelines to help conform to our style. Occasionally I enclose an article that seems important for the author to include, but to which he or she may not have access.

All of our reviewers receive feedback as well, including a copy of my decision letter and the other reviews. Reviewers seem to like this a great deal, as it helps them to learn to be better reviewers, and to get a sense about the current publication standards of the journal.

Decision Criteria

Accept with Minor Revisions

What are the bases for articles being either accepted, rejected with encouragement to resubmit, or rejected without encouragement to resubmit? A decision to accept with minor revisions indicates that the manuscript just needs fine tuning, possibly including cutting it down. If it is a 40-page manuscript, and it needs to be reduced to 30 pages, I may give the authors a lot of leeway about how to do this, although I usually try to give suggestions. The reviewers have often made such suggestions as well. But, basically, a manuscript accepted with minor revisions has the elements of a good paper described above. It may need a little more of this, and a little less of that, or a little better organization, style changes, or elimination of jargon. It must also seem clear that the authors are capable of accomplishing these changes. The editor reviews the revisions, but the paper is not sent out again to reviewers.

Reject with Encouragement to Resubmit

A decision to reject with encouragement to resubmit, on the other hand, is made for manuscripts that need more of a major overhaul. It still has to be a basically solid study, with a reasonable design and no fatal flaws, and it needs to be a potential contribution to the field. There are many reasons why people are asked to revise articles, including writing style. Sometimes we ask people to do more analyses. Sometimes they have just missed important aspects of the literature that they need to not just cite, but to integrate into their thinking. The authors may not have put their findings in sufficient context, or they may not have discussed their findings well enough. Authors may not have acknowledged or been clear enough about the problems with their study. However, authors will not be invited to resubmit unless the editor feels relatively certain that the authors are capable of making the revisions required.

Resubmit as a Brief Report

Sometimes authors are asked to resubmit a paper as a Brief Report. We get a number of articles that have data that probably would be of interest to our readers but they are not quite worth a full-length article because their findings are more preliminary or make only a modest contribution. Studies that are preliminary, or those that are essentially replications, would fall into these categories. This is sometimes a difficult task for people, cutting a full-length article into a brief report. But often it results in a better article, since it is more succinct and the appropriate length for what is reported. Of course Brief Reports is one of our formats, so a number of articles are submitted initially as Brief Reports.

Rejected without Encouragement to Resubmit

Finally, some articles are rejected without encouragement to resubmit. Occasionally, I send articles back unreviewed since I judge them to be inappropriate for *JTS*. Even some really excellent articles are rejected for this reason, although I may not always catch them ahead of time. Other reasons for rejection are that the study has a fatal flaw; for example, the confounding of primary study variables, making it impossible to interpret the results. Studies are rejected for poor design, poor rationale, little or poor discussion or interpretation, occasionally because of ethical concerns, and often for not being seen as making a significant contribution to the traumatic stress field. Some articles are rejected because the editor and/or reviewers do not feel that the author is capable of making the needed changes. I sometimes have reviewers who seem to be thinking "Boy! If this were written up better, it would be a really interesting study," and so recommend resubmission. Indeed, that reviewer might be able to write a great paper from that study, but the authors may not be able to do this. I do not like to ask people to do a revision unless they have a good shot at having their revision accepted or accepted with just a few more revisions. So even if there is potential, but the editor feels that the authors are not going to be able to turn it into an acceptable manuscript, then he or she (or I) will not encourage a resubmission.

Conclusion

Hopefully these suggestions and descriptions will be helpful to you as you write up your research for publication. There are many professional journals, so you have a good chance of finding an appropriate outlet for your work if you evaluate the contribution realistically and write up the study well. This is reason to approach the task optimistically. Keep your audience in mind as well as how reviewers and editors might view what you write. Be sure to have someone else, more than one person if possible, review your first few articles before they are submitted. This is the best time to correct them. Even those of us with a great deal of publishing experience need to review these points, and still benefit greatly from having colleagues go over our work.

Good luck and happy publishing!

Reference

American Psychological Association (1994). *Publication manual of the American Psychological Association* (4th ed.). Washington, D.C.: Author.

12

Writing a Grant Proposal

Malcolm Gordon

In developing a trauma research program, there comes a time when a researcher needs support for larger scale or more complex research than can be accomplished with a small or no research budget. This chapter briefly discusses sources of funding for research. The rest of the chapter explains the National Institute of Mental Health (NIMH) grant review process and provides detailed advice about how to develop a competitive research grant application for trauma research.

Sources of Research Support

There are four primary sources for support of research: (1) universities and research organization funds, (2) professional and civic organizations, (3) foundations, and (4) government agencies. Each of these sources of funding has a role in research support.

Universities and Research Organizations

Universities or research organizations may provide relatively limited in-house research funds for smaller scale studies. Often the intent of this type of funding is to allow you to collect pilot data that can be used in grant applications to outside sources. Usually such funding is only sufficient to support a very small research project.

Professional and Civic Organizations

Professional organizations of psychologists, social workers, or mental health professionals may have programs that award limited amounts of research funds for small scale projects. Often such funds are awarded competitively to organization members or new investigators. Some civic organizations may support research projects in areas that are of particular relevance to the organization's civic or charitable activities. They also may provide volunteer help in fund-raising or provide other supportive services. For example, I know of one instance in which a state women's service organization provided volunteers to be trained by an investigator as data collectors in a statewide study of abused children.

Foundations

A significant source of funding is provided by foundations. A major difficulty in obtaining foundation support for a research project is locating those foundations among the many thousands of foundations that have an interest in funding a particular research project. It is often difficult to identify a foundation that will fund research in the area that an investigator is proposing to investigate. Many foundations do not support research projects, but fund only direct service projects or provide donations to arts or civic organizations.

There are three primary types of foundations: (1) foundations established by individuals or families that fund in certain substantive areas of interest (e.g., research on particular diseases or other health or social issues); (2) local or regional foundations that offer grant support in a certain geographical area, often to civic or social service organizations, and (3) corporate foundations, which often fund interests of their employees (e.g., scholarships), but may fund activities related to interests of their customers (e.g., a toy company foundation funding child related activities) or fund civic or service activities in their plants or business locations.

There are two main ways to locate foundations that support research in the area of trauma. (1) Search reference works on foundation funding published by The Foundation Center. The Foundation Center is a clearinghouse on foundation information that annually publishes reference volumes listing types of foundation giving, including research grants. Many of these publications are by topical area (e.g., publications on foundation support for children's or women's issues). These publications often provide information on application procedures to individual foundations. The Foundation Center is headquartered in New York City, but has branches in other cities and a network of resource libraries in most areas of the country, so these references are readily available. (2) Review journal articles in the research area in which funding is sought for citations of foundation support. Such citations will identify foundations that are likely to support research and that may have a priority of funding in the area in which the researcher is conducting studies.

If you are seeking foundation support for a research project, you should be prepared to contact a large number of foundations to locate the one or a few foundations that might express an interest in funding your particular research project. In seeking foundation support, it is usually helpful to directly contact a program officer at the foundation to inquire about a foundation's interest in supporting the particular research project. Some foundations require an initial letter of inquiry and then submission of a grant application only if they express an interest in the topic outlined in the initial letter.

There are two major advantages of foundation support. (1) In general, foundations do not require a lengthy, detailed description of the research plan. The application may be just a brief statement of the research goals and methodology. Many foundations do not use a peer review system, but will fund projects that interest their board of directors. (2) The turnaround time from submission of an application until funding by foundations may be relatively brief, allowing you to begin a study fairly soon after applying.

Some disadvantages of foundation support are: (1) It may be difficult to locate a foundation that is interested in the particular research topic proposed. A great deal of time may be spent locating foundations willing to support a particular research project. (2) Foundations usually provide only a small amount of money for any research project, typically under $20,000; they usually do not pay indirect support to your institution; and they may be reluctant to provide support for a multiple-year research project. Foundations typically want their own staff or consultants to control or collaborate on larger-scale research studies that they may support. Many researchers who rely on foundation support find it necessary to stitch together support from more than one foundation in order to fund larger research projects. Researchers also may seek to develop a continuing interest in their research among foundation staff, which may lead to funding of additional related research projects in the future.

Government Agencies

Governmental units can support larger scale research projects for longer periods than other funding sources. With some exceptions, local and state governments primarily fund direct service delivery programs and do not fund much research. Some agencies in the more populous states do fund research projects, but often such funding is in the form of a contract rather than a grant. The governmental unit funding the contract will usually specify the scope of work to be conducted. Some state and local governmental agencies will also fund research and evaluation projects, especially in the area of direct service delivery, using pass-through funds from the Federal government. Such funds usually derive from Federal set-asides for evaluation or research in specific areas of categorical funding. These funds are given to the states to administer and award as part of state block grants.

The Federal government is the largest provider of funds for basic and many areas of applied research. In order to avoid overlap, there are usually just a few Federal agencies that fund research in any particular area and, when more than one agency funds research in an area, each agency is often more likely to support research that emphasizes the agency's primary area of responsibility. For example, the NIMH and the National Institute of Justice both fund research on domestic violence, but NIMH tends to focus more on research on the mental health consequences or on prevention and treatment of abusers and victims, whereas NIJ will more likely focus on police and judicial system response to domestic violence.

Federal agencies announce funding availability in two ways. Some agencies (e.g., NIJ, The Centers for Disease Control and Prevention, and the National Center on Child Abuse and Neglect) publish annual or periodical announcements of research funding priorities in such publications as the *Federal Register*. Most such agencies keep mailing lists for their research funding announcements and will mail them to researchers on their mailing list so they don't have to continually monitor Federal publications for research announcements. You should contact such agencies to be placed on their mailing list. Other agencies (e.g., the NIH institutes) have standing program announcements, which identify substantive research areas in which they provide research support. Often such programs fund "investigator initiated" research (i.e., a research idea that is developed by the researcher rather than specified by the funding agency). These agencies usually have a standardized application form, such as the Public Health Service Form 398 (PHS 398) for Department of Health and Human Services Public Health agencies, and one or more fixed deadlines during the year for submission of grant applications, and they often use a standing peer review system. In a peer review system, the quality of the proposed research is evaluated by research experts who are usually not Federal employees. The evaluation of the application by these outside experts plays a major determining role in the awarding of a research grant. It is highly advisable to contact program officials in the Federal agency to which you would like to apply for funding. Such officials can provide you with further information on funding availability and recent changes in application requirements. Some programs may provide technical assistance to applicants that may be useful in developing a more competitive grant application.

The disadvantages of Federal funding are: (1) there is usually a great deal of competition for Federal research funds, such that most agencies fund only a relatively small proportion of the applications submitted to them; (2) application forms usually require a detailed statement of the research goals and study design such that the time and energy required to develop an application is quite substantial; and (3) the application process from submission to funding may be quite lengthy. Nevertheless, Federal agencies are often the only source of funding for larger scale and multi-year research projects in a substantive area.

While each of these funding sources has its own procedures and requirements for applying for research support, in the remainder of this paper I will discuss the procedures and requirements for applying for funding support from one federal program, the NIMH, which is one of the prime funders of behavioral research on the prevalence, characteristics, course, consequences, treatment, and prevention of traumatic events and their mental health impact.

The NIMH Grant Review Process

The NIMH is a component of the National Institutes of Health (NIH) in the Department of Health and Human Services Public Health Service. Applications for research support to Public Health Service agencies are submitted using the PHS 398 grant application form. These application forms may be obtained from the office of sponsored research at universities, medical schools, and research organizations or directly from the Office of Grants Information, Division of Research Grants, NIH. Completed research grant applications are initially submitted to a central research grant application processing office, the Division of Research Grants (DRG) of the NIH. Those grant applications having direct *mental health relevance* or proposing to study basic behavioral, psychological, social, or biological processes of relevance to mental health are assigned by DRG to the NIMH. Within NIMH, a submitted grant application is referred both to an appropriate Initial Review Group (IRG), which is responsible for reviewing the application, and to a Program Branch, such as the Violence and Traumatic Stress Research Branch (VTSRB), which is responsible for developing and funding research in a specific area, such as the mental health aspects of traumatic events.

The IRG is composed of reputable scientists working in various mental health-relevant research areas. They review the scientific merits of proposals. Proposals in the substantive areas of victimization, traumatic events, individual violent behavior, and natural and manmade disasters are usually referred to the Violence and Traumatic Stress Research Review Committee. Members of the review group are nominated and the review sessions are run by a Scientific Review Administrator from the NIMH Division of Extramural Activities. Staff from NIMH programs that fund research cannot participate actively in the deliberations of the review committee, but usually try to attend, as observers, reviews of grant applications assigned to their program.

Review committees assign numerical scores to applications based on a set of descriptors of the scientific merit of the application. The impression that a proposal makes on the research experts composing the committee (as reflected in their numerical rating) is the most important factor in determining whether an NIMH grant proposal will be funded. The evaluation of an application is communicated to the applicant in the form of a written "Summary Statement," which consists of a brief summary of the committee's discussion and written critiques of assigned reviewers.

Developing a Grant Application to Submit to NIMH

In general an NIMH review committee will consider three aspects of the proposed research: its *importance* (e.g., Is it worthwhile studying what the proposal plans to study? Will the field learn anything of value from the study? Will this study advance methodology or conceptualization in the field?); its *feasibility* (e.g., Is it likely that the researcher can accomplish the proposed research? Does the researcher have the necessary expertise and prior experience to accomplish the work? Will the researcher be able to recruit enough subjects?); and its *technical merits* (e.g., Is the researcher using the best measures available? Is the proposed data analysis technically sound and does the researcher have the expertise to perform the analysis? Has the researcher incorporated the important previous research in the area into the design, conceptualization, and analysis of the research?).

Proposals that are not rated highly usually have such problems as (a) having a "fatal flaw" (i.e., an error in design or a feasibility problem such that it is unlikely that the researcher would be able to draw valid conclusions from the data), (b) failing to adequately describe important aspects of the research (i.e., not enough detail is provided on the measurement of variables, the way data will be analyzed, or the conceptual framework or rationale guiding the research for reviewers to gauge the potential quality of the results), (c) providing an inadequate rationale for aspects of the research (e.g., inadequate development of a rationale for the relationship between hypothetical constructs, between constructs and measured variables, or for the choice of a particular measurement instrument), (d) having a serious human subjects concern, or (e) proposing research that is technically sound but not of great significance or not likely to significantly advance the particular field of research.

The PHS 398 grant application form has a face page, abstract, budget section, key personnel biographical sketches, research plan, and appendices. The research plan section has five main subsections: specific aims, background and significance, progress report/preliminary studies, research design and methods, and human subjects. In writing a grant application using this form, you should strive to accomplish certain expository goals in each section. Thus, in the budget section, you should clearly specify and justify a research budget adequate to accomplish the goals of the research. Similarly, in the biographical sketch section, you should document your research experience and publication record to indicate that you have the background and experience to conduct the proposed study. When reviewers evaluate each of these sections, they have in mind a set of evaluative criteria. Many of these criteria arise from good methodological practice in research, others arise from the social history of the review committee (namely, methodological or conceptual criteria that have developed from prior reviews of applications in a subject matter area), and other criteria are peculiar to individual reviewers. How to develop these sections of the application and the criteria reviewers use to evaluate these sections will be the topic of the remainder of this chapter.

How to Develop the Budget

Reviewers assess the project budget separately from the evaluation of the scientific merit of the proposed research. Nevertheless, questions about the budget can influence the evaluation of the overall merits of the proposal.

For most applied behavioral research, approximately 70%–80% of the budget will be personnel costs; therefore, estimating and justifying the number of staff positions and the amount of time for each position is the primary task in developing a budget. The budget will be examined by reviewers to determine if it is reasonable for the scope of work proposed; this is often evaluated on the basis of whether the cost per participant or cost per task is reasonable.

You can estimate the number of staff positions required to conduct the research by developing a flow chart for the various tasks in the research, especially the recruitment and assessment of the research subjects. Other research tasks include time for staff training, data entry and coding, and coding reliability checks. When a project involves a large number of staff positions, it is especially important to justify each staff position by some indication of what activities each staff member will engage in and an indication of how much time such activities will require (e.g., "research assistant X will conduct an assessment with each of 100 subjects @ four hours per assessment and, in addition, he/she will ..."). Estimating number of staff positions and time per position will be more accurate if rates of subject recruitment, amount of time to completely assess all subjects in the study, time to locate previously recruited subjects in longitudinal research, and time to accomplish all proposed data analysis tasks are realistically estimated. Often a small pilot study in which subjects are recruited and assessed with the full research battery can both aid in the estimation of the time and resources needed to complete the research and convince reviewers that the research can be accomplished in the time period and with the resources proposed. It is also important that the budget timeline of the study be clear and reasonable in terms of subject processing and research tasks. For example, a review committee may wonder why a study requires three years to recruit and test 60 subjects or takes two years to analyze the data collected.

Often researchers who are submitting their first application skimp on their budget estimates on the (faulty) assumption that the more economical the research, the more likely it will be funded. Although an exorbitant budget can create a negative impression on a reviewer, it is just as likely that an overly frugal budget can raise questions about the feasibility of the project such as: Do the researchers really understand how much it is going to cost to get this kind of data? One common error in underbudgeting is failure to allocate staff time or resources to an important research task which is overlooked in developing a budget. For example, if the project involves longitudinal data collection and all staff time is computed on the basis of assessing subjects and no resources are allocated to tracking and contacting subjects, reviewers are likely to think that the project will not have sufficient resources to manage subject attrition (which is a major problem in longitudinal research) over the course of the project.

Other categories of expenses also must be carefully estimated. Often the office of sponsored research at the applicant institution or knowledgeable colleagues who have conducted similar studies can aid in estimating such expenses as secretarial and office expenses, rent, and subject recruitment expenses. Other important budget categories are described below.

Participant fees. Such fees can often help in recruiting participants and in decreasing dropout rates, especially in longitudinal studies. With difficult-to-recruit participants, the amount of the participant payment should be set high enough to serve these functions, but not so high as to appear to be economically coercive to low-income participants. Participant fees must be paid for any participation in the research (i.e., participation fees may not be paid only to participants who complete the entire research protocol).

Consulting fees. Allocating funds for subject matter and methodological experts is often a relatively cost-efficient means for bolstering both the expertise of the project staff and the feasibility of the project.

Costs associated with participant tracking or record searches. To collect longitudinal data or data from official records it will often be beneficial either to add additional staff solely for this purpose or to include funds in the budget for procedures (e.g., periodic call backs) to maintain contact with participants or to extract data from records (e.g., subcontract with agency personnel).

Subcontracts. Subcontracts can be used to help overcome feasibility problems. For example, one might subcontract to a survey research firm to collect survey data or to a service delivery agency because it has access to subjects who would be difficult to recruit.

How to Write the Biographical Sketch

The purpose of the biographical sketch is to assure the reviewers that the Principal Investigator(s) will be able to successfully conduct and complete the project as proposed. Reviewers examine the listed experience and publications of the Principal Investigator(s) for evidence that he or she is productive and has the experience and expertise to conduct research in the proposed area. In this regard, research publications *in the proposed area of research* in major, peer-reviewed journals are considered by reviewers to be the primary indicator of the investigator's qualifications and count much more heavily than do publications in minor journals, talks and presentations, and nonresearch papers. If you do not have such publication credits, it might improve your chances of approval to conduct at least some pilot research in the proposed area, which you can report in detail in the "Preliminary Studies" section, to demonstrate your research competence in this area. If you are proposing to conduct research in a field unrelated to your own area of research expertise or if you are using a type of methodology you haven't used before (e.g., you have conducted basic research and now propose to develop and/or evaluate an intervention program), you should attempt to collaborate with an individual or team who does have considerable experience in the related field or with the particular research methodology.

How To Develop the Research Plan

Specific Aims. The aims of the research are the goals that the research is seeking to accomplish. Your stated aims should make clear the reasons why the research is being conducted. The aims of the research usually fall into the categories of (a) developing knowledge (e.g., "to understand the individual, familial, and social factors that determine the impact of sexual abuse on children"), (b) filling gaps in knowledge (e.g., "although many emergency workers do not experience burnout, we do not know what factors determine their resistance to burning out"), (c) to test an established or proposed model or theory of a phenomenon (e.g., "the study will test the learned helplessness theory in a sample of women who return to a battering relationship") or (d) to test interventions or factors that are relevant to clinical intervention (e.g., "the study will assess cognitions concerning use of physical force in sexual relationships among early adolescents because such cognitions may be relevant to early interventions").

The aims of the research should be *clearly* stated. In general, no single research study can hope to completely accomplish the larger scientific aims, but the review committee will assume that you are intending to contribute to the accomplishment of the stated goals of the study and will judge the adequacy of the conceptual framework, the research design, and the data analysis to accomplish these aims, at least in part. Material not directly relevant to the statement of the aims of the research should be placed in other sections of the applications, (e.g., background justification and references in the literature review section). Reviewers will also assess whether, in their opinion, the stated aims of the research are important enough to justify supporting the research.

Background and Significance. The primary purpose of the Background and Significance section is to provide a justification for the importance of the research and to develop the theoretical framework that guides the research.

Reviewers prefer research in areas that are clearly of great significance to mental health and that are *theoretically driven.* This means that the selection of variables to measure, the sampling plan, the research design, the data collection procedures, the research hypotheses, and the data analysis plan should be based on a set of theoretical constructs and their interrelationships. You should use the Background and Significance section primarily to document the mental health importance of the research and to develop the conceptual framework of the study.

Importance of the Proposed Research. You should explain the importance to the research field of the proposed research and its *mental health relevance.* Also, in the review of previous research in the field, you need to present an adequate rationale for the mental health significance and for the particular conceptualization guiding the research. A proposal may not receive a very favorable review if reviewers feel that the fundamental question underlying the study is not very important or interesting. Therefore, you should emphasize the importance of the proposed research both in terms of its implications for filling gaps in and advancing the research and theory construction in the research field and implications for public mental health in general or for specific population subgroups.

Development of a Conceptual Framework. Development of a conceptual framework requires the selection and specification of a set of key constructs and hypothesizing of a set of relationships among these constructs.

SPECIFYING CONSTRUCTS. The theoretical framework for the study should include identification of the conceptual domains you are investigating (e.g., the relation between the domain of "family support" and the domain of "responses to trauma in children"). The framework should also identify the *specific* constructs within each domain (e.g., "parental acceptance/rejection" or "parental modeling of coping behavior" within the domain of "family support" or "regressive behavior" or "physical aggressiveness" in the domain of "response to trauma in childhood"). Pay particular attention to the conceptualization and operational definition of the most important specific constructs in each of the conceptual domains. This is especially true of constructs that encompass categories of individuals, behavior, or other phenomena with a variety of manifestations or that cover an extensive range on a continuum, (e.g., "abused children," "aggressive behavior," or "self-esteem").

You should cite the important literature in the field that has implications for the definition, differentiation, or subcategorization of broad general constructs (e.g., factor analytic studies of general scales measuring the global construct). Reviewers expect a thoughtful and critical evaluation of the extant research literature; that is, the literature should be more than a summary of what has been reported in other studies. In particular, you must lay an adequate foundation for your conceptual framework and research hypotheses. Your literature review should be oriented toward the *specific* questions or hypotheses with which your research is concerned. One of the common weaknesses of literature reviews in proposals is the inclusion of a survey of the research that is too general and provides no justification for the particular hypotheses or concepts that you put forward (e.g., a general discussion of the outcome literature on child abuse, but no focus on particular studies of increased aggressiveness, when that is your major hypothesized outcome variable). In particular, this discussion must provide adequate justification for the two most important choices relating to conceptual issues made in the research: (a) Why were the particular concepts being focused on chosen? Why are these concepts important (as opposed to other concepts)? and (b) What is the justification, in terms of previous research, pilot research, or a theoretical framework, for specific hypothesized relationships among constructs to be investigated in the research? The review of previous research need not be encyclopedic, but should weigh the evidence for and against the particular theoretical framework or the hypotheses you are proposing. In particular, you should critically evaluate research findings that may be interpreted to contradict your hypotheses or theoretical framework.

A theoretical framework may be viewed as more sophisticated to the extent that constructs are better differentiated and/or better defined operationally than previous research in an area. Many behavioral and psychic constructs have multiple components or multiple manifestations or are multidimensional For example, "depression" is manifested emotionally (e.g., anhedonia, sadness), cognitively (e.g., low sense of self-efficacy, hopelessness), and behaviorally (e.g., low activity level, irritability). It is not usually the case that the various manifestations, components, or dimensions of these complex constructs are perfectly correlated (at one extreme) or are independent (at the other extreme). The specific manifestation or dimensions of multiple component constructs that are included in the research should be specified and operationalized. For example, years ago, research on "abused" children often defined the construct of "abused child" only on the basis of a child being identified by a protective services agency case report. With growing conceptual sophistication, the construct of "abuse" is now often differentiated into different types of abuse (e.g., physical or sexual abuse) or characterized by reported severity of abuse on the basis of narrative account of abusive episodes. "Abused children" are identified with more elaborate confirmatory operationalizations (e.g., independent confirmation by coding of investigative records or interviews with a parent about the types of abusive incident(s)). Furthermore, more evidence than "absence of a protective service agency confirmation" is required to warrant accepting a child as a "nonabused" control.

Operationalization of constructs that represent categorical study populations (e.g., victim or perpetrator groups) can differ considerably in terms of who is included in each category and their characteristics. Your operationalization of constructs that delineate study groups should be consistent with the specific inclusion and exclusion criteria you intend to use in your study. For example, "sexual abuse" can be variously defined with regard to type and severity of sexual acts involved (e.g., contact versus noncontact sexual acts, age difference of victim and perpetrator) and can be identified from various sources (e.g., various levels of confirmation from protective service agencies or from self-reports using questions at varying levels of specificity).

SPECIFYING RELATIONSHIPS AMONG CONSTRUCTS. A conceptual framework includes not only the identification and operationalization of constructs, but also the specification of the important interrelationships among the identified constructs. Behavioral research uses a heterogeneous collection of different types of relationships among constructs, including deterministically causal (i.e., one construct is necessary and sufficient for the occurrence of another construct), probabilistically causal (i.e., the occurrence of one construct increases or decreases the probability of another construct, as in the case of "risk" or "protective" factors), or cooccurrence (i.e., occurrence of constructs is correlated with no specification of causal direction). The most important hypothesized relationships among constructs in the theoretical framework of the study should be either supported by citation of prior research or identified as new or innovative ideas about how constructs are related.

You must *justify* hypothesized relationships among constructs with either your previous research, the deductive logic of the conceptual framework, or a literature review. In general, a conceptual framework

is considered more "sophisticated" to the extent that the specified relationships function as "linkage" or "mediating" variables between
"input" and "output" variables. Possible problems with the proposed
conceptualization should also be discussed, such as alternative conceptualizations of the specific constructs in a domain, alternative hypotheses about the relationships among the constructs, or important
moderating or confounding variables that are not accounted for in
your conceptualization. You should also give attention to the temporal relationship among constructs. For example, if you propose that social support decreases the probability of (moderates) depressive symptoms in women sexually abused in childhood, it makes a difference
whether you propose that this relationship is temporally true of social
support (a) at the time of the abuse (in which case, some adequate assessment of this construct at that time is needed), (b) ongoing since the
abuse, or (c) at the time you are assessing depressive symptoms in
adulthood. The length of time between occurrence or assessment of related constructs is also of importance. Temporally distant input and
output variables are harder to justify as being linked than are contem-
poraneous or temporally contiguous variables.

STATING HYPOTHESES. The relationships among the specific
constructs described in the conceptual framework are the basis for the
formulation of the research hypotheses guiding the research. Proposed
research that does not explicitly state the hypotheses derived from relationships posited in the conceptual framework is unlikely to be highly
evaluated or funded. You should clearly state these hypotheses, the
measures that you will use to test the hypotheses, and how your data
analysis will confirm or disconfirm the hypotheses. Your hypotheses
should be specific enough that they can be disconfirmed and not so
general as to be uninteresting. They should also not be so implausible
as to lead reviewers to question their "face validity" (e.g., "All sexually
abused children will develop serious mental health problems in adulthood," or "Physical aggression in intimate relationships almost always
escalates into battering"). Moreover, some prioritizing or ranking in
terms of importance of hypotheses should be done. Proposals including a long "laundry list" of "hypotheses" between variables (especially
when many are obvious or uninteresting) are viewed negatively by re-

viewers. The crucial or interesting hypotheses that would have the greatest impact on your research field should be the ones highlighted in the application.

It is also important to provide some basis for the validity of the proposed hypotheses. It must not appear that hypotheses are arbitrary or drawn out of thin air. Rather, you should present some rationale for why the study hypotheses are likely to be confirmed by the research. The types of justification for hypotheses that can be marshaled include (in order of decreasing cogency) (1) your previous research that has tested this or similar hypotheses, (2) previous research reported in the scientific literature by other researchers, (3) pilot studies that provide some data on the likely validity of the hypotheses, (4) studies conducted by you or others that confirm related hypotheses in the area or analogous hypotheses in other areas, (5) a firm basis for the hypotheses in the conceptual framework for the study (such that the particular hypotheses would largely confirm or disconfirm the particular conceptual framework proposed), and (6) clinical or informal observations.

You should assess your research design, sampling plan, measurement plan, and data analysis plan to determine their adequacy to actually test the specific hypotheses derived from the conceptual model. There can be many limitations in the research that compromise the ability to test the proposed hypotheses. Examples of such limitations include selection bias in sampling and use of a cross-sectional design to test posited longitudinal relationships. You should acknowledge and discuss these kinds of limitations in the application. Alternative explanations should be entertained for (causal) relationships among variables, especially the existence of "confounding" variables, which can wholly or partly explain the relationships among the variables of interest.

Common Weaknesses in the Conceptual Framework of Proposals:
1. Conceptual framework not clearly specified.
2. Too many constructs included in the conceptual framework.
3. Conceptual framework overly simple.
4. No specific hypotheses about relationships among constructs.
5. Too many hypotheses, especially when many are uninteresting or uninformative.

6. Failure to consider alternative hypotheses to explain the results of the study.
7. Failure to discuss temporal relationships among variables or to justify hypothesized temporal relationships.

Preliminary Studies. This can be one of the most important parts of the application, because successful completion of relevant and technically competent work in the research area of the proposal can convince reviewers that the proposed research is also likely to achieve its goals. One type of preliminary study that can be helpful is psychometric development of new measures intended to be used in the research. You should give enough detail of prior studies to convince reviewers of its technical competence. It is important to describe the results obtained from prior research that are relevant to the proposed research, including results that bear on the feasibility of the proposed research, on the adequacy of sample sizes that are available, and on the likelihood that the major hypotheses of the study will be supported. As with the literature review, your discussion of previous research results should focus on their relevance to the research proposed in the application, especially the specific hypotheses or conceptual framework guiding the research.

Research Design and Methods. This section includes detailed descriptions of the measures to be used in the study, the sampling plan you intend to use, the procedures planned for data collection, and descriptions of the statistical analyses you plan to do.

Measurement. The measures of the independent and dependent variables used in the research should operationalize the key constructs in the conceptual framework underlying the research. You should identify the specific measures to be used, give a rationale for the selection of the specific measures, and describe the psychometric adequacy of each measure (reliability and validity).

SELECTION OF MEASURES. The two major problems seen in the measurement plan of research proposals are (1) failure to adequately measure the key constructs on which the research is based and (2) inclusion of measurement instruments or procedures that measure variables that do not correspond to constructs in the conceptual framework.

Inadequate measurement can include absence of an identified measurement instrument or procedure for a key construct, use of a measure that does not correspond conceptually to the theoretical construct to be measured, failure to justify use of a particular measure among alternative measures, or use of a measurement instrument or procedure with inadequate or problematical psychometric properties. Examples of such inadequate measurement include use of a single question or a few items on a scale to measure a key construct, use of an instrument that measures a heterogeneous collection of constructs rather than focusing on the specific construct of interest in the research (e.g., use of a very general child problems measure, such as the Child Behavior Checklist, when the major construct in the research is peer aggressiveness), or use of an instrument or procedure of unknown validity or reliability.

You should justify the choice of a particular measure and provide evidence that it is a good indicator of the construct of interest in the target population. If available measures have a number of subscales, ratings, or coding categories, the specific measures that will be used in the data analysis should be identified. Sometimes it is permissible to omit superfluous subscales, ratings, or coded categories from the data collection and analysis, if such omissions do not affect the psychometric properties of the measurement instrument or procedure. If there is more than one possible instrument available to measure constructs (e.g., measures of self-esteem or structured psychiatric interviews to determine diagnoses), and particularly, if there is controversy or disagreement in the field about which among various available measures are most valid, it is important to justify the choice of one particular measure over other possible measures. Such a justification can be developed either from your own knowledge or experience or from consultation with other researchers who have knowledge of the adequacy of the available, competing measures.

In general, multiple source/multiple method measures of the key constructs in the conceptual framework of the study are preferable. However, use of multiple forms of the same measurement procedure or use of multiple measures of a construct obtained from the same data source or reporter can introduce distortion or bias into the relationship among variables due solely to the measurement process. Thus, use of multiple self-report measures can lead to a consistency bias in self-report ratings, making variables appear more related than they are. Use of multiple measures for individual constructs can also create difficulties in the analysis of the data, especially when there are discrepancies between informants or low agreement among measures. Thus, when multiple measures and informants are used, one needs to thoughtfully consider how such potential difficulties will be handled. Expert consultation from design, measurement, or data analysis consultants may be helpful in formulating strategies to manage these potential difficulties.

The second common problem seen in the measurement plan of research proposals is the inclusion of a large number of measurement instruments in the research protocol that do not correspond to constructs discussed in the theoretical framework of the study. Usually, these additional measures are included for "exploratory" purposes (i.e., to see if anything turns up in the data from these measures). Such data mining studies are unlikely to receive a high priority score from a review committee because the committee won't know if anything will, in fact, turn up from these exploratory analyses.

There are a few circumstances in which a larger number of variables can be usefully included in the research design and data collection. One of these circumstances is the use of multiple indicators of an underlying construct. Another circumstance is when additional information is collected from subjects to aid in the interpretation of results of the study. This might take the form of collecting background information on subjects to determine if the research groups differ in important ways; this information can then be used to temper interpretation of results or incorporated into the data analysis.

PSYCHOMETRIC ADEQUACY OF MEASURES. There are three ways to obtain measures to operationalize the constructs which play a role in a research project: (1) use an instrument or procedure already developed, (2) adapt an existing instrument, or (3) construct your own instrument or procedure.

For any measurement instrument or procedure, whether already developed, adapted, or developed for the research, the reliability of the measurement instrument or procedure needs to be documented or established. Low reliability reduces the ability of such measures to indicate valid relationships among the constructs in the study. For many often-used measurement or assessment instruments there are published studies of the psychometric adequacy of the measure (especially of reliability). This literature should be cited in the justification for the choice of a measure for constructs in the study.

Assessment of reliability of a measure can take several different forms, depending on the type of measurement and the procedure by which the measure is obtained. Thus, for items making up a (continuous) scale, some indication of adequate scale reliability should be presented (e.g., item-total correlations or Cronbach's alpha); for classification procedures some indicators of the reliability of classifications should be presented (e.g., sensitivity and specificity); and for coding procedures some indication of inter-rater reliability should be presented (e.g., percent agreement or Cohen's kappa).

The implications of published or pilot studies of the psychometric adequacy of the measures proposed for use in the research should be carefully weighed. It is not enough to simply report that there have been studies of the psychometric adequacy of a measure; the results of such studies should be used to evaluate the adequacy of proposed measures for the study. For example, if a proposed key measure in the form of a multi-item scale has been reported to have an internal consistency (Cronbach's alpha or split-half reliability) of around .60 or lower in samples similar to the proposed research, the adequacy of the scale as a measure of a proposed underlying unidimensional construct is questionable. Either the instrument has to be improved or a better measure should be selected.

Often available measures, especially standardized assessment instruments, are not appropriate measures for the important constructs in the proposed research. In such cases, adaptation of an existing instrument by modifying its contents or measurement procedures may be proposed or the development of a new measure proposed. Use of an instrument or measurement procedure that has been developed or modified for use in a specific research project can be problematic, especially if the instrument measures an important independent or dependent variable. Such instruments are of unknown validity and reliability. In such cases, the steps that will be taken in the research to develop and evaluate the proposed instrument should be specified. It is preferable to develop a preliminary version of the instrument and at least collect some pilot data on the reliability and validity of the new or modified instrument.

Though for many variables there are few studies available on the validity of measurement scales, invalid instruments may lead to erroneous conclusions about the relationships among the constructs in the conceptual framework. Evidence for measure validity can include factor analyses or item response analyses of potentially multidimensional constructs, correlations of a scale assessing a construct with other recognized scales assessing the same construct, correlations of scale scores with other indicators of the underlying construct, or scale scores differentiating criterion groups differing on the underlying construct.

Absent a literature on the validity of a particular key instrument or measurement procedure, reviewers will sometimes assess the *face validity* of the assessment instrument. They might form an opinion about whether the content and number of items in your assessment instrument or procedure is likely to adequately assess the underlying construct. The proposed research instruments should be scrutinized from this same perspective. For example, some researchers have criticized the widely used Conflict Tactics Scale, which assesses verbal and physical aggression in relationships, in terms of the adequacy of the content of the items for certain types of research (e.g., the items don't differentiate defensive or retaliatory aggression from offensive aggression). Additionally, attention should be paid to *demand characteristics* of items or measurement procedures, especially involving socially desirable responses by informants or a press for consistency in responses (e.g., parents seeking treatment for their child are unlikely to rate their child as not having any problems on a behavior problem checklist).

Another issue in the validity of measurement of constructs is the quality of the data available from various sources, especially the potential for informant bias. Thus, certain informants may have agendas that bias their responses (e.g., individuals seeking treatment may want to portray themselves as worse off than they really are), or certain informants may have limitations in terms of exposure, mental state, or observational ability affecting their ability to make informed judgments or to report reliable observations (e.g., foster parents or teachers may be poor informants if they have limited experience with a particular child). You should incorporate strategies to reduce the influences of these biases on the research or acknowledge in the discussion section the limitations arising from this source.

The adequacy of the measures for the particular populations being investigated should be considered (e.g., a measure with psychometric adequacy on a normative sample might not be adequate with, for example, younger or older subjects, subjects of different ethnicity, or members of special populations, such as psychiatric patients). You should also consider the appropriateness of the measures with regard to the intelligence, reading ability, ethnicity, and social class of the subjects. In research involving assessment of children and adolescents, developmental issues in assessment should be addressed, especially the appropriateness of measurement and interpretation of responses given by children from a wide age range (e.g., 6 to 17).

If you propose to use "official" records in your research, you should provide some documentation of your access to such records and an indication of the quality of information that can be obtained from such records. Furthermore, when using questionnaires, (semi-)structured interviews, and coding schemes, your should describe the procedures you intend to use to establish inter-rater (or interviewer) reliability.

If you are not knowledgeable about the technical aspects of psychometric properties of measurement instruments, you should consult measurement experts when developing your measurement plan.

Common Weaknesses in the Measurement Plan of Proposals.
1. Key constructs not adequately measured.
2. Measures not linked to constructs in the conceptual framework.
3. Failure to provide information about the psychometric properties of measures.

4. Failure to consider the psychometric adequacy of measures for the specific proposed study.
5. Uncontrolled measurement biases.

Sampling Plan. The sampling plan of the study includes a characterization of the population of eligible subjects, an explanation of how such subjects will be recruited, and identification of specific, operational criteria for selecting *and* excluding subjects from the sampling population.

POPULATION SAMPLED. The generalizability of the results is important. You should give consideration to the representativeness of your study's subjects. For example, if you propose to study sexual assault among women, and a sample of college women is recruited, you cannot validly claim that the results of this study will generalize to all women who have been sexually assaulted (e.g., women who don't attend college). Such a study may be valuable in its own right (e.g., as a study of a population at a high risk for sexual assault), but the sample limits the conclusion that can be drawn about the effects of sexual assault with other nonrepresented populations.

Samples representative of larger, more general populations are preferred over samples from more restricted populations. Thus, national samples, community samples, multi-site clinical samples, and single-site clinic or institution samples represent declining generalizability. Often, however, in trauma research, samples representative of larger, general populations are unsuitable when the intent of the study is to study low-base rate behaviors (e.g., exposure to severe types of trauma). In such cases, general population samples are unlikely to yield sufficient numbers of subjects exhibiting the low-base rate behaviors. Thus, it may be necessary for you to adopt sample recruitment procedures to increase the number of individuals exhibiting the low-base rate behavior (e.g., recruitment at a facility providing services to such individuals, such as a rape crisis center for sexual assault victims, or screening a more general population, such as screening high school students for severe victimization experiences). Even in such cases, it is important to consider and discuss sampling limitations in the proposal. Low percentages of potential subjects who agree to participate in the study or differential rates of consent to participate in different research groups can seriously affect the representativeness of samples vis-a-vis the populations they represent. This is particularly true of hard-to-recruit populations, such as child and spouse abusers, sex offenders, or psychiatric patients.

The question of the representativeness of a sample should be particularly addressed for "convenience" samples (i.e., samples available at a particular clinic or in a school system chosen solely because of investigator access). Reliance on convenience samples is usually considered a weakness of the sampling plan of the study. At a minimum, data describing the characteristics of the convenience sample(s) should be collected (e.g., demographic characteristics, referral reason for clinic samples, and diagnostic information on psychiatric inpatients), so that these characteristics can be compared to the population or to other samples.

You should address sample attrition in the sampling plan, particularly if it is likely to differ for the different research groups (e.g., a clinical vs. a control sample). Realistic estimates of attrition together with an explanation of how the estimates were derived should be provided. If possible, you should propose procedures for characterizing refusers and dropouts and comparing them to sample subjects. For longitudinal studies, especially that collect data over a period of a year or longer, you should include discussion of tracking procedures to reduce sample attrition over time.

RECRUITMENT. Procedures used to recruit subjects into the study should be detailed, including how access to potential subjects will be obtained, how subjects will be recruited, and who will obtain consent from subjects for participation. To demonstrate the feasibility of proposed recruitment procedures, you should provide documentation that the numbers of subjects specified can be recruited, such as by providing figures on the number of subjects available in the total subject pool and in pools for various subgroups. Figures or estimates from previous research of the percentage of subjects in the various subject pools who are likely to choose to participate in the research would be helpful.

Some sample recruitment procedures result in samples that are considered less than optimum because of biases introduced by the recruitment procedures. Such cases include self-selected samples (e.g., subjects who respond to newspaper or other advertisements) and "nominated" samples (e.g., subjects nominated to be in a study by therapists or teachers). Such samples are considered to be biased to some unknown extent by unique characteristics of individuals who volunteer or are nominated for the research as compared to a random sample of individuals from the target population. In general, reviewers strongly favor sample recruitment strategies that allow all individuals in the targeted population an equal opportunity to participate in the research (e.g., locating subjects in a community sample who meet criteria for participating in the study by means of random digit dialing or identifying potential subjects randomly from an institutional or agency database).

INCLUSION AND EXCLUSION CRITERIA. Within the total population of available subjects, there may be valid reasons for including or excluding potential research participants (e.g., children who have been "confirmed" for sexual abuse by a protective service agency investigation may be included in a study of "sexual abuse" or psychiatric patients in acute distress, who might not be able to provide reliable self-report data, may be excluded). Such inclusion and exclusion criteria should be clearly stated and justified and their operationalization in the recruitment procedures should be specified. Particular attention should be paid to avoiding false positives and false negatives in study and control groups. For example, subjects selected as "battered women" from self-reports would be false positives if, in fact, they actually had not been physically abused by their partners. Conversely, subjects selected as a "non-battered control" from the community would be false negatives, if they had been physically abused, but did not report it.

INCLUSION OF GENDER AND MINORITY GROUPS. NIMH review committees are required to examine the participation of both genders and of minorities in the sampling plan for most research studies. If one gender and/or minorities are excluded or under-represented in the study for any reason, an explicit rationale for the exclusion or under-representation of these groups must be provided, specifically indicating why this sampling is justified or not remediable. In addition, prevention and treatment studies are required to include sufficient numbers of males and females and minorities such that the effectiveness of the intervention for these different groups can be assessed. This requirement is waived only in cases where the disorder or problem does not occur in one or more of the gender and/or minority groups or occurs so rarely that recruitment of a sufficient number of subjects in that group would not be feasible (e.g., women Vietnam veterans exposed to *direct* combat).

Common Weaknesses in the Sampling Plan of Proposals:
1. Failure to adequately describe the population to be sampled.
2. Failure to adequately describe sample recruitment procedures.
3. Use of convenience samples.
4. Failure to address sampling bias issues.
5. No documentation to support sample size estimates.

Procedures for Data Collection. The procedures that will be used to collect data should be detailed, including an indication of which measures are going to be collected from which subjects on which occasions, the order of administration of the measures, and the time required of each subject on each assessment occasion. If data is being collected at more than one point in time, you need to justify the particular time points chosen and the intervals between data collection points. Such a justification might include evidence from the literature on the amount of time symptoms typically take to develop or remit in a trauma group. Several additional issues in data collection that should be considered are discussed below.

DATA COLLECTION IN SPECIALIZED SETTINGS OR WITH SPECIAL POPULATIONS. Collecting data in specialized settings (e.g., inpatient mental health facilities or social service agencies) or with special populations (e.g., psychiatric patients, refugees, abused children and their families) may present difficulties in terms of gaining access and obtaining quality data. Reviewers may judge the feasibility of the research proposal by the prior experience of the research staff in collecting data in these settings or with these subjects. The significant difficulties in accessing and collecting data in these settings or with these subjects collecting data in these settings or with these subjects should be discussed and how such difficulties will be addressed should be clarified.

RESPONDENT BURDEN. You should estimate the amount of time required to collect data from each research participant and carefully consider the effect of the burden on the respondent (with respect to inconvenience, fatigue, and stress) and on the quality of data obtainable from potentially overburdened respondents. You should make an effort to reduce excessive respondent burden by thoughtfully selecting the minimum number of instruments to achieve research goals, using short forms of research instruments, and using more than one information source. In addition, any physically or emotionally aversive procedures (e.g., drawing blood for serum assays or questioning about recent victimization experiences) should be carefully justified from both the human subjects protection perspective and the perspective of the willingness of subjects to participate in the research.

REACTIVITY TO MEASURES. A subject's responses to measurement instruments can be affected by his or her awareness of being assessed (e.g., responding in socially desirable ways) or by a response consistency set across multiple instruments (e.g., subject introducing more consistency into his or her reports of different behaviors than would exist if the behavior were assessed directly). You should carefully consider the order of administration of research instruments to assess whether it introduces error in the form of sequential or carryover effects in subjects responses.

RECRUITMENT AND TRAINING OF DATA COLLECTORS. Data collection procedures requiring complex clinical judgments, development of rapport with subjects, or collection of information concerning sensitive topics are likely to require recruitment of data collectors with more training, experience, or personality qualities than are required for less demanding data collection tasks. Qualifications of these types of data collectors and recruitment procedures to obtain such individuals should be specified. You should describe a training plan that will ensure adequate data collection and which includes assessment of the adequacy of the training procedures.

BLINDNESS OF DATA COLLECTORS. To avoid experimenter bias, data collectors, to the extent possible, should be blind to characteristics of subjects that play a role in the research hypotheses of the study, such as group membership (e.g., abused versus control status), or assignment to treatment or control group. If data collectors cannot be made completely blind to subject characteristics (e.g., a questionnaire on contacts with Protective Services is included in the data gathering instruments), it is often possible to plan data collection procedures to minimize the influence of potential data gathering bias (e.g., have the interview on Protective Services contacts be the last data collected from the subjects during the interview session).

Common Weaknesses in the Data Collection Procedures in Proposals
1. Failure to clearly specify how data will be collected.
2. Reliance on a single data source.
3. Excessive respondent burden.
4. Introduction of measure reactivity in the data collection procedures.
5. Failure to specify training procedures for data collectors.
6. Failure to specify procedures to prevent experimenter bias from affecting research.

Statistical Analysis.
STATISTICAL PROCEDURES. The statistical analyses should be detailed, not just outlined. You should describe the particular statistical methods you will use to verify each specific hypothesis or expected relationship among variables as opposed to merely listing general techniques to be used in the data analysis without specifying which particular variables will be analyzed by such techniques. If there are multiple measures of the same construct (e.g., child-reported, parent-reported, and teacher-reported measures of child aggression), or multiple measures in the same conceptual domain (e.g., various dimensions of family functioning), you should provide a data reduction plan to use, reduce, or combine these multiple measures.

Certain statistical procedures are generally accepted as appropriate for analyzing certain types of data, so that their use is usually not questioned. Thus, some procedures, such as ANOVA, MANOVA, and multiple regression analysis, are considered standard procedures with certain types of data and reviewers usually do not question their appropriateness as long as the actual variables being analyzed are specified. On the other hand, other procedures need more justification and specification. Thus, for example, cluster analysis is considered a group of related procedures rather than one standard procedure. Unless the statistical analysis is very simple and straightforward, it is advisable to obtain a statistical consultant to help formulate the statistical analysis for the proposal and to be included as personnel or as a consultant on the grant.

If the research includes the collection and analysis of "qualitative" data, the procedures for analyzing this type of data should be specified in detail. Although a combination of quantitative and qualitative analysis is often viewed as a strength in a proposal, a study proposing only qualitative data analysis is not as readily accepted by review committees as a study using quantitative methods of analysis. Reviewers are often concerned about the "subjectivity" of qualitative methods and must be convinced that the qualitative analysis that will be used is "objective" enough so that the obtained results could be replicated by another investigator. If qualitative techniques of analysis are proposed, it is usually preferable to use qualitative techniques that have been standardized or otherwise validated.

POWER. Review committees usually require some type of statistical "power analysis" for the research design to insure that the sample sizes proposed are sufficient to adequately detect group differences or relationships among constructs (see Cohen, 1988; Kraemer & Thiemann, 1987).

For a number of reasons, often such a power analysis is not feasible for the actual data analysis that will be performed. For example, to compute a power analysis for a multivariate analysis of variance design requires *a priori* knowledge not only of the variance-covariance matrix of the groups by dependent variables design matrix, but also the "alignment" of the multivariate group means in the multivariate measurement space. Faced with the difficulty of computing a power analysis for the actual (complex) statistical analysis to be used in the research, applicants typically adopt one of 3 strategies: (1) compute a power analysis for a similar, though simpler, analysis than the one they are actually conducting in the research (e.g., compute a power analysis for a univariate analysis of variance as opposed to a multivariate analysis of variance); (2) compute a power analysis for the proposed statistical analysis under a set of simplifying assumptions that allow the power to be calculated (e.g., Stevens [1992] has published tables of statistical power for multivariate analysis of variance using a set of reasonable simplifying assumptions for behavior research); or (3) refer to references in the statistical literature which present power tables for particular complex statistical procedures; these are often based on computer simulation studies of the statistical procedure on different types of hypothetical data sets (see, for example, Vonesh and Schork, 1986).

Regardless of the type of power analysis proposed, there are a number of rules of thumb that reviewers use in evaluating the adequacy of the proposed sample size:

(1) The number of subjects in the smallest *significant* cell of the design. Thus, if it is proposed to compare the effects of two different interventions with males and females from two different ethnic groups, the review committee is not as likely to focus on the total number of subjects recruited, but on the number of subjects in the smallest cell about which inferences will be made (here, the subjects of one sex in one of the ethnic groups).

(2) The ratio of number of variables collected to the number of subjects. If 30 measures are collected from each of 30 subjects, the review committee is liable to feel that, because of the common source variance and the large number of variables collected, there is a high probability of "discovering" spurious relationships among variables in the research.

(3) The number of subjects typically recruited in studies in the area. For example, if, in studies of nationally representative samples, 2000 subjects are typically included and a study with only 500 subjects is proposed, the review committee is likely to think that the sample is too small. In contrast, if comparison of different treatments is typically

based on studies using 20 subjects in a group, and the proposed study will recruit 50 subjects in each group, the sample size will appear adequate to the committee.

Common Weaknesses in the Data Analysis Plan of Proposals
1. Failure to describe how specific hypotheses will be tested or analyses will be conducted.
2. Lack of congruence between how data will be analyzed and the aims of the study.
3. Use of complex statistical procedures that are not well understood by the investigator.
4. Use of simple statistical procedures when more complex procedures are necessary or commonly used.
5. Use of statistical procedures that are not state-of-the-art.

Human Subjects. All research supported by the Department of Health and Human Services must meet certain requirements for protection of human subjects from risks associated with participation in research. There are four main concerns in human subject protection: (a) obtaining voluntary consent; (b) informing participants of potential risks; (c) attending to potential adverse effects of the research; and (d) safeguarding the confidentiality of information obtained from participants. A research proposal in which there are substantial concerns about safeguarding the well-being or confidentiality of subjects will not be funded unless corrected.

Often applicants do not realize some of the intricacies involved in human subject protection procedures in the area of trauma research. This is particularly true, if the proposed research involves certain populations (e.g., children, crime victims, or disaster victims) or on certain sensitive issues (e.g., criminal behavior, child abuse, spouse abuse, or rape). In such cases, I would recommend talking to knowledgeable colleagues, especially researchers who have had Federal research funding, or NIMH staff about the best available human protection protocols being used in the research field.

Informed Consent. Obtaining informed consent is a process consisting of the following components: (1) apprising potential participants of the general nature of the research, the number and length of data collection sessions, the type of information to be collected, and potential risks associated with participation clearly enough so that potential participants can decide whether or not they wish to participate in the research; (2) ensuring that the participants understand the explanation of the research procedures and risk well enough to consent to participate in the research; and (3) obtaining voluntary consent to participate. Although typically informed consent is documented by asking participants to sign a voluntary consent form, it is important to realize that informed consent is *not* a document, but rather a process whereby the investigator attempts to guarantee that potential participants have enough knowledge of the research to truly make informed decisions about whether they want to participate in the research project. You should include the consent form that will be used in the research and a description of the process used to obtain voluntary consent in the application.

The explanation of the research in your consent form should be targeted toward the level of understanding of potential participants. It is important to remember that subjects' level of understanding may be affected by their age, education, and emotional stability. Brief, abstract, vague, or overly general accounts of the research are not acceptable means of providing adequate information to potential participants on which to base their voluntary consent. Particular aspects of the research which might be problematic for some participants (such as sensitive topics the applicant will be asked about, burdensome or stressful assessment instruments, or invasive or intrusive procedures) should be clearly identified and explained to the subject together with their options for participating or withdrawing from the research or particular procedures.

In research involving children and adolescents, you are generally required to obtain voluntary consent to participate from the parent or legally responsible caregiver and to also obtain some type of consent or permission from the child or adolescent, depending on his or her age and cognitive and emotional maturity.

Any appearance of coercion, no matter how subtle, must be avoided. For example, one should avoid unusually large subject payments, a perception that receipt of services at an agency is dependent on participation in the research, or parental coercion of reluctant children to participate in research. Participants should be informed of their freedom to withdraw from the research at any time and to refuse to participate in any particular aspect of the research that makes them uncomfortable.

Research Risks. You must clearly explain any potential risk from participating in the research to the potential participant before consent is obtained. For example, if information is obtained from a family member that could lead to an abuse report, reporting requirements must be explained to family members prior to obtaining consent. There also may be limitations to confidentiality of data obtained from subjects. For example, data obtained from adolescents may be legally accessible to their parents unless some waiver is obtained from parents. You should think through and address such potential limitations to confidentiality either with additional protective procedures or by advising potential participants of the limitations to confidentiality. It may be advisable to seek legal advice about such limitations and to institute additional protective procedures.

You must make provisions for potential adverse reactions due to participation in the research either of informants or by others directed towards the informant; this is especially true of adverse emotional reactions of participants (e.g., of crime or disaster victims) and potential retaliation against victims by abuse perpetrators for abuse reporting. These provisions usually include adequate staff training to detect such reactions and procedures to provide clinical services for problems related to the research or identified during the research, for referral to adequate helping resources, or for adequate physical safety. In research on sensitive issues, research involving invasive or intrusive procedures, or research with high risk populations, debriefing and follow-up procedures should be planned to assess whether participants experienced any discomfort or difficulties from participating in the research immediately after participation and after some delay. Adequate provision should be made to address such discomfort or difficulties.

Confidentiality. At a minimum, safeguarding of confidentiality requires numerically coded data forms, locked files, and restricted access to data records. When research data might be subject to subpoena, you can apply for a DHHS Certificate of Confidentiality through NIMH. As described above, any limitations on confidentiality must be clearly explained to the subject (e.g., mandated child abuse reporting, parents' access to children's or adolescents' research data, *Tarasoff* limitations).

Review of Human Subjects Protections. Institutions applying for NIMH support for research involving human subjects must meet certain requirements for conducting an institutional review of the proposed procedures to protect human subjects from risks associated with participating in the research project. Most large universities, medical schools, and research institutions have an agreement with the Department of Health and Human Services concerning conducting such reviews by an Institutional Review Board (IRB). IRBs must meet certain requirements concerning their composition and operation. If such an agreement is in place, the institution is issued a Multiple Project Assurance allowing the IRB at the institution to review research projects submitted for DHHS funding. Usually this review takes place prior to submission of the application. If an institution does not have such a standing review board approved by DHHS, it must negotiate with the Office for Protection from Research Risks (OPRR) at the NIH to establish such a board to review each specific project.

Approval of the human subjects protection provisions of a research project by an institutional IRB is not sufficient in itself to meet human subjects requirements for research supported by NIMH. IRBs vary greatly in the criteria they use to evaluate provisions for human subjects protections, sometimes underprotecting subjects from significant risks and sometimes overprotecting subjects from minimal risks. Human subjects protections will also be reviewed by review committees and by NIMH program staff for their adequacy. Sometimes this can create difficulties for an applicants when there is a conflict between human subjects protection requirements of the IRG or program staff and the institutional IRB; changes in the human subjects protections procedures made by an applicant in response to an IRG review or program staff requirements must be reapproved by the institutional IRB.

Some research is exempt from human subjects protection requirements, but applicable Federal regulations granting exemptions from human subjects protections and DHHS interpretation of such regulations are very narrow. Exempted research usually falls in the category of research on extant records or research on data routinely collected in public agencies, educational institutions, or clinics.

Common Weaknesses in Human Subjects Protection in Proposals:
1. Failure to clearly describe consent procedures.
2. Failure to attend to potential risks of research participation.
3. Failure to attend to ethical and legal requirements that apply to professionals.
4. Failure to specify procedures for confidentiality of data.
5. Assumption that institutional IRB approval satisfies human subjects protection requirements.

Intervention Research

Research on preventive or treatment interventions has additional research design criteria that are evaluated in a grant review. Intervention research is concerned with establishing whether an intervention effected a change in individuals (sometimes groups) that resulted in a significant change in some desired outcome. As with other types of research, proposed intervention research should be based on a strong conceptual model. The elements of a conceptual framework for intervention research include: (1) a conceptualization of *what to change*, (2) a conceptualization of *how the intervention changes the target of the intervention*, and (3) a conceptualization of *what factors affect variation in intervention outcome*, and (4) a conceptualization of *how to maintain intervention gains over time*.

The methodology of intervention research is concerned with how to ensure the validity of the inference that the change in outcome resulted from the intervention per se, to eliminate or control alternative explanations for change in outcome (internal validity of the intervention inference), and to establish the robustness or variability of the intervention effect across clients, treatment administration, and settings. Many of the issues raised in this brief discussion of intervention research are discussed in greater depth in Kazdin (1992). Some issues in developing intervention research are described below.

Assessment of Intervention Effects

Assessment of intervention effects should focus on precisely what the intervention is designed to change. Often, interventions for mental health problems or dysfunctional behavior are not designed to directly affect these problems or behavior, but to change cognitive, emotional, or behavioral processes that are hypothesized to mediate the problems or behavior (e.g., negative cognitions in depressed individuals) or to modify other types of risk factors associated with the problems or dysfunction (e.g., poverty or drug usage in parents neglectful of their children). Evaluation of intervention effectiveness should assess the mediating or risk factors that are hypothesized to be changed by the intervention. Assessment of the mental health or behavioral outcomes that are the ultimate goal of the intervention is usually also assessed in intervention research. If the intervention positively affects both the mediating or risk factors targeted by the intervention and the ultimate mental health problems or dysfunction, the intervention trial not only demonstrates the effectiveness of the treatment, but also tends to validate the mediation or risk factor model, linking the processes modified by the intervention and the ultimate problem or dysfunction. It may also be the case that the intervention effectively changes the hypothesized mediating targets, but shows nonsignificant improvement in the ultimate problem or dysfunction for a number of reasons (e.g., difficulty in assessing change in the problem or inadequacy of the mediational model). With complex, long-term or sequential types of interventions, assessment of effectiveness at various critical transition points in treatment is recommended.

Intervention Specification

To assess whether an intervention effected change in targeted outcomes requires that the intervention be specified clearly enough and adequately implemented, such that it can be determined whether the research trial adequately tested the intervention approach in the sense that the clients actually received the proposed intervention. This determination is usually based on (1) a clear specification of how the intervention is to be implemented in the form of a manual and/or other training material, (2) procedures to adequately train intervention providers in the implementation of the intervention, and (3) procedures to assess whether intervenors are actually implementing the intervention as designed (they are *adhering* to the treatment plan), possibly with corrective feedback procedures. Related to this is the assessment of *differential intervention fidelity*, which consists of procedures to assess whether therapists are faithfully administering an intervention as intended in the treatment condition, but also are not using the target treatment interventions in other intervention conditions or in the control condition. This might particularly be a problem when the same therapists are administering more than one intervention condition or when therapists in the same setting might communicate or otherwise pick up the target intervention procedures and apply them to the control or other treatment groups. Such contaminations adversely affect the estimation of the efficacy of the target intervention process compared to other interventions or controls.

Additional insight into the effectiveness of interventions can be gained by assessment of the process of intervention. Such assessment can take the form of linking various characteristics of the intervention process to measures of intervention outcome (e.g., characteristics of the intervenor's or client's behavior during sessions). One important form of this type of assessment is an assessment of *dose-response* relationship. This concept, borrowed from pharmacological studies, can involve various measures of the quantity or intensity of intervention received. For example, assessment of dose-response relationship could include the relationship of outcomes to such measures as number of intervention sessions administered or attended, completing versus dropping out of treatment, and level of client involvement in treatment (e.g., "homework" assignments completed, active participation in intervention sessions).

Factors Affecting Variation in Intervention Outcome

Factors affecting variation in intervention outcome can include client .characteristics, intervenor characteristics, interactions between client and intervenor characteristics, and intra-session and extra-session processes and conditions that affect the administration of the intervention or response to intervention. The impact of some of these factors might be either controlled experimentally or assessed during an intervention trial.

Among client characteristics that might affect intervention outcome are the severity of presenting problem, co-occurring problems (e.g., alcohol abuse in spousal assaulters), and motivation for treatment (e.g., help seekers versus mandated clients). The level of severity of the presenting or target problem should, particularly, be considered in terms of the representativeness of the intervention trial subject to the target clinical population, the difficulty of demonstrating clinically significant change in client samples with only mild or moderate levels of impairment, the refractoriness of clients with severe levels of dysfunction or multiple types of difficulties, and the possibility of overestimating treatment effects by using extreme groups. If intervention trial participants have not been selected with regard to their level of severity of target problems, it is often useful to *post hoc* stratify subjects by level of problem severity to gauge the relationship between intervention effectiveness and problem severity.

Among intervenor characteristics that can affect intervention outcome are intervenor competence, which is often assessed as years of experience or amount of training, intervenor adherence to the intervention protocol, or intervenor bias toward an intervention. Similarly, some clinical research has focused on the match between client characteristics and therapist characteristics, especially on such characteristics as race, ethnicity, sex, age, and personality style.

Many intra-session factors that influence intervention outcome are assessed in studies of intervention process. Among these are development of a "working alliance" between therapist and client, the "quality" and timing of interventions by the intervenor in sessions, and the response to interventions by the client in sessions. Among extra-session conditions or factors that can influence intervention outcome are support for intervention participation by significant others, experience of extra-therapeutic crises and life stressors, and other interventions received in addition to the target intervention.

Often conditions for administration of treatment are not ideal. Some writers on intervention research distinguish between intervention trials of the *efficacy* of intervention versus trials of the *effectiveness* of interventions. Supposedly, in an *efficacy* trial, the researcher can control the selection and assessment of subjects, of therapists, and of the administration of treatment such that the trial is an adequate test of *effectiveness* of the intervention model under near ideal conditions (in other words, of the internal validity of the inference that the intervention model can effect change in the target of the intervention). *Effectiveness* studies, which often follow *efficacy* trials, then attempt to assess whether interventions that have been shown to be efficacious in controlled trials maintain their efficacy in real-world clinical settings. My own view is that the categorical distinction between *efficacy* and *effectiveness* trials is artificial. Rather, I think there is a continuum of control that researchers have over aspects of the intervention (i.e., the researcher may or may not be able to adequately control various factors in the intervention such as selection of subjects and of intervenors, of assignment of subjects to treatment groups, and of administration of interventions) and that any intervention trial falls somewhere on this continuum. Moreover, I think that the assessment of factors that influence intervention outcome is part of a complete intervention model.

Research Designs in Intervention Research
There are a number of research designs used in intervention research. They can be split into multiple group and single group designs. Multiple group designs include (1) intervention versus control or comparison groups and (2) comparisons of alternative interventions, often also including control or comparison groups. Special cases of the latter include comparing groups receiving a standard intervention with those receiving the standard intervention plus additional components, to determine if the additional components will enhance treatment efficacy of a known effective intervention, and disaggregation of multifaceted interventions, which usually attempt to determine what elements of

complex interventions are actually instrumental in effecting change.

Single group designs are usually regarded as weaker research designs than multiple group designs because outcomes can not be compared to no-treatment or to alternative interventions. Nonetheless, there are occasions on which such designs are necessary and may even be superior to standard multiple group studies. Among single group designs are single subject designs in which treatment efficacy is inferred from synchrony between administration of treatment and change in outcome target from a baseline. Often single case results are aggregated in an intervention study. Another form is single sample pre-, post-designs which measure change in the time period covered by an intervention. Such designs are usually most persuasive when the target of the intervention is strongly resistant to change so that it is unlikely that change in the targeted outcome could result from factors other than intervention. Another form of single sample design is when a series of stages of improvement in difficult outcomes (e.g., personality change, recovery from serious trauma) are defined and the subject advances through these stages in synchrony with interventions targeted at outcomes characteristic of that particular stage. Outcomes characteristic of other stages may also be assessed to indicate that improvement is not general, but is restricted to the outcomes targeted for intervention.

Randomization plays an important role in supporting the validity of the inference that the intervention effected change in some outcome measure against alternative explanations. Thus, random assignment of potential subjects to treatment or control groups guards against the possibility that differential effects of interventions, or of interventions over control, are due to preexisting differences between the groups prior to intervention or in response to intervention. Similarly randomization can be used to control other factors that might affect outcome besides administration of treatment (e.g., random assignment of therapists to different treatments to guard against therapist competence as affecting outcome). However, it is important to realize that randomization is a design *strategy* to control for nontreatment factors; there are situations in which randomization does not serve this function well (e.g., randomly assigned groups may become biased by differential attrition during treatment administration) and in which randomization adversely affects valid inference about treatment effectiveness (e.g., when treatment efficacy is maximized by matching treatment with client characteristics).

Ethical Issues in Intervention Research

In addition to the general issues concerning informed consent, confidentiality, and human subjects protection previously discussed, there are additional human subject issues specific to intervention research.

An important issue in informed consent is that if potential subjects are to be randomly assigned to different intervention groups or to interventions and no treatment or placebo groups, they must be informed about this random assignment. This disclosure can significantly impact the willingness of potential subjects to participate in the study, particularly, if they feel that they might not receive effective intervention. Other consent issues arise with potential subjects who may be coerced into interventions (e.g, children by their parents or individuals court-mandated for intervention).

Additional human subject safeguards are required in intervention research associated with the issue of the demonstrated efficacy of treatments. So, for example, it might be difficult to justify administering experimental interventions to subjects in place of interventions known to be effective in a study in which the intent is to demonstrate that an experimental approach is even more effective. Similarly, human subjects protection usually requires that harmful intervention be terminated as soon as the harm is known and that, if a particular intervention is conclusively demonstrated to be superior to other interventions during the course of a trial, then the less effective interventions should be terminated, and the effective intervention substituted for all subjects.

Conclusion

The process of obtaining support for research has changed dramatically in the last few years. It used to be the case that a researcher could focus on a single source of support for research in a certain area, often a Federal agency that funded in the research area. As long as a researcher could develop a very good research proposal, he or she could be fairly optimistic that the research project would be funded. Because research funding has not kept pace with the increased costs of doing sophisticated research and increasing competition for relatively scarce research dollars, this situation no longer holds.

Currently, most funding sources cannot fund all of the excellent research proposals that they receive. Thus, you can no longer assume that there is a high probability that you will be funded by a single funding source for a particular research project. You must become knowledgeable about alternative funding sources for research such as government agencies, private foundations, professional and civic organizations, and other private sources of research funding, and you need to submit proposals to several different funding sources to maximize the chances of having your research funded. To increase the chances of a research project being funded, you need to be persistent in locating potential funding sources, interacting with staff at the funding sources to learn about application requirements, developing research applications, and learning about and following through on the application process of funding sources. Although onerous, this process is now almost essential in order to obtain funding to conduct the kind of sophisticated research that requires a significant research budget.

In this competitive environment, trauma researchers have some advantages over researchers in many other areas due to the social salience and importance of this area of research, but it is essential that you give careful attention to the conceptual and methodological issues discussed in this chapter in developing a research plan. The level of sophistication in addressing these conceptual and methodological issues defines the relative merits of the research in developing reliable and valid scientific knowledge of phenomena associated with traumatic experiences. A high level of research sophistication in a proposal not only improves your chances of having your research proposal funded, but also ensures that your research will maximize the value of the knowledge about trauma gained from the research.

References

Cohen, J. (1988). *Statistical power analysis for the behavioral sciences* (2nd ed.). San Diego: Academic Press.

Kazdin, A. E. (1992) *Research design in clinical psychology* (2nd ed.). New York: Macmillan.

Kraemer, H., & Thiemann, S. (1987). *How many subjects?* Newbury Park, CA: Sage.

Stevens, J. (1992). *Applied multivariate statistics for the social sciences* (2nd ed.). Hillsdale, N.J.: Erlbaum

Vonesh, E. F., & Schork, M. A. (1986). Sample sizes in the multivariate analysis of repeated measures. *Biometrics, 42,* 601–610.

Contributors

Judith G. Armstrong, Ph.D.
Sheppard Pratt Health System

Stephen L. Bieber, Ph.D.
Department of Statistics
University of Wyoming

J. Douglas Bremner, M.D.
Department of Psychiatry
Yale University School of Medicine
and
West Haven VA Medical Center

Eve B. Carlson, Ph.D.
Department of Psychology
Beloit College

John A. Fairbank, Ph.D.
Social and Behavioral Research Center
Research Triangle Institute
and
Department of Psychiatry and Behavioral Sciences
Duke University Medical Center

Malcolm Gordon, Ph.D.
Violence and Traumatic Stress Branch
National Institute of Mental Health

Bonnie L. Green, Ph.D.
Editor, *Journal of Traumatic Stress*
Department of Psychiatry
Georgetown University Medical School

B. Kathleen Jordan, Ph.D.
Social and Behavioral Research Center
Research Triangle Institute
and
Department of Psychiatry and Behavioral Sciences
Duke University Medical Center

Danny G. Kaloupek, Ph.D.
Department of Psychiatry
Tufts University School of Medicine
and
National Center for PTSD
Boston VA Medical Center

Terence M. Keane, Ph.D.
National Center for PTSD
Boston VA Medical Center

Fred Lerner, D.L.S.
National Center for PTSD
White River Junction, VT

Elana Newman, Ph.D.
National Center for PTSD
Boston VA Medical Center

Fran H. Norris, Ph.D.
Department of Psychology
Georgia State University

Frank W. Putnam, M.D.
Unit on Developmental Traumatology
National Institute of Mental Health

William E. Schlenger, Ph.D.
Social and Behavioral Research Center
Research Triangle Institute
and
Department of Psychiatry and Behavioral Sciences
Duke University Medical Center

Elizabeth M. Smith, Ph.D.
Department of Psychiatry
Washington University School of Medicine

Susan D. Solomon, Ph.D.
Office of Extramural Research
National Institutes of Health

B. Hudnall Stamm, Ph.D.
Department of Psychology
University of Alaska

Beginning with the assumption that caring for people who have experienced highly stressful events puts the caregiver at risk for developing similar stress-related symptoms, this book brings together some of the best thinkers in the trauma field to write about the prevention and treatment of **Secondary Traumatic Stress.**

Contributors include pioneers in the study of secondary traumatic stress, such as Charles R. Figley, Ph.D, Laurie Anne Pearlman, Ph.D, Mary Beth Williams, Ph.D, Jonathan Shay, M.D., Ph.D, and Sandra Bloom, M.D.

This "cutting edge" material not only reflects the current state of knowledge about secondary traumatization, but in a personal way explores our ethical obligations to each other, to our communities, and to future trauma research.

STSS. December 1995, 280 pp., paper, ISBN 0-9629164-9-8, $18.95.

"A *must* for the practicing clinician."
—Martin Seligman, Ph.D., University of Pennsylvania

"Both practical and deeply personal....a necessary companion for all those who do the work."
—Tom Williams, Psy.D., President, International Association of Trauma Counselors

For information about *Sidran* Foundation programs and publications, call, fax, write or email: Sidran Foundation, 2328 W. Joppa Rd., Suite 15, Lutherville, MD 21093. FAX (410) 337-0747; Phone (410) 825-8888; Email, sidran@access.digex.net.

- -

☐ Please send a free copy of the **Sidran Foundation Bookshelf** catalog.
☐ ____ copies of *Secondary Traumatic Stress* @ $18.95.
Shipping: Add $4.50 for the first book, $1 each additional. MD residents only, add 5% sales tax.
Canadian residents, add $3.50 to your order. U.S. funds only.

☐ VISA ☐ MasterCard ☐ Check or Money Order Enclosed   Total _____

Credit Card Number _____ Exp _____ / _____ Signature_____

Name _____

Address _____

City _____ State _____ Zip _____

Daytime Phone Number: _____

Sidran Foundation, 2328 W. Joppa Rd., Suite 15, Lutherville MD 21093.
FAX (410) 337-0747; Phone (410) 825-8888; Email, sidran@access.digex.net.